Mastering
Word 5.0
for the
IBM PC

Mastering Word 5.0 for the IBM PC

Pamela S. Beason

BANTAM BOOKS
NEW YORK · TORONTO · LONDON · SYDNEY · AUCKLAND

I am dedicating this book to Alice Foster —
my grandmother and my friend.

MASTERING WORD 5.0 FOR THE IBM PC
A Bantam Book / March 1989

This book was produced by Publishing Synthesis, Ltd., New York, NY.

ISBN 0–553–34670–9

Contents

P A R T II *Revising*

C H A P T E R 4

Editing Your Document   45

P A R T III   *Changing the Appearance of Text*

C H A P T E R 7
Character Formatting   123

C H A P T E R 8
Paragraph Formatting   137

CHAPTER 12

Incorporating Graphics and Drawing Lines   227

P A R T   IV   *Page Layout and Printing*

CHAPTER 13

*Adding Page Numbers, Running Heads and Running Feet, and
Footnotes   245*

C H A P T E R 15

Printing   305

P A R T V   *Working With Complex Documents*

C H A P T E R 16

Calculating and Sorting   321

C H A P T E R 17

Working With Long Documents   331

P A R T VI *Customizing Word*

C H A P T E R 22
Using Macros   431

C H A P T E R 23
Changing Word to Suit You   447

Acknowledgements

I'd like to thank all my friends at Microsoft who were always willing to help me keep in touch with new developments. I'd also like to thank Jono Hardjowirogo, my Editor at Bantam, for his patience in dealing with this book and its author; and Bruce Sherwin, the Managing Editor for Bantam Electronic Publishing, who saw the book through production.

P A R T   I

The Basics

This part of the book teaches you the basic tasks that you need to know to create files with Microsoft Word: how to start and quit Word, how to use commands, and how to manage your files. If you're an experienced Word user, you probably know how to do many of these tasks already, and you may want to read only some sections and skip over others. If you're new to Microsoft Word, you'll find all the information you need to get started right here.

1

WELCOME TO MICROSOFT WORD

This Chapter Contains the Following:

What's New In Version 5 of Word
The Many Views of Microsoft Word

Microsoft Word is a powerful word processing program and desktop publishing program, rolled into one. You can use Word to create any type of document you can imagine, form letters, calculations, sorting—any writing task you want to perform for your personal writing or for your office. You can import graphics or spreadsheets, create multiple columns and complex tables, and link information in your Word documents to other documents. Then you can check the page layout, make any final alterations to the formatted pages, and print your document.

WHAT'S NEW IN VERSION 5 OF WORD

This book deals with version 5 of Microsoft Word, although much of the information presented is applicable to previous versions as well. If you've used any of the earlier versions of Word, you may be surprised at how much version 5 has changed. With Word 5, you can now:

- Integrate text and graphics
- View and edit multiple columns on the screen
- Repaginate continously while you work (background repagination)
- Create cross-references that Word will update for you
- Link text in a Word document to its original spreadsheet or other file
- Save automatically at specific time intervals
- Save all files at once with one command
- See miniature versions of your pages before you print (print preview)
- Specify an exact position for text or graphics on a page and make text "wrap" around a positioned object
- Add annotations

There are many improvements to existing Word features as well; such as easier tab setting, better OS/2 support , installable video drivers, better use of color to show character formatting, an integrated spelling checker, line drawing, and extensive macros that you can run to automate your word processing tasks.

Of course, Word still has all of its previous capabilities such as the ability to create outlines, tables of contents, and indexes; the ability to use revision marks and hidden text, the ability to work with multiple documents, the ability to use styles and glossaries to save formatting, text, and graphics, as well all the usual word-processing features you would expect to find in a state-of-the-art program.

Overall, you'll find that Word 5 is more powerful than previous versions of Word, but not more difficult to use.

THE MANY VIEWS OF MICROSOFT WORD

The most outstanding difference in version 5 of Word is that now you can look at a document in several different ways. Here's a list of Word's four different views and the uses of each.

View	Use
Document view (also called *galley view* or *normal view*)	To enter, edit, and format text and graphics, and to work with multiple documents at one time
Show layout view	To view and edit multiple columns and positioned objects on full-sized pages
Print preview	To view all elements of a page (multiple columns, running heads and feet, footnotes, and positions of objects) on miniature pages
Outlining view	To create outlines, and to view and rearrange a document according to its heading levels

Figures 1-1 through 1-4 show a sample of what a document might look like in each of Word's views.

You'll find out more about how to use Word's different views, as well as its powerful features, in the chapters ahead.

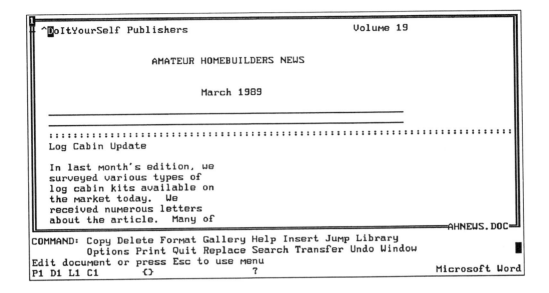

```
^DoItYourSelf Publishers                          Volume 19


                    AMATEUR HOMEBUILDERS NEWS


                        March 1989
   _____


:::::::::::::::::::::::::::::::::::::::::::::::::::::::::::::::::::::::::
Log Cabin Update

In last month's edition, we
surveyed various types of
log cabin kits available on
the market today.  We
received numerous letters
about the article.  Many of
                                                      AHNEWS.DOC
COMMAND: Copy Delete Format Gallery Help Insert Jump Library
        Options Print Quit Replace Search Transfer Undo Window
Edit document or press Esc to use menu
P1 D1 L1 C1        {}                  ?            Microsoft Word
```

Figure 1-1.   **Document view.**

Figure 1-2.   **Show layout view.**

```
Log Cabin Update              Stair Design Tips

In last month's edition, we    Those of you who are
surveyed various types of      constructing staircases
log cabin kits available on    should be aware of the "rise
the market today.  We          and run" theory of building
received numerous letters      steps.  For each vertical
about the article.  Many of    step (rise), there is a
the letters pointed out that   recommended horizontal
log cabins may not meet        measurement (run) to the
building codes in some         next step.  The rise and run
areas.  Be sure to check       work together to create the
with your local planning       slope of the staircase.  And
department before you order    we all know what happens if
a kit or start harvesting      the slope of the stairs is
logs for your cabin.  Take a   too steep!
lesson from the experience
of George Bushes, who          Here are some basic rules
finished his log cabin in      for building staircases:
                                                      AHNEWS.DOC
COMMAND: Copy Delete Format Gallery Help Insert Jump Library
        Options Print Quit Replace Search Transfer Undo Window
Edit document or press Esc to use menu
P1 D2 L17 C35      {u}                 ?            Microsoft Word
```

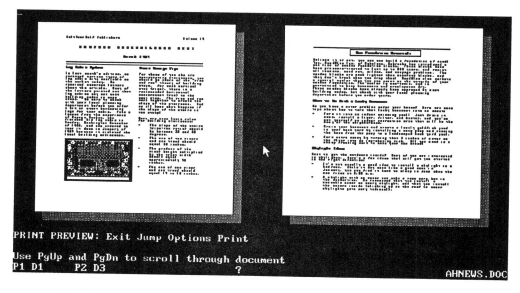

Figure 1-3.   **Print preview.**

Figure 1-4.   **Outline view.**

```
Log Cabin Update
     Violation of Building Codes
     Harvesting Your Own Logs
Stair Design Tips
     Basic Rules
     Situations to Avoid
New Foundation Materials
What to Do with a Leaky Basement
     Indoor Swimming Pool
     Goldfish Pond
     Ice Skating Rink
Skylight Ideas
     Not in the Bedroom!
     Covers for Skylights



COMMAND: Copy Delete Format Gallery Help Insert Jump Library
         Options Print Quit Replace Search Transfer Undo Window
Edit document or press Esc to use menu
Level 1              {}              ?
                                          Microsoft Word
```

2

GETTING STARTED

This Chapter Contains the Following:

Starting Word
A Survey Of the Word Screen
Using Keys In Word
   How to Read Key Combinations in This Book
Using the Mouse In Word
Choosing Commands
   Choosing Commands with Keys
   Choosing Commands with the Mouse
   Choosing Subcommands and Options
   Carrying Out a Command
   Canceling a Command
Using the Learning Word Lessons
Getting Help
Running Other Programs From Word
Quitting Word

This chapter describes the basics you need to know to operate Word: how to start and quit Word, how to choose commands and options, and how to use Word's help system. If you're new to Word, you'll want to read through this chapter in sequence.

STARTING WORD

You can start Word several ways by typing one of the following commands at the operating system prompt (usually A> or C>), then pressing Enter.

Type	To
word	Start Word.
word /l	Start Word and open the last file on which you worked.
word filename	Start Word and open the file you specify.

If you have a graphics card installed in your computer, you can also type the following commands to start Word in different modes:

Type	To
word /c	Start Word in character (text) mode for fastest operation and to see more lines of text on the screen.
word /g	Start Word in graphics mode for the display most similar to the printed document (the "what-you-see-is-what-you-get" mode).
word /h	Start Word using a smaller character size to display more lines of text on the screen
word /m	Start Word in high resolution monochrome mode (useful only if you have an EGA card with 64K of memory and an Enhanced Color Display monitor).

You can combine the switches (the */x* combinations) to get the result you want. For example, you could type *word /l /g* to start Word in graphics mode and load the last file on which you worked. The combination you use has to make sense for your computer setup—you can't use the switches for a graphics card if your computer doesn't have a graphics card.

If you have a graphics card, you can press Alt+F9 to switch between graphics and character modes while running Word. This feature allows you to get the most from your machine; or example, you might want to run Word in the character mode most of the time to make the program faster, but switch to the graphics mode occasionally to see your formatting more clearly. You can also switch modes by choosing the Options command and choosing a new option in the "display mode" field.

You could also start Word by putting an appropriate *Word* command at the end of an AUTOEXEC.BAT file, which would start Word when you turn on your computer. See your DOS manual for more information about AUTOEXEC.BAT files.

A SURVEY OF THE WORD SCREEN

Word opens in document view, the view you'll use most often. Take a look at the Figure 2-1, which points out different parts of the screen. You'll see these terms used throughout this book.

Figure 2-1.   **The Word screen in document view.**

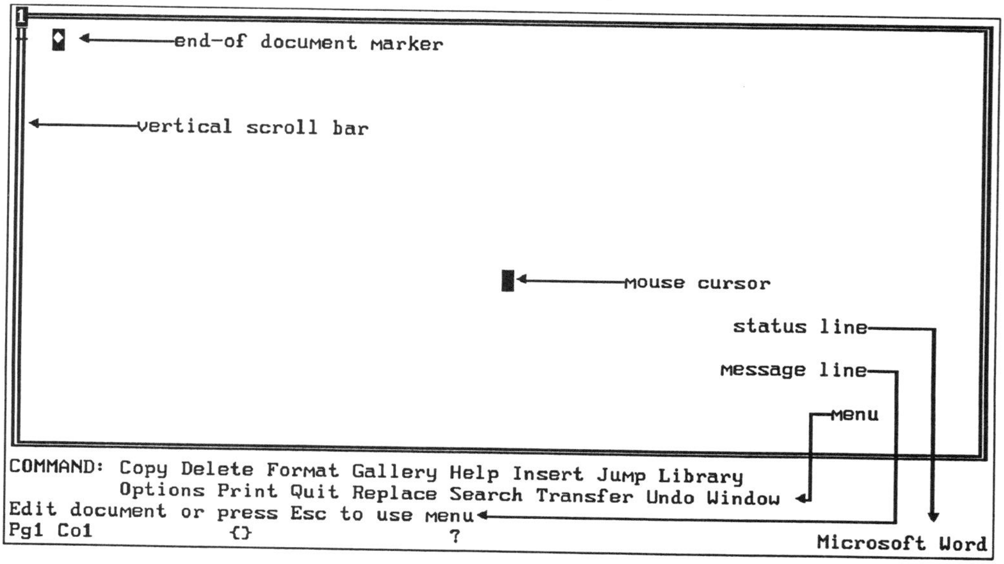

```
┌─────────────────────────────────────────────────────────────────┐
│ ┌───────────────────────────────────────────────────────────┐   │
│ │ ◙ ◀──────end-of document marker                            │   │
│ │                                                             │   │
│ ◀──────vertical scroll bar                                   │   │
│ │                                                             │   │
│ │                                                             │   │
│ │                              █◀──────mouse cursor           │   │
│ │                                            status line──────┐   │
│ │                                          message line──────┐│   │
│ │                                                  ┌─menu     ││   │
│ └──────────────────────────────────────────────┘  │         ││   │
│ COMMAND: Copy Delete Format Gallery Help Insert Jump Library  ││   │
│          Options Print Quit Replace Search Transfer Undo Window ◀┘│
│ Edit document or press Esc to use menu◀───────────────────────┘   │
│ Pg1 Co1              {}                    ?                       │
│                                                   Microsoft Word  │
└─────────────────────────────────────────────────────────────────┘
```

USING KEYS IN WORD

If you're more comfortable using the keyboard instead of the mouse, you can use keys to do everything in Word, or you can switch between the keyboard and the mouse, using whichever is more convenient. Keyboard procedures are presented along with mouse procedures throughout this book. In cases where it's actually faster to use the keyboard to perform an operation, we've listed special techniques as "Keyboard Shortcuts." To make sure you won't be confused by the keyboard instructions in this book, you should know the locations and the names this book uses for important keys:

Key Name	Description
Alt	Labeled "Alt."
Ctrl	May be labeled "Control" or "Ctrl."
Shift	May be labeled "Shift," or may have an up arrow symbol.
Enter	Sometimes called "Carriage Return" or "Return" key. May be labeled "Enter," "Return," or have a bent arrow symbol to indicate a line break.
Del	May be labeled "Delete" or "Del."
Backspace	May be labeled "Backspace" or have a left arrow symbol.
Ins	May be labeled "Insert" or just "Ins."
Arrow keys	Sometimes called direction keys. Marked with arrows pointing up, down, right, or left.
Numeric keypad keys	Keys in the "calculator" portion of the keyboard to the right of the keys used for typing text.
Function keys	Keys labeled with F followed by a number: F1, F2, etc. Found at the left or the top of a keyboard.

How to Read Key Combinations in This Book

When this book tells you to press several keys at once, the key combination is shown with plus signs (+) between the key names. For example, Alt+B means hold down the Alt key while you press the B key.

Key combinations with commas between them mean to press one key, then release it and press the next key. For example, Esc, F, E means press Esc, then release it and press F, then release it and press E.

Uppercase letters are used to show alphabetic keys in key combinations, but you don't need to press Shift to to make the letter uppercase—the lowercase letter works just as well.

USING THE MOUSE IN WORD

When you use a mouse with Microsoft Word, the left and right mouse buttons may perform different functions, so be sure to pay attention to "left" and "right" in the instructions in this book.

You may already be familiar with using the mouse. But just in case you need a reminder, here are the mouse terms used in this book:

Term	Description
Point	Roll the mouse on your desk to move the mouse pointer to a specific location on the screen.
Click	Quickly press and release the mouse button while the cursor is in a specific location. For example, "Click the word" means move the mouse pointer to the word, then press and release the mouse button.
Drag	Hold down the mouse button while you move the mouse. For example, "Drag the split line" means point to the split line, then hold down the mouse button while you move the mouse to drag the split line to a new location.

CHOOSING COMMANDS

When you start Word, you see a menu of commands at the bottom of the screen; this screen is the main menu. You can use either the keyboard or the mouse to choose a command.

Choosing Commands with the Keyboard

When you use Word with the keyboard, it's important to remember that there are two modes in Word: a typing or edit mode, where you can enter or change text in a document, and a command mode, where you can choose commands and options. Every time you want to switch modes, press the Esc key.

To choose a command with keys:

1. Press Esc to switch to the command mode. In command mode, Word highlights the Copy command at the bottom of the screen.
2. Press the capitalized letter of the command name (usually the first letter). For example, press T to choose the Transfer command.

If you choose a command by mistake, you should press the Esc key to get back to the main menu.

Choosing Commands with the Mouse

To choose a command with the mouse: Point to the command name and click the left mouse button. For example, to choose the Transfer command, point to the word Transfer in the command menu and click the left mouse button. Figure 2-2 shows an example of choosing a command with a mouse.

If you click a command by mistake, just click both mouse buttons simultaneously to get back to the main menu.

Choosing Subcommands and Options

Only a few Word commands take effect as soon as you choose them. Other Word commands display a menu of subcommands, from which you can choose, or display a list of options to ask you for more information about what you want to do. For example, when you choose the Format command from the main menu, it displays a menu of subcommands, as shown in

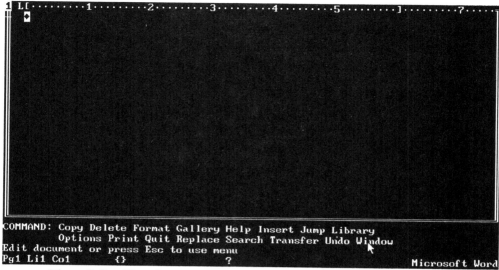

Figure 2-2.   Choosing a command with the mouse.

Figure 2-3.   The Format command displays another menu of subcommands.

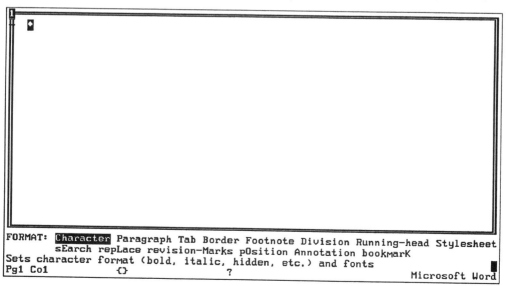

Figure 2-3. The name of the original command, Format, is displayed in capital letters at the left side of the menu.

You choose a subcommand the same way you choose a command from the main menu, by pressing the capitalized letter in the command name or by clicking the left mouse button on the command.

Speed Tip for Mouse Users: To choose a command from the main menu and choose the first subcommand (such as Format , then Character) in one step, you point to the command name in the main menu and click the right mouse button.

In this book, just like in the Word manuals, we use a kind of shorthand terminology when referring to commands. If you need to choose two or three commands in quick succession, we combine their names. For example, when we say to choose the Format Tab Set command, we mean to choose the Format command from the main menu, then choose the Tab command from the Format menu, then choose the Set command from the Tab menu.

There's another level lower than subcommands. When Word needs more information to carry out a command, it displays command fields.

Figure 2-4.   **Fields for the Format Tab Set command.**

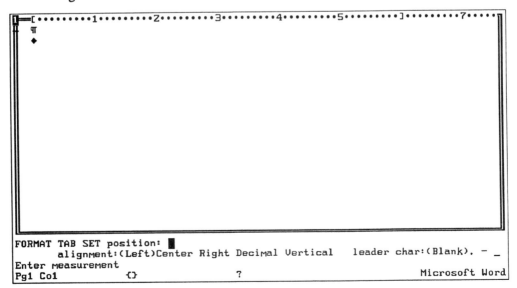

For example, if you choose the Format Tab Set command, you'll see the command fields shown in Figure 2-4.

Word has two types of command fields:

- "Fill-in" command fields, in which you type a response.
- "Menu" command fields, in which you choose an option from a list.

When you choose a command, you'll see that some options are selected (surrounded by parentheses), and sometimes you'll see a file name or a measurement displayed in a fill-in field, even if you've never used the command before. These selections come from Word's *default settings*—the settings Word assumes you'll want to use most of the time. These settings are kept in the MW.INI file. You can accept the default settings in the command fields by leaving them alone, or you can change the initial settings to the options you want. To move from one command field to the next field:

- Use the arrow keys (or the Tab key) to move the highlight to the field you want.
  or
- Point to the field and click the left mouse button.

The message line gives you clues about how to use command fields. If the message line begins with "Enter. . .," you can type a response. If the message line contains ". . . or press F1. . .," you can press the F1 key to display a list of choices from which to pick, or you can type a response. When the message line says "Select option," you select an option from a "menu" command field.

To type a response in a fill-in command field, just start typing. You don't need to first erase a response that's already there.

To choose an option from a menu command field:

- Press the first letter of the option you want. (If there are two options with the same first letter, press the spacebar to highlight the option you want.) Word puts parentheses around your choice.
  or
- Point to the option you want and click the left mouse button.

Carrying Out a Command

When you have chosen the options you want in a command's fields, you're ready to carry out the command.

Speed Tip for Mouse Users: To choose an option in a command field and carry out the command at the same time, point to the option and click the right mouse button.

To carry out a command:

- Press Enter.
  or
- Click the capitalized name at the left of the command area, as shown in Figure 2-5.

Canceling a Command

If you change your mind anytime before you carry out a command, you can press the Esc key, or point to the bottom of the screen and click both mouse buttons simultaneously to cancel a command.

Figure 2-5.   **Clicking the capitalized command name carries out the command.**

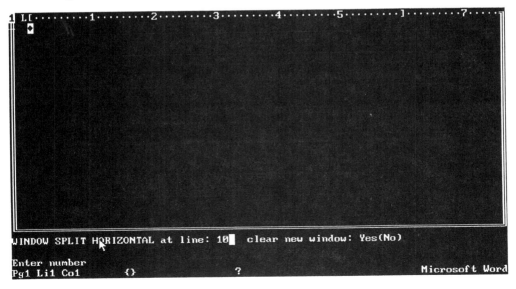

USING THE LEARNING WORD LESSONS

If you're new to Word, you'll probably find that the fastest way to learn to use the basic program features is to get hands-on practice with the Learning Word lessons, which came with the Word package. You can get to the lessons in two ways:

- Outside of Word, you use DOS or OS/2 to go to the directory or drive containing the Learning Word lessons and type *learn*.
- In Word, you choose the Help Tutorial command, as explained in the following section. You must have 384K of available memory to use the Learning Word lessons in this way.

GETTING HELP

Word's help system is available any time you need it. You can quickly get specific help about a command or command field, you can peruse the extensive help system at your leisure, or you can jump to the Learning Word tutorial to see a lesson and get hands-on practice. There's even a form of minihelp that's on the Word screen at all times. When you use the arrow keys to highlight a command name in the command area, Word displays a brief description of that command at the bottom of the screen, as shown in Figure 2-6.

To get quick help about a command or command field:

1. Use the arrow keys to highlight the command or command field you want to see for help information.
2. Press Alt+H or point to the question mark (?) at the bottom of the screen and click the left mouse button.

To get quick help about editing:

- When you're typing or editing (when the cursor is in the document window), press Alt+H or point to the question mark (?) at the bottom of the screen and click the left mouse button.

When you ask for help, Word closes the document window and opens a Help window, as shown in Figure 2-7, that displays the information you requested.

The Help system is one long file, full of topics you can scroll through at your leisure. To peruse the help topics:

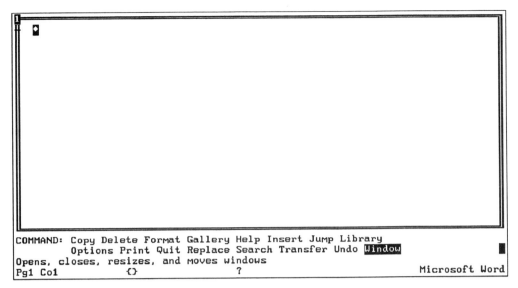

```
COMMAND: Copy Delete Format Gallery Help Insert Jump Library
         Options Print Quit Replace Search Transfer Undo Window
Opens, closes, resizes, and moves windows
Pg1 Co1            {}                    ?              Microsoft Word
```

Figure 2-6.   **Word displays a description of the highlighted command in the message line. Press the arrow keys to move the highlight to a different command.**

Figure 2-7.   **A Word help screen.**

```
HELP     Screen 1 of 3
Every Help screen lists name of topic and number of
screens related to topic in upper-left corner.

To get Help on a      1. Use direction keys to move highlight to command
command or command       or field you want help on.
field                 2. Hold down Alt key while you press H (Alt+H).

To browse in Help     1. Press Escape key (Esc), then press H.
                      2. Press N (next) or P (previous) to view Help
                         information.

To view Help Index    1. Start Help (Press Esc, H, or Alt+H).
                      2. Press I to choose Index from Help menu.



                        ═══ Tutorial: Getting Quick Help
                            Using: Ch. 6, "Getting Help"

HELP: Exit Next Previous Basics
      Index Tutorial Keyboard Mouse
Returns to location or menu where Help was requested
Pg1 Co1            {}                    ?              Microsoft Word
```

1. Choose the Help command from the main menu, or click the question mark (?) in the status line if you're using a mouse. Word closes the document window and opens a help window like the one shown in Figure 2-7.
2. Choose the appropriate command:

Choose	To Do This
Basics	Display information about how to use the help system.
Index	Display a list of help topics from which you can select.
Tutorial	Suspend Word and use the Learning Word lessons for instruction and hands-on practice. Choose Lesson to start the lesson displayed on the screen, or choose Index to see an index of lessons you can select from.
Keyboard	Display information about how to use keys in Word.
Mouse	Display information about how to use a mouse in Word.
Next	Display the next screen of information.
Previous	Display the previous screen of information.
Exit	Get out of the help system and back to Word.

Word displays a screen with the information you requested.

RUNNING OTHER PROGRAMS FROM WORD

If your computer has enough available memory, you can temporarily suspend Word and run other programs or use an operating system command. This feature is especially handy if you want to use DOS or OS/2 to find a file or check disk space.

To suspend Word and run another program:

1. Choose the Library Run command.
2. In the "run" field type the DOS command or OS/2 command you need to run another program.
3. Press Enter. After the command is completed or you've exited the other program, you'll see the "Press a key to resume Word" message.
4. Press any key to return to Word.

Helpful Hint

The Library Run command allows you to use only one operating system command at a time. If you think you may need to use several DOS commands to find a file or rearrange files, you can use the DOS COMMAND command or the OS/2 CMD command, which put all operating system commands at your disposal (in computer talk, these commands create a "shell" by running the executive program, so you really have two instances of the executive running at one time).

To use the DOS COMMAND or the OS/2 CMD command from Word:

1. Choose the Library Run command.
2. Do one of the following:

   • If you see command or cmd in the "run" field, press Enter.
   • Type *command* for DOS or *cmd* for OS/2 in the "run" field, then press Enter.

Word disappears, and you'll see the operating system version message appear on the screen, followed by your usual operating system prompt (C>, for example).

3. Use any operating system commands as usual.
4. When you're finished using operating system commands, type *exit* at the prompt, then press Enter. (The EXIT command terminates the shell.) You'll see the "Press a key to resume Word" message.
5. Press any key to resume Word.

Note: It's *not* a good idea to use operating system commands to delete .BAK or .TMP files while Word is suspended in this way. If you delete a .BAK or .TMP file that Word needs to finish the file you're working with, Word won't be able to continue because you destroyed information the program needs.

QUITTING WORD

To quit Word:

• Choose the Quit command from the main menu.

If you've made any changes (even if you only pressed the spacebar or the Enter key), Word asks you if you want to save the file before quitting.

CREATING, SAVING, AND MANAGING FILES

This Chapter Contains the Following:

Because all of your documents are saved in files, file management is an essential part of working with Word. This chapter teaches you the basic skills you need to create and manage Word files on your computer.

ABOUT DOS AND OS/2 FILENAME RULES

When you name a Word file, you must obey the operating system's rules for filenames. If you try to type an invalid filename in Word, or any other program running on DOS (MS-DOS or PC-DOS) or OS/2, you'll see a message something like:

Not a valid filename

The names of all files you use with these operating systems must conform to these rules:

- Your filenames must contain no more than eight characters in the basic filename before a period, and no more than three characters in the filename extension after the period. No spaces are allowed in filenames. For example, you could use FILE.MY, INVOICE.601, FOSTER.LET, LETTER, but not MY FILE (which contains a space) or THISISMINE.DOC (which has too many characters).
- You can't use an asterisk (*) or a question mark (?) in a filename. These characters are reserved for use as *wildcards* when searching for files. You'll learn more about that later in this book.

HOW WORD NAMES FILES

If you don't specify an extension or a period after the basic filename, Word adds a .DOC extension to a filename. For example, if you tell Word you want a file named MIKE, it assumes you want the file named MIKE.DOC. If you want a file with no extension, type a period (.) after the basic filename; for example, if you want a file named just MIKE, type *MIKE.* when saving or asking for the file.

When you want Word to find or put a file in a directory or a disk drive that's different than the one you're working in, you need to type a pathname in front of the filename (or choose directories or drive letters in a list, as explained in "Opening Existing Files" later in this chapter). For example, to use a file named MIKE.DOC in a directory named LETTERS on drive B:, you'd type B:\LETTERS\MIKE.DOC when referring to the file.

For more information about filenames, pathnames, disk drives, and operating sytem rules, see the operating system manual that came with your computer.

CREATING A NEW DOCUMENT

When you start Word by typing *word* at the operating system prompt, Word opens a new, empty document so you can start typing right away. When you save your document, you give it the name you want and Word displays that name in the lower right corner of the screen.

If you have already started Word and opened an existing document, you can use the Transfer Load command to open a new, empty document.

To create a new document:

1. Choose the Transfer Load command.
    Word displays the command fields shown in Figure 3-1.
2. Type a name for your document in the "filename" field.
3. Press Enter or click the capitalized command name.
4. When the message line displays "Press Y to create document," press Y to open a new empty document.
    If you've made any changes to an existing document on the screen (even if the changes are invisible, as when you press the spacebar or the Enter key), Word asks you if you want to save the changes first.

ENTERING TEXT

Entering text is easy—just type! You don't need to press Enter when you come to the end of a line: Word automatically begins a new line when the text reaches the right margin. This feature is commonly called *wordwrap*.

To begin a new paragraph, press Enter. To erase errors, press the Backspace key. You'll learn more about editing in Part II, "Revising."

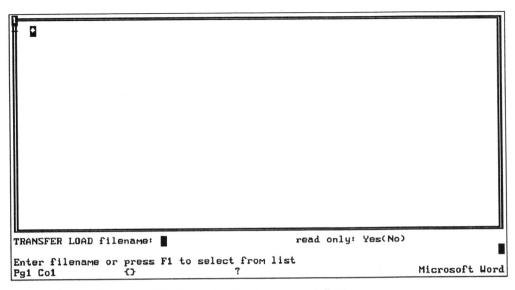

Figure 3-1   **The Transfer Load command fields.**

OPENING EXISTING FILES

To open an existing file:

1. Start Word.
2. Choose the Transfer Load command.
3. Type the name of the file you want to open, or press F1 to see a list of names like those shown in Figure 3-2. Word automatically displays the names of the files ending with .DOC in the active directory on the active disk drive. To see the names of other files, you may need to do one of the following:

To See a Listing of
Files with .DOC extensions on a different drive (B:, for .example)

Do This
Type the drive name (B:, for example), then press F1
or
Press F1, then use the arrow keys or the mouse to highlight the drive name in the list ([B:], for example), then press Enter.

```
C:\WORD5\*.DOC
AHNEWS.DOC        JREPORT.DOC       STUFF.DOC         ZEST.DOC
COLUMNS.DOC       MAILTEST.DOC      TABLES.DOC        ZEST1.DOC
EXP-FORM.DOC      MEMO.DOC          TABS.DOC          ZEST2.DOC
FRED.DOC          OUTTEST.DOC       TEST.DOC          [..]
FREPORT.DOC       PRICELST.DOC      TESTWF.DOC        [DEMO]
GRTEST.DOC        REPORT.DOC        TYPOS.DOC         [A:]
GTEST.DOC         SALES1.DOC        WORDDEMO.DOC      [C:]
INVOICE.DOC       SALES2.DOC        ZERK.DOC          [D:]

















TRANSFER LOAD filename: AHNEWS.DOC              read only: Yes(No)
Enter filename or press F1 to select from list (194043712 bytes free)
Pg1 Co1              {}                   ?                Microsoft Word
```

Figure 3-2.   **When you press F1, Word displays a list of files to choose from.
Highlight a file, then press F1 to get back to the other command fields.**

Files with .DOC extensions
in a different directory
(\INVOICES, for example)

Type the directory pathname
(\INVOICES, for example), then
press F1. (Early versions of DOS may
not allow you to do this.)
or
Press F1, then use the arrow keys or the
mouse to highlight a directory name
in the list ([..] (root) or [INVOICES],
for example), and press Enter. Repeat
until you find the file you want.

Files with extensions other
than .DOC (.LET extensions,
for example)

Type an asterisk (*) followed by a
period and the extension (*.LET, for
example), then press F1.

All files in a directory

Type the name of the directory (if it's
not the current directory), then
type *.* (\LETTERS*.*, for example).

Speed Tip for Mouse Users: You can point to the name of a file in the list and click the right mouse button to select the file and get back to the "filename" field all at once.

If you accidentally display a list you don't want, press Esc or click both mouse buttons simultaneously to get back to the "filename" field, then try again.

4. If you typed the filename in the "filename" field, press Enter. If you used F1 to display a list of filenames, press the arrow keys or point and click the left mouse button to highlight the name of the file you want to open, then press Enter. If the file is an RTF file, Word displays a message asking if you want to convert the file to Word format, or load it in RTF format.

SAVING A DOCUMENT

Word doesn't save the text you've typed until you choose the Transfer Save command, whose command fields are shown in Figure 3-3. To minimize the risk of losing your work, it's a good idea to save frequently.

If Word is almost out of memory or disk space, it displays "SAVE" in the status line. This message means "Save NOW!" If you see this "SAVE" message frequently, you're probably working with large files that are overloading your computer's capabilities. Try doing one of the following:

• Choose the Transfer Save or the Transfer Allsave command to save the document, then choose the .Transfer Clear All command to free memory, then use the Transfer Load command to load your file again.

Keyboard Shortcut

To choose the Transfer Load command and display a list of .DOC files in the current directory at the same time, you press Ctrl+F7.

Helpful Hint

If you want to suspend Word temporarily and use the operating sytem to find a file or rearrange files, you can use Word's Library Run command in combination with the DOS COMMAND command or the OS/2 CMD command, which put all operating system commands at your disposal. (In computer talk, these commands create a "shell" by running the executive program, so you really have two instances of the executive running at one time.)

To use the DOS COMMAND or OS/2 CMD command from Word:

1.   Choose the Library Run command.
2.   Do one of the following:

   • If you see *command* or *cmd* in the "run" field, press Enter.
   • Type *command* for DOS or *cmd* for OS/2 in the "run" field, then press Enter.

   Word disappears, and you'll see the operating system version message appear on the screen, followed by your usual operating system prompt (C>, for example).
3.   Use any operating system commands as usual.
4.   When you're finished using DOS or OS/2 commands, type exit at the prompt, and press Enter. (The EXIT command terminates the shell.) You'll see the "Press a key to resume Word" message.
5.   Press any key to resume Word.

Note: It's *not* a good idea to use DOS or OS/2 commands to delete or move .BAK or .TMP files while Word is suspended in this way. If you delete a .BAK or .TMP file that Word needs to finish the file with which you're working, Word won't be able to continue because you destroyed information the program needs.

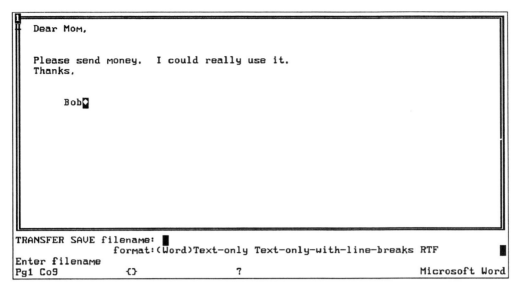

```
┌┬──────────────────────────────────────────────────────────────────────┐
│‖  Dear Mom,                                                            │
│‖                                                                       │
│‖                                                                       │
│‖  Please send money.  I could really use it.                          │
│‖  Thanks,                                                              │
│‖                                                                       │
│‖       Bob▯                                                            │
│‖                                                                       │
│‖                                                                       │
│‖                                                                       │
│‖                                                                    │   │
│‖                                                                    │   │
│‖                                                                       │
│‖                                                                       │
├────────────────────────────────────────────────────────────────────────┤
│ TRANSFER SAVE filename: ▮                                               │
│               format:(Word)Text-only Text-only-with-line-breaks RTF  ▮  │
│ Enter filename                                                          │
│ Pg1 Co9              {}              7                 Microsoft Word   │
└──────────────────────────────────────────────────────────────────────┘
```

Figure 3-3. **The Transfer Save command fields.**

- Break large files up into smaller files while you're in the creating and editing stages, then—if necessary—merge them into one large file when you're ready to print. See Chapter 4 for more information about copying and moving text, and see "Merging Files" later in this chapter for more information about merging files.

Saving a Document for the First Time

To save a document for the first time:

1. Choose the Transfer Save command.
2. Type a name for your document in the "filename" field.
3. Press Enter or click the command name to save the file.
   If you typed a filename that's already been used for another file, Word asks you if you want to replace that file with the one you're saving. If you typed a filename that doesn't meet the rules, Word will display a message telling you it's an invalid filename.
   Word displays a summary sheet, as shown in Figure 3-4.

4. If you want to keep a summary sheet to help you find files in the docu-
    ment retrieval system, fill out the summary information command
    fields as follows, then press Enter to save the file. For more informa-
    tion about using the document retrieval system, see Chapter 21.

Field Name	Type This
Title	A descriptive title for the document (up to 40 characters).
Author	The name of the person that created the document (up to 40 characters).
Operator	The name of the person typing the document or making revisions, if different from the author, (up to 40 characters).
Keywords	Words or phrases that will help in identifying this document. If you wanted to keep track of all documents that involved a certain customer, product, legal case, or other topic, you could type the customer name, product name, legal case name, or words to identify a certain topic (up to 80 characters).
Comments	Any further information you want to add to clarify the document. For example, you might type something like *his letter responds to a suggestion from a customer about lowering the sugar content in our cookies.* (You can type up to 220 characters.)

If you don't want to fill out the summary sheet fields, press Esc or click
both mouse buttons simultaneously to skip the summary sheet and save
the document. (If you don't want to use Word's retrieval features, you can
instruct Word not to display the summary sheet fields by choosing the Options command, then choosing No in the "summary sheet" field. When
Word finishes saving the document, it displays the number of characters
in the file in the lower left corner of the screen.

Saving an Edited Document

You can use the Transfer Save command to save a document, or the Transfer Allsave command to save a document and the associated style sheet
and glossary files at the same time.
    To save a document with the same name:

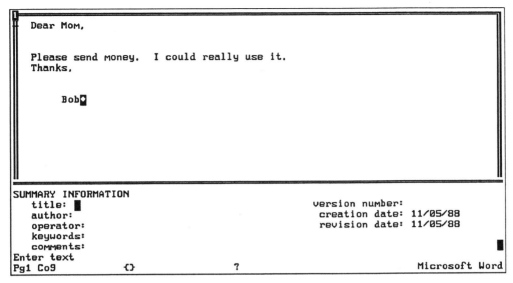

Figure 3-4.   **The summary sheet fields**.

- Choose the Transfer Save command.

    or

1. Choose the Transfer Allsave command.
2. Press Enter or click the capitalized command name.
   Word displays the Transfer Save command fields as usual, but you
   don't have to look at them if you don't want to change the filename.
   You can just press Esc, T, S, Enter (Esc for command mode, T for
   Transfer, S for Save, Enter to carry out the command) to save the file
   quickly.

Keyboard Shortcut

Instead of choosing the Transfer Save command, then pressing
Enter to save a file with the same name, you can just press
Ctrl+F10. Word will save the file without displaying the command
fields.

Saving a Document in a Different File

Sometimes you'll want to save a version of a document with a different name and leave the original document intact. For example, if you work on invoices, you might open a file called APRIL.INV, then update it for May, and save the updated file as MAY.INV. Then you would have both files for your records: APRIL.INV and MAY.INV.

To save a document with a different name:

1. Choose the Transfer Save command.
2. Type a new name for the document in the "filename" field.
3. Press Enter or click the capitalized command name. Word saves the file with the new name, and leaves the original file intact.

Saving a Document in a Different File Format

Word allows you to save your documents in different file formats so you can use them with other programs.

1. Choose the Transfer Save command.
2. If necessary, type a new filename in the "filename" field.
3. Choose an option in the "formatting" field.

Choose	To Create an
Text-only	ASCII file without Word formatting (preserving only the text, tab characters, and paragraph marks in the file).
Text-only-with-line-breaks	Same as Text-only file, but with ASCII carriage-return characters at the end of each line to preserve line breaks.
RTF	Rich Text Format file (used by some applications).

4. Press Enter or click the command name. Word displays a message, "Enter Y to confirm loss of formatting," just to make sure you really mean it. After all, once you remove the Word formatting, you can't get it back without reentering all the formatting.
5. Press Y.

Saving Automatically

Because what you see on the computer screen is not written to a disk until you save it, it's always a good idea to save frequently so that you won't lose any of your work in the event of a power failure, a program crash, or other disaster. Word lets you set an autosave option that saves your work at regular intervals.

Using the autosave feature does not take the place of using the Transfer Save command. The autosave feature stores changes in temporary backup files with these extensions:

File Type	Autosave Extension
document	.SVD
style sheet	.SVS
glossary	.SVG

In the event of a power failure or other problem, you can recover your work from these files. The Transfer Save command, on the other hand, completely updates the file on disk and deletes the autosave files when it's done. The first time Word performs an automatic save, it saves the entire document, so this might take a few seconds. Thereafter, Word saves only the parts of the document that you've changed, so automatic saving is very fast. You'll see the message "Saving file. . ." in the message line whenever Word is performing an automatic save.

Turning on Autosave

To turn on autosave:

1. Choose the Options command.
2. In the "autosave" field, type the number of minutes you want for a time interval between saving. For instance, if you want Word to save your work every five minutes, type 5.
3. If you want Word to display a message before saving to ask you if you want to save, choose Yes in the "autosave confirm" field. Otherwise, choose No. This option determines whether Word displays a message to which you must respond at the interval specified in the "autosave" field. For example, if you've set the "autosave" field to five minutes and you choose Yes in the "autosave confirm" field, Word will display this message every five minutes:

About to backup changes with autosave. Enter Y to backup or Esc to cancel

Restoring Autosave Files

If you're using Word's autosave feature when lightening strikes or when a colleague walks by and trips over your power cord, pulling it out of the wall, you can recover your work from the temporary autosave files. When you start Word again, Word displays a message asking you if you want to recover the autosave files. If you choose to recover, Word saves each autosave file and restores them with the appropriate extensions (.DOC, .STY, .GLY).

Turning Off Autosave

To turn off autosave:

1. Choose the Options command.
2. In the "autosave" field type a zero (0) or press the Del key.
3. Press Enter or click the command name.

MERGING DOCUMENTS

If you want to merge two or more documents into one file, Word makes it easy.

To merge documents:

1. Open the first document.
2. Move the cursor to where you want to insert the second file.
3. Choose the Transfer Merge command.
4. In the "filename" field, type the name of the file you want to merge, including any pathnames Word needs to find it, or press F1 and select from a list of filenames.
5. Press Enter or click the command name.

You can repeat this process to merge as many files as your computer or disk can handle. Be sure to save soon after merging.

CLOSING DOCUMENTS AND FREEING MEMORY

Word automatically closes an open document when you quit Word or when you load another document (unless you've opened another window, as described in Chapter 4). You can also close a document any time you like—this causes Word to clean up any temporary document files it has created when working with that document. You can also choose to close all temporary files, such as style sheet files and glossary files—this frees up more memory for future work.

To close a document in the Word window:

1. Choose the Transfer Clear Window command.
2. Press Enter or click the command name. If you've made any changes since you last saved the document, Word asks you if you want to save the changes before closing the document.

To close all temporary files Word is using:

1. Choose the Transfer Clear All command.
2. Press Enter or click the command name. If you've made any changes since you last saved the document, the glossary or style sheet files, Word asks you if you want to save the changes before clearing the memory.

FILE MANAGEMENT

You can rearrange, rename, and copy files using the DOS or OS/2 MOVE, RENAME, and COPY commands, Word's Transfer Rename command, or using Word's document retrieval system (explained in Chapter 21). You can delete files with Word's Transfer Delete command or with the DOS or OS/2 DEL command. The following sections give you general instructions. For more information on using DOS or OS/2 commands, see your operating system manual.

Renaming Documents

You can rename a document with Word's Transfer Rename command or with the DOS or OS/2 RENAME command.

To rename a document with Word:

1. Use the Transfer Load command to open the document you want to rename.
2. Choose the Transfer Rename command.
2. Type a new name for the file in the "filename" field.
3. Press Enter or click the command name. Word changes the name of the file in the lower right corner of the screen.

To rename a document using the DOS or OS/2 RENAME command:

1.   Quit Word if necessary.
2.   At the DOS prompt, type:

rename oldfilename newfilename

For example, to change the name of the BEGIN.DOC file to INTRO.DOC, you would type:

rename BEGIN.DOC INTRO.DOC

3.   Press Enter. Unless you typed a name that's invalid or has already been used (make sure you're in the right directory and using the right disk drive), the operating system changes the filename immediately. Don't wait for a message: when the prompt reappears, the change has been made.

Deleting Documents

To delete a document, you can use Word's Transfer Delete command or the DOS or OS/2 DEL command. You can also use Word's document retrieval system to delete several documents at once. (See Chapter 21 for more information about that.) You can't delete a file that you have open at the time.
   To delete a document with Word:

1.   Choose the Transfer Delete command. (Don't use the Delete command on the main menu which is used to delete text within a document.)
2.   Type the name of the file you want to delete in the "filename" field, or press F1 to see a list of names like those shown in Figure 3-2. Word automatically displays the names of the files ending with .DOC in the active directory on the active disk drive. To see the names of other files, you may need to do one of the following:

To See a Listing of	Do This
Files with .DOC extensions on a different drive (B:, for example)	Type the drive name (B:, for example), then press F1; or

	Press F1, use the arrow keys or the mouse to highlight the drive name in the list ([B:], for example), then press Enter..
Files with .DOC extensions in a different directory (/INVOICES, for example)	Type the directory pathname (/INVOICES, for example), then press F1. Oolder versions of DOS may not allow you to do this.) or press F1, use the arrow keys or the mouse to highlight a directory name in the list ([..] (root) or [INVOICES], for example), and press Enter. Repeat until you find the file you want.
Files with extensions other than .DOC (.LET extensions, for example)	Type an asterisk (*) followed by a period and the extension (*.LET, for example), then press F1.

If you accidentally display a list you don't want, press Esc or click both mouse buttons simultaneously to get back to the "filename" field, then try again.

3. If you typed the filename in the "filename" field, press Enter. If you used F1 to display a list of filenames, press the arrow keys or point and click the left mouse button to highlight the name of the file you want to delete, press F1 to get back to the "filename" field, then press Enter again to delete the file.

    Speed Tip for Mouse Users: You can point to the name of a file in the list and click the right mouse button to select the file and get back to the "filename" field all at once.

    Because deleting a file is serious business, Word asks you to confirm your choice by displaying this message: "Enter Y to confirm deletion of file."

4. Press Y to delete the file.

It's frighteningly easy to delete a file with the DOS or OS/2 DEL command, so be sure that you really want to get rid of the file before you use this next procedure.

To delete a document with the DEL command:
1.   Quit Word if necessary.
2.   At the operating system prompt, type:

del filename

For example, to delete a file named MISTAKE.DOC, you'd type:

del mistake.doc

3.   Press Enter. Unless you've typed a filename that doesn't exist (make sure you're in the right directory and using the right disk drive), the operating system deletes the file immediately. Don't wait for a message. When you see the prompt again, the file has been deleted.

Copying Documents

You can copy a document by using Word's Transfer Save command to save a version with a different name, leaving the original copy intact, or you can use the DOS or OS/2 COPY command. You can also copy several files at once by using Word's document retrieval system. See Chapter 21 for more information about that.
To use the COPY command:

1.   Quit Word if necessary.
2.   At the operating system prompt, type:

copy filename1 filename2

For example, to make a copy of a file named MYFILE.DOC and name the copy YOURFILE.DOC, you'd type:

copy myfile.doc yourfile.doc

To make a copy with the same name on another drive or in another directory, you'd use the same filename, but precede it with a different drive name or directory path. For example, to make a copy of CHAPTER1.DOC in the BOOKS directory on drive C and put the copy in the BACKUP directory on drive B, you'd type:

copy c:\books\chapter1.doc b:\backup\chapter1.doc

3. Press Enter. Unless you've typed an incorrect filename, the operating system copies the file immediately and displays the message "1 file(s) copied."

USING WORD ON A NETWORK

Because many users can open the same file on a network, it's necessary to control the changes each user makes to a file. To do this control, the network assigns one of two attributes to files:

Attribute	Meaning
Read-only	The file can be opened but not changed.
Read-write	The file can be opened and changed.

To prevent making multiple changes to the same file at the same time, only one user on a network may open a file as a read-write file. If Word displays a message telling you that the file is in use when you attempt to open a file, this message means that another user has opened the file for read-write. You can either load the file as a read-only file and save it with a different filename, creating a new file on which you can work, or wait until the file has been closed, then open it to make your changes. When you have opened a file as read-write, you should keep in mind that others cannot use that file until you have closed it.

PART II

Revising

Not many of us are so skilled that we can create a perfect document the first time we enter text. We usually want to go back and edit our documents to delete, add, and rearrange text. Sometimes we have to review the work of others, and add revision marks and annotations. When we're finished making changes, we want to check spelling, maybe use a thesaurus to add variety, and count the words or characters in the finished piece. This part of the book shows you how to do all of these tasks.

EDITING YOUR DOCUMENT

This Chapter Contains the Following:

In addition to adding, deleting, and rearranging your document, you might want to copy text from another document, or work with multiple document windows to view different parts of a long document at the same time. This chapter shows you how to do all these tasks.

SCROLLING AND MOVING THE CURSOR

If your document has more text than will fit in the window, you need to scroll (move the text in the Word window) to see all of your document. You can scroll using keys or the mouse.

Moving the Cursor with Keys

When you scroll with keys, you move the cursor (the highlight) at the same time. To scroll with keys, you'll use the keys on the numeric keypad:

To Scroll	Press This Key
One line up or down	Up or Down arrow
One character right or left	Right or Left arrow
One word right or left	Ctrl+Right or Ctrl+Left arrow
Beginning or end of the line	Home or End
Beginning or end of the text displayed in the window	Ctrl+Home or Ctrl+End
One paragraph up or down	Ctrl+Up or Ctrl+Down
One windowful up or down	PgUp or PgDn
Beginning or end of document	Ctrl+PgUp or Ctrl+PgDn

Using the Numeric Keypad to Type Numbers

You can use the numeric keypad at the right of the keyboard to move the cursor, as described in the previous section, or to type numbers (like on a 10-key calculator). Use the NumLock key to switch between the two uses.

To type numbers on the numeric keypad:

1. Press the NumLock key. "NL" appears in the status area.
2. Type numbers or symbols on the keypad.

To switch back to using the keypad for cursor movement, press the NumLock key again. "NL" disappears from the status area.

Moving with the Mouse

If you're using a mouse, you can click the button on the left and bottom borders of the document window scroll through a document, as shown in Figure 4-1. The left border always serves as a scroll bar, but the bottom border serves as a scroll bar only when your document is too wide to fit in the document window.

If you're running Word in the graphics mode, the mouse pointer becomes a two-headed arrow when it's on one of the scroll bars.

In character (text) mode, the mouse pointer stays a rectangle, no matter where it is on the window.

Figure 4-1.   **The scroll bars allow you to scroll through a document using the mouse.**

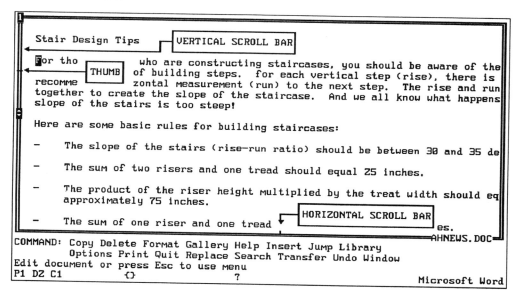

To Scroll	Point to
Down	The left window border, then click the right mouse button.
Up	The left window border, then click the left mouse button.
Right	The bottom window border, then click the right mouse button.
Left	The bottom window border, then click the left mouse button.
To a relative position	The position on the left window border relative to where you want to scroll to in your document, then click both mouse buttons at the same time. For example, if you want to scroll to the middle of your document, point to the middle of the left window border, then press both mouse buttons to scroll to that position.

When you scroll with the mouse, be sure not to confuse the mouse pointer and the text cursor (the highlight)—they're two different objects, as shown in Figure 4-1. The cursor stays in the same location until you click in the document window or use keys to reposition it.

Whether you use keys or the mouse to scroll, the thumb (the tiny horizontal line in the left window border) moves to reflect the position of the text in the window relative to the entire document. For example, when the thumb is near the bottom of the left window border, the text you see in the window is near the end of your document.

USING COMMANDS TO MOVE TO A NEW LOCATION

You can use two of Word's commands, Jump Page and Search, to move the cursor to a new location quickly.

To use the Jump Page command, Word must have already divided your document into pages. Word paginates documents before printing, displaying pages in show layout view or in print preview, or when creating an index or table of contents. If you haven't done any of these things, you'll need to paginate your document with the Print Repaginate command before using the Jump Page command. (You can find out more about controlling pagination in Chapter 14.)

To jump to a specific page:

1. Choose the Jump Page command.
2. In the "page number" field type the page number that you want the cursor to move to.
3. Press Enter or click the command name.

The Search command looks for the next occurrence of a specific word or phrase. You can use this command to jump to a specific spot in your document.

To move the cursor to specific text:

1. Choose the Search command.
2. In the "search for" field, for which you want to search.
3. Press Enter or click the command name.

You can learn more about searching for text later in this chapter.

TYPING OVER EXISTING TEXT

If you want to type new text over existing text, you can use Word's over-type mode. It's this easy:

1. Move the cursor to the beginning of the text you want to type over.
2. Press F5 to turn on overtype mode.
   Word displays "OT" in the status line to remind you that you're in overtype mode.
3. Type over the text.
4. Press F5 to exit from overtype mode.

INCLUDING FOREIGN AND SPECIAL CHARACTERS

If your printer can print the IBM Extended Character Set, you can insert its foreign characters and graphic symbols in your document. If you don't know what your printer can handle, you can run the *character_test.mac* macro, which prints out all characters your computer is capable of in a font you choose. See "Testing the Capabilities of Your Printer" in Chapter 15 for more information about using this macro.

To enter a character from the IBM Extended Character Set, hold down the Alt key and type the number code for the character on the numeric keypad.

SELECTING TEXT: TELLING WORD WHERE TO MAKE CHANGES

Whenever you want to change text (edit or format it) in Word, you:

1. Select the text you want to change.
2. Choose a command or use a key combination to change the selected text.

Selecting text highlights the text so you can easily see what you've selected, as shown in Figure 4-2. The commands you choose affect that text as long as it's highlighted.

Figure 4-2.   **Selecting text.**

```
┌─────────────────────────────────────────────────────────────────────┐
│█                                                                      │
│                                                                       │
│  Stair Design Tips                                                    │
│                                                                       │
│  For those of you who are constructing staircases, you should be aware of the│
│  and run" theory of building steps.  for each vertical step (rise), there is │
│  recommended horizontal measurement (run) to the next step.  The rise and run│
│  together to create the slope of the staircase.  And we all know what happens│
│  slope of the stairs is too steep!                                    │
│                                                                       │
│  Here are some basic rules for building staircases:                   │
│                                                                       │
│  -    The ▓slope of the stairs▓ (rise-run ratio) should be between 30 and 35 de│
│                                                                       │
│  -    The sum of two risers and one tread should equal 25 inches.     │
│                                                                       │
│  -    The product of the riser height multiplied by the treat width should eq│
│       approximately 75 inches.                                        │
│                                                                       │
│  -    The sum of one riser and one tread should equal 17 to 18 inches.│
│                                                          ═══AHNEWS.DOC═│
│COMMAND: Copy Delete Format Gallery Help Insert Jump Library           │
│         Options Print Quit Replace Search Transfer Undo Window      █ │
│Copies selected text to scrap or to a named glossary entry             │
│P1 D2 C28        {}              ?                    Microsoft Word    │
└─────────────────────────────────────────────────────────────────────┘
```

Selecting with Keys

Here's the basic method for selecting text with keys:

• Hold down the Shift key while you move the cursor. See "Moving the Cursor with Keys", earlier in this chapter, for the list of keys that move the cursor.

Here are some other shortcuts:

To Select	Press
Previous word	F7
Next word	F8
Previous sentence	Shift+F7
Next sentence	Shift+F8
Previous paragraph	F9
Next paragraph	F10
Current line	Shift+F9
Entire document	Shift+F10

If you change your mind while selecting and want to start over, just release all the keys, then press an arrow key to remove the highlight.

Extending the Selection Over a Large Area

An alternative to holding down the Shift key is to turn on extend mode, which selects all text over which the cursor moves. This method is especially useful when selecting several pages of text.

To use extend mode:

1. Move the cursor to the beginning of the text you want to select.
2. Press F6. Word displays "EX" in the status area to tell you that extend mode is on.
3. Move the cursor to the end of the text you want to select.
4. Choose a command or action to affect the selected text. If you've made a mistake while selecting and want to start over again, press F6 again to cancel extend mode. Word removes "EX" from the status area, and you're free to move the cursor again without highlighting text.

Selecting a Block of Text

To select a rectangular block of text, such as a column:

1. Move the cursor to one corner of the rectangle you want to select.
2. Press Shift+F6 to turn on column selection. Word displays "CS" in the status area to tell you that you're using column selection mode.
3. Move the cursor to the end of the text you want to select.
4. Choose a command or an action to affect the selected text. If you've changed your mind and want to start over again, press Shift+F6 to turn off column selection mode. Figure 4-3 shows selecting a column of text.

Selecting with the Mouse

Here's the basic procedure to select text with the mouse:

1. Click to position the cursor at the beginning of the text you want to select.
2. Hold down either mouse button while you move the cursor to the end of the text you want to select.

Figure 4-3.   **Selecting a column of text.**

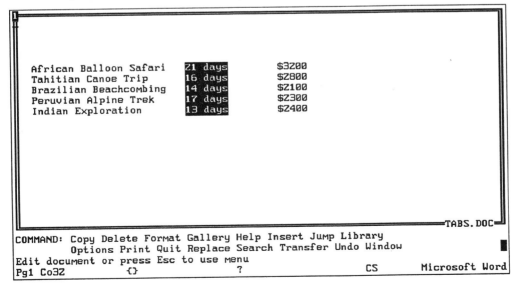

3. When all the text you want is highlighted, release the mouse button.

If you change your mind while selecting and want to start over again, just release the mouse button, then click to remove the highlight and set the cursor at a new location.

Word has many variations for selecting text with the mouse. The procedures for the most useful variations are:

To Select	Do This
One word	Point to the word and click the right mouse button, which selects the word and the following space (if any).
A sentence	Click to set the cursor anywhere in the sentence. Press both mouse buttons simultaneously.
Lines of text	Move the mouse pointer into the selection bar, beside the line you want to select, as shown in Figure 4–4. Click the left mouse button to select one line, or hold down the left button and drag the mouse cursor down the selection bar until you've selected all the lines you want, then release the button.
Paragraphs	Move the mouse pointer into the selection bar, beside the paragraph you want to select, as shown in Figure 4–4.Click the right mouse button to select one paragraph, or hold down the right button and drag the mouse cursor down the selection bar until you've selected all the paragraphs you want, then release the button.
The entire document	Move the mouse pointer into the selection bar. Click both mouse buttons simultaneously.

Extending the Selection Over a Large Area

To select a large amount of text, such as several pages:

1. Position the cursor at the beginning of the text you want to select.
2. Press F6. Word displays "EX" in the status area to tell you that extend mode is on.

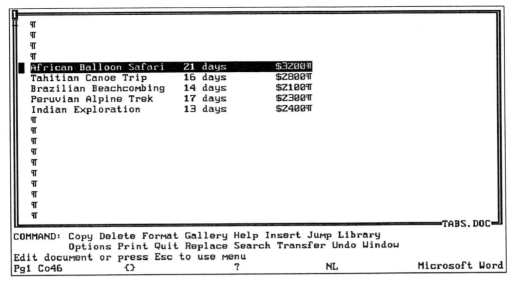

Figure 4-4.   **Using the selection bar to select text with the mouse.**

3. Point to the end of the text you want to select and click either mouse button to highlight the text.

4. Choose a command or action to affect the selected text, or, if you've made a mistake while selecting and want to start over again, press F6 again to cancel extend mode. Word removes the "EX" from the status area, and you're free to move the cursor again without highlighting text.

Selecting a Block of Text
To select a rectangular block of text, such as a column:

1. Click to set the cursor at one corner of the rectangle you want to select.

2. Press Shift+F6 to turn on column selection. Word displays "CS" in the status area to remind you that you're using column selection mode.

3. Point to the end of the text you want to select and click either mouse button to highlight the text.

4. Choose a command or an action to affect the selected text or, if you've changed your mind and want to start over again, press Shift+F6 to turn off column selection mode.

DELETING TEXT

Deleting text in Word is easy. You:

1. Select the text.
2. Press the Del key to erase the text.

If you want to delete text and insert it elsewhere, you should use the Delete command as described in the following section, "Moving Text." If you want to delete text from your document, but save it for later use, you can define it as a *glossary entry*. Then you can use that text again wherever and whenever you want, or delete it at a later time if you decide not to use it. (For more information see "Saving Text and Graphics for Repeated Use: Using Glossaries" later in this chapte.r)

MOVING TEXT

When you move text, you'll use the Delete and Insert commands. When you use the Delete command to remove text, Word moves that text to a temporary holding area called the scrap, where it stays until the next text you remove replaces it. The scrap is represented by the two curly brackets ({ }) shown at the bottom of the window. Word displays the beginning of the scrap's contents between these brackets (Figure 4–5). As long as the text is in the scrap, you can move the cursor to a new location in the same document, or to a different document, then insert the text.
To move text:

1. Select the text you want to move.
2. Choose the Delete command.
3. Press Enter or click the command name. Word removes the selected text from your document and places it in the scrap. You can see the text, or at least the first few words, between the scrap's curly brackets ({ }) at the bottom of the window.
4. Place the cursor where you want to insert the text.

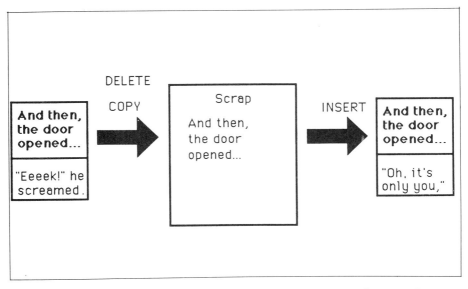

Figure 4-5.   **The Delete, Copy, and Insert commands use the scrap to move text.**

5. Choose the Insert command.
6. Press Enter or click the command name. Word inserts a copy of the text from the scrap.

Replacing Existing Text with Inserted Text

If you want to replace existing text with the new text you insert:

1. Select the text you want to move.
2. Press the Del key.
3. Select the text you want to replace
4. Press Shift+Ins to insert the new text.

Note: If you want to delete text but preserve the information that's in the scrap, select the text to delete, then press Shift+Delete.

COPYING TEXT

If you've typed a phrase, paragraph, or several pages of text that you want to use in another location, you can copy that text and insert it in another

---

Keyboard Shortcut

You can quickly move text without choosing commands. To insert new text in front of existing text:

1.   Select the text you want to move.
2.   Press the Del key.
3.   Place the cursor where you want to insert the text.
4.   Press the Ins key to insert the text.

Mouse Shortcut

To use the mouse to move text quickly without using the scrap:

1.   Select the text to move.
2.   Insert the text using the following table as a guide:

To Insert in Front of	Point Here	Hold Down the Ctrl key and Click This Button
Character	In window	Left
Word		Right
Sentence		Both
Line	In selection bar	Left
Paragraph		Right
Beginning of document		Both

place without affecting the original text. You can copy text to a new location within the same document or to a different document.
   To copy text and insert the copy in a new location:

1.   Select the text you want to copy.
2.   Choose the Copy command.

3. Press Enter. Word places a copy of the selected text in the scrap. You can see the text, or at least the first few words, between the scrap's curly brackets ({ }) at the bottom of the window.
4. Place the cursor where you want to insert the copy.
5. Choose the Insert command.
6. Press Enter. Word inserts a copy of the text from the scrap.

Speed Tip: You can press the Ins key to quickly insert text from the scrap instead of using the Insert command. As long as the text you want is in the scrap, you can use the Insert command (or press Ins) to insert a copy as many times as you like.

If you want to use the same text often, you can save that text as a glossary entry and insert it wherever and whenever you like. (See "Saving Text and Graphics for Repeated Use: Using Glossaries" later in this chapter for more information.)

Helpful Hint

Deleting text to the scrap is always somewhat risky, because the text in the scrap is replaced when you delete something else. You can easily and safely move text to a new location by temporarily assigning text to a key as follows:

1. Select the text to move.
2. Choose the Delete command.
3. In the "to" field, press a key that's easy to remember, such as the zero (0) key, then press Enter. This step assigns the deleted text to that key (you're actually creating a glossary entry, which you'll learn more about later in this chapter).
4. Move the cursor to the new location.
5. Choose the Insert command.
6. In the "from" field, press the key you assigned the text to, then press Enter. Word inserts the text assigned to that key.

When you quit Word, you'll see the message "Type Y to save changes to glossary, N to lose changes, or Esc to cancel." Word is asking you if you want to save the text -to-key assignments you made using this procedure. Press N to throw away the temporary assignments.

Keyboard Shortcut

To quickly copy text without using a command:

1. Select the text you want to copy.
2. Press Alt+F3.
3. Move the cursor to where you want to insert the text.
4. Press the Ins key.

Mouse Shortcut

To use the mouse to quickly copy text without using the scrap:

1. Select the text to copy.
2. Insert the text using the following table as a guide:

To Insert in Front of	Point Here	Hold Down the Shift Key and Click This Button
Character	In window	Left
Word		Right
Sentence		Both
Line	In selection bar	Left
Paragraph		Right
Beginning of document		Both

UNDOING A CHANGE

Everyone knows that "oh, no!" feeling that you get when you've made a mistake. You've just deleted text you should have kept, moved a phrase to the wrong place, or chosen the wrong command. When this happens to you, don't panic. Word has made allowances for mistakes, and there is practically nothing you can do in Word that can't be undone.

If you realize your mistake immediately after you've made it, you can use Word's wonderful Undo command. The Undo command can, in most cases, reverse your last action.

To undo the last action:

• Choose the Undo command.

If you've just done something that Word can't undo, Word beeps and displays a message telling you the action can't be undone. In that case, you can probably choose a different command to correct the problem. If you haven't made many changes since you last saved the file, you could also use the Transfer Clear All command to clear the file from Word's memory without saving the changes, then load the last version of the file and start over.

SAVING TEXT AND GRAPHICS FOR REPEATED USE: USING GLOSSARIES

Do you have an address, a letterhead, or a complicated phrase that you need to use over and over again in your documents? Word lets you save a few characters, a couple of paragraphs, or even several pages of text as entries in a *glossary*. Using a glossary is like renting a safety deposit box—you can put the entries you want to keep in it, then open it up and take out the entries any time you like.

Almost anything can be kept in a glossary, from one character to a whole document. You can store graphics by copying the .G. paragraph that creates them (you'll learn more about graphics in Chapter 12). You can even store formatting in glossaries by storing paragraph marks, division marks, and so forth. You'll learn more about that in later sections of this book. Keep in mind, though, that the more information Word has to keep track of, the slower the program runs, so you should only store those entries that you really want to save. You can always delete entries from glossaries, if they become too full.

You'll use Word's Delete, Copy, and Insert commands to work with glossary entries.

Creating Glossary Entries

To save text as a glossary entry:

1. Select the text you want to save as a glossary entry.
2. Choose the Copy command to put a copy of the text in the glossary (and leave the original in your document), or choose the Delete command to erase the text from your document and put it in a glossary.
3. In the "to" field, type a name for your glossary entry. For example, if you were saving your company logo, you might type *logo*. Keep the name short (you can use just one character, or up to 31 characters in a name), but descriptive enough so that you can remember it or recognize it in a list.
4. Press Enter or click the command name.

Displaying Glossary Entries

You can display a list of glossary entries from which to choose by using the following procedure:

1. Choose the Insert command.
2. In the "from" field, press the F1 key.

Word displays a list of glossary entries, as shown in Figure 4-6, even if you've never saved any entries of your own. These are entries that come with Word in its standard glossary file—you can see a description of what they do below.

Word comes with a standard glossary file, NORMAL.GLY, which contains the following glossary entries you can use in all your documents:

Name	Description
Page	Inserts (page), which Word replaces with a page number when printing.
Footnote	Inserts an automatic footnote number (used when you've accidentally deleted one).
Date	Inserts the current date.
Dateprint	Inserts (dateprint), which Word replaces with the date when printing.
Time	Inserts the current time.

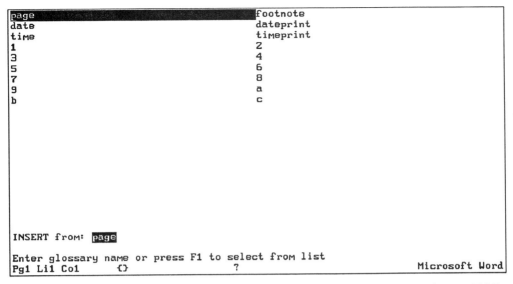

```
page                                     footnote
date                                     dateprint
time                                     timeprint
1                                        2
3                                        4
5                                        6
7                                        8
9                                        a
b                                        c




INSERT from: page

Enter glossary name or press F1 to select from list
Pg1 Li1 Co1      {}                    ?              Microsoft Word
```

Figure 4-6.   **A list of glossary entries supplied with Word in the NOR-MAL.GLY file.**

| Timeprint | Inserts (timeprint), which Word replaces with the time when printing. |
| Clipboard | Inserts the contents of the Clipboard (used only when running Word from Microsoft Windows). |

You'll learn more about how to use these entries, as well as how to add your own entries, later in this chapter. We'll also mention the use of these glossary entries throughout this book.

Glossary entries are kept in glossary files. You can create many different glossary files. For example, you might create one containing legal phrases, called LEGAL.GLY, one containing math symbols, called MATH.GLY, and so forth. Then you can open the glossary file you want and use the entries in it for your documents.

Saving a Glossary File

You can choose to add the entries you've defined to Word's standard glossary file, NORMAL.GLY (which automatically makes them available to all documents), or you can save them in a different glossary file you name.

If you save your entries in a different glossary, you'll have to open that file when you want to use those entries.

Saving Glossary Entries in the NORMAL.GLY File
To save glossary entries in the NORMAL.GLY file:

1. Choose the Transfer Glossary Save command.
2. Make sure the "filename" field contains "NORMAL.GLY."
3. Press Enter or click the command name.

If you quit Word without saving changes to the glossary, Word displays the message "Enter Y to save glossary, N to lose edits, or Esc to cancel." Press Y to save your entries in the current glossary file.

Saving Glossary Entries in a File You Specify
If you don't want to save your entries in the NORMAL.GLY file, but you want to create a new, specialized glossary file instead:

1. After defining all the glossary entries you want, choose the Transfer Glossary Save command.
2. Type a name for your glossary in the "filename" field. Use the .GLY extension to let Word know this is a glossary file, or don't type an extension and let Word automatically add .GLY to the filename. For example, you could type *math.gly* to name a mathematics glossary file, or you could just type *math* and let Word add the .GLY extension to name the file MATH.GLY.
3. Press Enter or click the command name, thereby saving in the new file all the entries that were in the NORMAL.GLY file, plus any entries you've added.

From now on, when you want to use your new glossary, you'll need to open it using the Transfer Glossary Merge command, as explained in "Opening a Glossary File" later in this chapter.

Inserting Entries from a Glossary

When you've saved an entry in a glossary, you can insert that entry into your documents any time you like.

To insert a glossary entry:

1. Place the cursor where you want to insert the entry.
2. Choose the Insert command.
3. Type the name of the glossary entry you want, or press F1 to see a list of glossary entries, then use the arrow keys or the mouse to select the one you want.
4. Press Enter to insert the entry in your document.

Keyboard Shortcut

If you know the name of the glossary entry you want, you can insert it without choosing any commands:

1. Place the cursor where you want to insert the entry.
2. Type the name of the entry. For example, if you want to put the date into your document, you could type *date*, or if you have your company logo stored in a glossary entry named "logo," type *logo*. Don't worry about inserting the entry name in your document—this will be fixed in the next step.
3. Press F3. Word replaces the entry name with the contents of the entry. Magic! If Word *doesn't* replace the name, you either mistyped the entry name, or that entry is not in the glossary file you're using.

Helpful Hint

Because you can save a complete document as a glossary entry, you might consider saving common forms such as memos, invoices, and letters as glossary entries. Just type and format the text that stays the same in a blank document, leave space for the information that changes, then save the entire document as a glossary entry.

Then, when you need to use the form again, just insert the entry, fill in the appropriate blank areas, and print. You'll always have the right format because the glossary entry doesn't change.

Example: Using a Glossary Entry

You frequently use your name and address in letters, so you'd like to save something similar to the following as a glossary entry:

> Dr. Peabody Peabrain
> 4905 Esquire Estates
> Upperclass, NY 87022

1. Type and format the name and address, then select them.
2. Choose the Copy or Delete command and type *address* in the "to" field.
3. Press Enter or click the command name.
4. Write your letters. At the end of each letter, choose the Insert command, type *address* in the "from" field, and press F3 to insert the glossary entry.
5. Save the glossary when you quit Word so that you can use the address entry the next time you write a letter.

Inserting the Same Glossary Entry Several Times

If you need to insert the same glossary entry several places in the same document:

1. Insert it once.
2. Move the cursor to the next location.
3. Press F4 or click the word COMMAND in the menu to repeat the insertion. (Pressing the F4 key or clicking COMMAND repeats the last action.)
4. Repeat steps 2 and 3 to insert the same entry as many times as you like.

Opening a Glossary File

Word automatically uses the NORMAL.GLY file, so if you've saved your entries in that file, you don't need to worry about opening a glossary file— Word does it for you.

Helpful Hints

Using Key Assignments to Speed Up Typing

Using a temporary glossary entry can be a real timesaver when you have to type a complicated group of words several times in a document.

For example, when you're typing a document in which the phrase "Consumer Conglomerate, Inc." appears several times. To save time, not to mention wear and tear on your fingers, type the phrase once, select it, then choose the Insert command and press an easy-to-remember key as the glossary name (the 8 key, for example). Think of this process as assigning the selected text to a key.

Then, when you need to type the phrase again, just use the Insert command to insert the text quickly. For example, if you assigned the text to the 8 key, you'd press Esc, I, 8, Enter (Esc=command mode, I=Insert command, 8=glossary entry named 8, Enter=carry out the command) to insert the glossary entry in a fraction of a second. You can assign as many entries to keys as you like (you may want to write down the key assignments if you use several), then use them when appropriate.

Using Key Assignments when Moving Text

Assigning text to a key is a safer way to move text than putting it in the scrap, especially if you're moving text between documents. Just select the text you want to move, choose the Delete command, press a key you want to assign the text to, then press Enter. Move the cursor to the new position, choose Insert, then press the key you assigned to the text to insert the text in the new position.

If you've saved entries in a specialized glossary file using the Transfer Glossary Save command, and you want to use those entries as well as the ones in NORMAL.GLY, you'll have to open that glossary file to use the entries.

To open a glossary file other than NORMAL.GLY:

1.   Choose the Transfer Glossary Load command.

2. In the "filename" field type the name of the glossary file you want to open, or press F1 to see a list of files ending with .GLY. Use the arrow keys or the mouse to highlight the file you want.
3. Press Enter or click the command name to open the file. Now you can use the entries in both the NORMAL.GLY file and in the specialized glossary file.

Merging Glossary Entries

If you want to combine two glossary files you've created (glossaries other than NORMAL.GLY), you can merge the entries using the Transfer Glossary Merge command. If any of the entries in the two files have the same name, the entries loaded last will take the place of already-loaded entries with the same name.

If you want to keep the two files merged, save the glossary file by using the Transfer Glossary Save command or by answering Yes to the "Enter Y to save glossary, N to lose edits, or Esc to cancel" message when you quit Word. Otherwise, the files remain combined only until you quit Word.

To merge two glossary files:

1. Use the Transfer Glossary Load command to load the first glossary file, as described in "Opening a Glossary File" earlier in this chapter.
2. Choose the Transfer Glossary Merge command.
3. In the "filename" field, type the name of second glossary file (including any drive and path names Word needs to find the file), or press F1 to display a list of glossary files, then select the file you want.
4. Press Enter to merge the two files.

Changing a Glossary Entry

You can change the contents of a glossary entry. You might want to make a change if you didn't select everything you wanted the entry to contain, or if you've decided to change the text or format of the entry.

To change a glossary entry:

1. Insert the glossary entry, if necessary, then make the changes you want and select the text you want the entry to contain.

2. Choose the Copy command to copy the selected text to the entry, or choose the Delete command to erase the selected text from your document and put it in the glossary entry.
3. In the "to" field, type the name of the entry you want to contain the selected text, or press F1, then highlight the name in the list.
4. Press Enter. Word displays a message asking you if you want to replace the glossary entry with the new text.
5. Press Y. Word replaces the entry's contents with the selected text.

Deleting a Glossary Entry

You can delete entries you no longer use from a glossary. Word does not allow you to delete entries that it supplies in the NORMAL.GLY file, such as "time" or "dateprint,"—the program doesn't even display these entries when you press F1 to see a list from which to delete.

To delete a glossary entry:

1. Choose the Transfer Glossary Clear command.
2. In the "names" field type the names, separated by commas, of the entries you want to delete or press F1 to display the list of glossary entries. Highlight the name of the entry you want to delete. To highlight several names at once, click the left mouse button on the names.
3. Press Enter. Word displays the message "Enter Y to erase glossary names."
4. Press Y.

If you've deleted entries from the NORMAL.GLY file, be sure to press Y when Word asks you if you want to save the glossary before quitting. If you've deleted entries from another glossary file, use the Transfer Glossary Save command to save the glossary file before quitting.

Printing Glossaries

To keep track of entries in glossaries, you can print glossary files for easy reference.
To print a glossary:

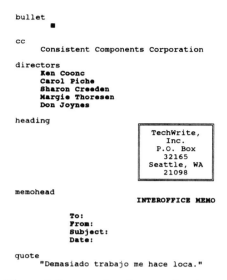

```
bullet
          ■

cc
          Consistent Components Corporation

directors
          Ken Coonc
          Carol Piche
          Sharon Creeden
          Margie Thoresen
          Don Joynes

heading
                        TechWrite,
                          Inc.
                        P.O. Box
                          32165
                        Seattle, WA
                          21098

memohead
                   INTEROFFICE MEMO

          To:
          From:
          Subject:
          Date:

quote
          "Demasiado trabajo me hace loca."
```

Figure 4-7.   **A printout of a glossary file.**

1. Use the Transfer Glossary Load command to load the glossary file
   you want to print.
2. Choose the Print Glossary command.

In the printed document, page breaks are indicated by <page> and
division marks by <division> . Figure 4-7 shows a printout of a glossary
file.

SEARCHING FOR AND REPLACING TEXT AND FORMATTING

Word has two commands that search for text and special characters:

Command	Description
Search	Searches for the first occurrence of text or special characters you specify.
Replace	Searches for the first occurrence of text or special characters you specify, and replaces it with the new text you specify.

You can quickly search for a word, a phrase, or even a hidden formatting character with these commands, and you can replace occurrences of the text one by one, or replace all occurrences at once.

Word also has six commands that search for formatting (bold, italic, indents, line spacing, etc.):

Command	Description
Format sEarch Character	Searches for the first occurrence of the character formatting you specify.
Format sEarch Paragraph	Searches for the first occurrence of the paragraph formatting you specify.
Format sEarch Style	Searches for the first occurrence of the style you specify.
Format repLace Character	Searches for the first occurrence of the character formatting you specify, and replaces it with the character formatting you specify.
Format repLace Paragraph	Searches for the first occurrence of the paragraph formatting you specify, and replaces it with the paragraph formatting you specify.
Format repLace Style	Searches for the first occurrence of the style you specify, and replaces it with the style you specify.

Word begins every search at the cursor position, so you may want to reposition the cursor before you begin a search. You can ask Word to search from the cursor position to the end of the document (down), or to search from the cursor position to the beginning of the document (up).

If you want to confine searches or replacements to a specific part of your document, select that part before choosing a command. If you want the search or replacements to apply to the entire document, make sure nothing is selected before choosing the command.

Searching for Text

Word can search for any text characters (letters, numbers, spaces, and punctuation you can type in a document. If you want to search for text that's formatted as hidden text, you need to display it first by choosing

Yes in the "show hidden text" field of the Options command. Word won't find any text in a document that doesn't appear on the screen.

To search for text:

1. Choose the Search command. Word displays the command fields shown in Figure 4-8.
2. Type the text which you want to search in the "text" field. To search for spaces, just press the spacebar once for each space. Be sure to type *exactly* the text you want to search. If you type two spaces between words in a phrase, for example, Word won't find the phrase with just one space between words in your document. Every rule has an exception: There is one case in which you don't have to type exactly the text you want to search. You can use a question mark (?) to take the place of any character in a word when searching. When you want to search for a question mark itself, however, you'll have to type a caret (^) before the question mark character as follows:

To Search for	Type
Any character in a word	? (For example, type t?o to find two and too.)
Question mark	^?

3. In the "direction" field, choose Down (the default choice) to search from the cursor position to the end of the document, or choose Up to search to the beginning of the document.
4. Choose the following options if desired:

Choose	If You Want to
Yes in the "case" field	Match uppercase and lowercase letters exactly when searching. For example, you might want to search for *United* or *UNITED* but not *united*. If you choose No in this field, Word searches for all occurrences of the letters you type.
Yes in the "whole word" field	Search only for a whole word, not just part of a word. For example, if you choose No in this field and you type *are* in the "text" field, Word might find and display matches such as hare, wares, arena, aren't, because all these words contain the letters you're searching.

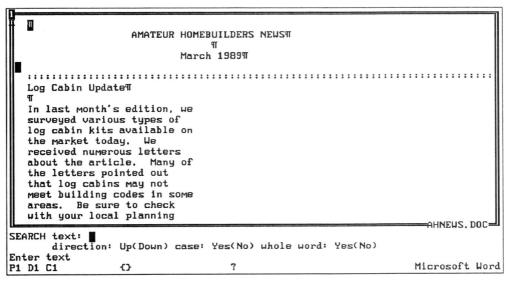

Figure 4-8.   **The Search command fields.**

4. Press Enter or click the command name to begin the search.
    Word highlights the first occurrence of the text you specified, or, if it
    reaches the end of the file before finding an occurrence, Word dis-
    plays the message "Search text not found."
5. If you want to search for the next occurrence of the same text, press
    Shift+F4.

Searching for Special Characters

You can search for a variety of special formatting characters by typing
the following in the Search or Replace command fields.

To Indicate	Type
Tab mark	^t
Paragraph mark	^p
Newline mark	^n
Section mark	^d
Optional hyphen	^-

Caret or circumflex   ^^

Nonbreaking space   ^s

Division mark or page break   ^d

White space (any combination   ^w
of spaces, tab characters,
paragraph marks, and page
break marks, etc.—the parts of
your document that are blank
when printed.)

Searching for Character and Paragraph Formatting

Word not only can search for specific characters, but it can also search for character formatting, such as bold, italic, or small capitals, and for paragraph formatting, such as indents, line spacing, and alignments. You'll learn more about character formatting in Chapter 7, and more about paragraph formatting in Chapter 8. To search for character and paragraph formatting, Word uses the Format sEarch Character and Format sEarch Paragraph commands.

To search for character or paragraph formatting:

1. Choose the Format sEarch command (Esc, F, E).
2. Choose Character or Paragraph. Word searches for either character formatting or for paragraph formatting. It can't search for both at the same time.

   When you choose Character or Paragraph, Word displays the command fields for the Format Character or Format Paragraph commands.
3. Choose options in the fields to specify the formats for which you want to search. For example, if you chose Character and you want to search for bold text, choose Yes in the "bold" field; or if you chose Paragraph and you want to search for a centered paragraph, choose Center in the "alignment" field.
4. Press Enter to begin searching.

   Word highlights the first text it finds with the same format.
5. Press Shift+F4 if you want to search again for the next occurrence.

Searching for Styles

Styles are named sets of character, paragraph, and division formats that you can create and apply to text in your documents. You can learn more about styles in Chapter 11.
   To search for styles:

1.   Choose the Format sEarch Style command (Esc, F, E, S).
2.   In the "keycode" field, type the letter code associated with the style.
3.   In the "direction" field, choose Up to search from the cursor position to the beginning of the document, or choose Down to search to the end.
4.   Press Enter or click the command name to begin the search.
      Word highlights the first paragraph it finds with the specified style.
5.   Press Shift+F4 to search for the next occurrence.

Replacing Text and Special Characters

To replace existing text or special characters:

1.   Choose the Replace command. Word displays the command fields shown in Figure 4-9.
2.   In the "text" field, type the text or special characters for which you want to search. Refer to the previous sections, "Searching for Text" and "Searching for Special Formatting Characters" if you need instructions about what you can type in this field.
3.   In the "with text" field, type the new text or special characters you want to substitute for the old text or characters. You use the same characters to indicate text and special characters whether you're searching for, or replacing with the characters you type. Refer to the previous sections, "Searching for Text" and "Searching for Special Formatting Characters" if you need instructions about what you can type in this field.
4.   In the "confirm" field, choose Yes if you want to approve each replacement before Word makes the change, or choose No if you want Word to make all the changes automatically.

5. Choose the following options if desired:

Choose	If You Want to
Yes in the "whole word" field	Search for and replace only a whole word, not just part of a word.
Yes in the "case" field	Match uppercase and lowercase letters exactly.

6. Press Enter to begin the replacements. If you chose Yes in the "confirm" field, Word highlights each occurrence it finds and asks you if you want to replace it. Press Y for Yes or N for No, and Word automatically goes on to the next occurrence. Press Esc if you want to quit the replacement process. If you chose No in the "confirm" field, Word makes all the replacements, then displays the number of replacements in the message line. If this number looks suspiciously high, either, choose the Undo command immediately or check your replacements, then reverse the text you typed in the "text" and "with text" fields to undo the replacements.

Figure 4-9.   **The Replace command fields.**

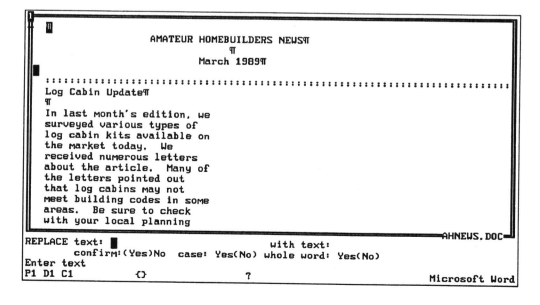

Example: Replacing Special Characters

Suppose you've pressed the spacebar four times at the beginning of each paragraph in your document to indent the first line of the paragraphs. Later, you decide to replace the spaces with tabs. Instead of deleting the spaces in each paragraph individually, you can:

1. Choose the Replace command.
2. In the "text" field, type ^*p*, then four spaces (press the spacebar four times) to search for the spaces. The ^p stands for the paragraph mark that ends the preceding paragraph—including ^p ensures that only spaces at the beginning of a paragraph will be replaced.
3. Type ^*p*^*t* in the text field to replace the spaces with a tab character. Including the ^p ensures that the paragraph mark ending the preceding paragraph is not deleted.
4. Press Enter to begin making the changes.

Helpful Hint

To enter text faster with fewer mistakes, substitute a two- or three-character code for long words or phrases that you type often. For example, instead of typing *Consistent Components Corporation* several times in a memo, just type *ccc* then use the Replace command later to replace *ccc* with Consistent Components Corporation.

When you choose a code like this, be sure to choose a letter or number combination that doesn't occur other places in your document, such as *qq, xx, p9*, or any character repeated several times: *www,]]], \\\, %%*, and so forth.

Replacing Character or Paragraph Formatting

To replace character or paragraph formatting, you'll use the Format replace command. For example, you might want to change all bold characters to italic, or change all double-spaced paragraphs to single-spaced.

To replace character or paragraph formatting:

1. Choose the Format repLace command (Esc, F, L).
2. Choose Character or Paragraph. Word searches for either character formatting or for paragraph formatting: It can't search for both at the same time. When you choose Character or Paragraph, Word displays the command fields for the Format Character or Format Paragraph commands.
3. Choose options in the fields to specify the formats for which you want to search. For example, if you chose Character and you want to search for bold text, choose Yes in the "bold" field; or if you chose Paragraph and you want to search for a centered paragraph, choose Center in the "alignment" field.
4. Press Enter. Word displays the command fields again, preceded by the words "REPLACE FORMATTING WITH." Choose the formats with which you want to replace the old formatting.
5. In the "confirm" field, choose Yes if you want to approve each replacement before it's made. Choose No if you want Word to make all of the replacements automatically.
6. Press Enter to begin the replacements.

    If you chose Yes in the "confirm" field, Word highlights each occurrence it finds and asks you if you want to replace it. Press Y for Yes or N for No, and Word automatically goes on to the next occurrence. Press Esc if you want to quit the replacement process.

    If you chose No in the "confirm" field, Word makes all the replacements, then displays the number of replacements in the message line. If this number looks suspiciously high, check your replacements.

Replacing Styles

To replace styles:

1. Choose the Format repLace Style command (Esc, F, L, S).
2. In the "keycode" field, type the letter code associated with the existing style.
3. In the "with keycode" field, type the letter code of the style with which you want to replace the existing style.

4. In the "confirm" field, choose Yes if you want to approve each re-
    placement before it's made. Choose No if you want Word to make all
    the replacements automatically.
5. Press Enter to begin the replacements.

   If you chose Yes in the "confirm" field, Word highlights each occurrence it finds and asks you if you want to replace it. Press Y for
Yes or N for No, and Word automatically goes on to the next occurrence. Press Esc if you want to quit the replacement process.

   If you chose No in the "confirm" field, Word makes all the replacements, then displays the number of replacements in the message line.
If this number looks suspiciously high, check your replacements.

WORKING WITH MORE THAN ONE WINDOW

There are times you'll want to have more than one document open at a
time. You might just want to refer to another document to see what you've
written, or you might want to copy or move text between documents.
When you're working with a long document, you also might find it convenient to be able to see more than one part of your document at a time.
Word lets you work with multiple documents or display multiple views
of the same document by splitting the Word window into several different
windows.

   You can have up to eight windows open on the screen, each displaying
different documents or different parts of the same document, as shown in
Figures 4-10 and 4-11. Normally, however, you'll probably just want to
have two or three windows open at a time so that you can easily read the
text in each window.

   You can use the keys or the mouse to scroll text in each of the windows.
All of Word's editing and formatting commands work just the same in a
small window as they do in the standard Word window. To make writing
and editing easier, you can make any of the windows full-size when you
want. (See "Making Windows Full Size" later in this chapter.) You can
also easily move text back and forth between documents by copying or
deleting text to the scrap or to a glossary in one window, then moving the
cursor to the next window and inserting the text.

```
1
  African Balloon Safari    21 days     $3200¶
  Tahitian Canoe Trip       16 days     $2800¶
  Brazilian Beachcombing    14 days     $2100¶
  Peruvian Alpine Trek      17 days     $2300¶
                                            ═══TABS.DOC═
2
  Log Cabin Update¶
  ¶
  In last month's edition, we
  surveyed various types of
  log cabin kits available on
                                          ═══AHNEWS.DOC═
3
      -    more vacation time (a minimum of 4 weeks per year)¶
      -    better benefits¶
      -    more office parties¶
  ¶
  If you don't meet our demands, we'll have to consider what
  to do next.¶
                                            ═══MEMO.DOC═
COMMAND: Copy Delete Format Gallery Help Insert Jump Library
         Options Print Quit Replace Search Transfer Undo Window
Edit document or press Esc to use menu
Pg1 Co12             {requests}         ?              MR    Microsoft Word
```

Figure 4-10.   **Horizontal windows.**

Figure 4-11.   **Vertical windows.**

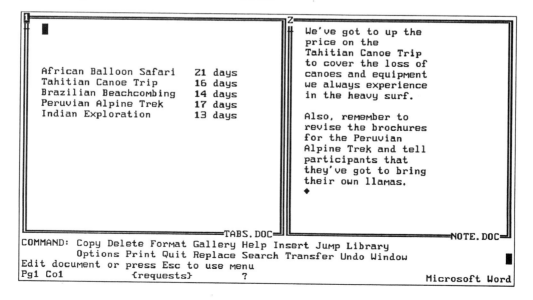

```
1                                    2
  ■                                    We've got to up the
                                       price on the
                                       Tahitian Canoe Trip
                                       to cover the loss of
  African Balloon Safari   21 days     canoes and equipment
  Tahitian Canoe Trip      16 days     we always experience
  Brazilian Beachcombing   14 days     in the heavy surf.
  Peruvian Alpine Trek     17 days
  Indian Exploration       13 days     Also, remember to
                                       revise the brochures
                                       for the Peruvian
                                       Alpine Trek and tell
                                       participants that
                                       they've got to bring
                                       their own llamas.
                                       ◆

                       ═══TABS.DOC═                  ═══NOTE.DOC═
COMMAND: Copy Delete Format Gallery Help Insert Jump Library
         Options Print Quit Replace Search Transfer Undo Window
Edit document or press Esc to use menu
Pg1 Co1             {requests}         ?                 Microsoft Word
```

Opening Another Window

You open another window by splitting an existing Word window into two. You can display up to three windows vertically or up to eight windows horizontally on the screen, provided that your screen has enough space to display the borders, selection bar and style bar, and at least one character. Word numbers all the windows on the screen. Each window's number is displayed in the upper left corner of the window.

Before you can split a window, you must have the window borders displayed. If you've removed window borders, display them again by choosing the Options command, then choosing Yes in the "show window borders" field.

Word displays the same document in the new window unless you clear the window before opening it, or load a new document into it after it's opened.

To split a Word window, into two, using the keys:

1. Choose the Window Split command.
2. Choose Horizontal if you want to create stacked windows like those shown in Figure 4-10, or choose Vertical if you want to create side-by-side windows like those in Figure 4-11.
3. In the "at line" field (for horizontal windows) or the "at column" field (for vertical windows), type the number of the line or column where you want Word to split the screen. For example, if your screen displays 30 lines of text and you're creating horizontal windows, you might type *15* in the "at line" field to make Word split the window in half horizontally. If your screen displays 80 columns of text and you're creating side-by-side windows, you might type *40* to make Word split the window in half vertically. You can also press F1 to display a highlight in the window border, then use the arrow keys to move the highlight to where you want to split the window.
4. If you want the new window to be empty so you can create a new document, choose Yes in the "clear" field. Otherwise, Word displays the same document in the new window. You can always clear the window or load a new document into it later, so in most cases you'll want to leave this field alone.
5. Press Enter to split the window.

To split a Word window, into two, using the mouse:

1. To split a window horizontally, point to the right window border where you want the split to appear. To split a window vertically, point to the top window border where you want the split to appear.
2. Click the left mouse button to split the window.

Working with Two or More Views of the Same Document

You can use multiple windows to see different parts of the same document, as shown in Figure 4-12. For example, you might want to see both the beginning and the end of your document to see if you've used the same phrasing, or view the location from which you want to delete text and the location to where you want to move that text.

You'll find that working with different views of your document is easier than scrolling through a long document. You should also keep in mind that you're working on the same document, even though you may see different parts of that document in different windows. If you make changes to your document using three different windows, you're still changing just one document. Any change you make in one window affects the same

Figure 4-12.   **Viewing two parts of the same document.**

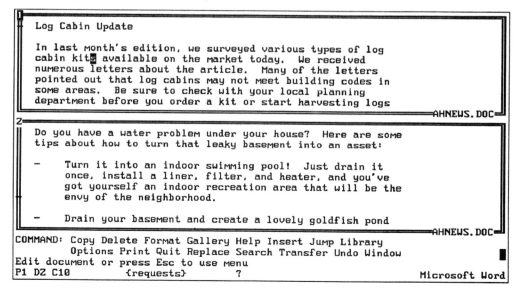

document in all windows, even though you may not see the change everywhere if you're looking at different parts of the document.

Moving the Cursor Between Windows

You can only make changes to the document in the window that contains the cursor—the active window.

To move the cursor to another window with the keys, you should make sure you're in edit mode (no commands are highlighted), then:

- Press F1 to move the cursor to the next window in the numerical sequence. Word highlights the number of the active window.

To move the cursor to another window using the mouse:

- Point to the window number in the upper left corner of the window and click the left mouse button. You can also move the cursor to a new window and select text at the same time by clicking the left button inside the text area in a window.

Loading a Document into a Window

To open a document in a window:

1. Move the cursor to that window. Word highlights the window number.
2. Use the Transfer Load command to create a new document or to load an existing document.

For more information about creating new documents or opening existing documents, see "Creating a New Document" or "Opening Existing Files" in Chapter 3.

If you've made any changes to the document in the window (even if you've only pressed the spacebar or the Enter key), Word asks you if you want to save it before loading the document.

Changing the Size of Windows

When you have multiple windows open, you can change the size of a window by moving its right and bottom borders if there is another window in an appropriate position to adjust to the changes. Word doesn't allow blank space around a window. In other words, you can't move the right border of a window unless there is another window to the right that will take up the remaining space. You can't move the bottom border of a window unless there's another window below.

To change the size of a window with keys:

1. Choose the Window Move command.
2. In the "window #" field, type the number of the window you want to change.
3. If you want to move the window's bottom border, move to the "to row" field, then:

    • Type a row number in the field.

    or

    • Press F1 to put a highlight in the window's right border. Use the arrow keys to move the highlight to where you want the border to be, then press Enter.

4. If you want to move the right window border, move to the "to column" field, then:

    • Type a column number in the field.

    or

    • Press F1 to put a highlight in the bottom window border. Use the arrow keys to move the highlight to where you want the border to be, then press Enter.

5. Press Enter to redraw the window.

To change the size of a window using the mouse:

1. Point to the lower right corner of the window.

2. Hold down either mouse button and drag the window to a new size.
3. Release the mouse button to redraw the window.

Note: Because you must move the lower right corner of a window, you can't change the size of the lower right window by moving the borders. You have to change the size of other windows above and to the left of it to adjust it to the size you want.

Making Windows Full Size

Why try to scroll around and select text in a teeny-tiny window? You can make any window on your screen full size (sometimes called *zooming a window*) when you want. When you make a window full size, the other open windows stay behind the full-size window. You can quickly switch a window back and forth between full-size and its original size.

You can't split a window that you've "zoomed" in this way. If you choose the Quit command while a window is zoomed, Word reduces the window to its original size and then asks you if you want to save changes before quitting.

To make a window full size using the keys:

1. Move the cursor to the window you want to change.
2. Press Ctrl+F1.
   Word displays "ZM" in the status area to remind you that the window has been "zoomed" and that other windows are behind it.
3. When you're ready to return the window to its original size, press Ctrl+F1 again.

To make a window full-size with the mouse:

1. Point to the window number in the upper left corner of the window.
2. Click the right mouse button.
   Word displays "ZM" in the status area to remind you that the window has been "zoomed" and that other windows are behind it.
3. When you're ready to return the window to its original size, click the right mouse button on the window number again.

Closing Windows

When you have multiple windows open on the screen and you close one, Word resizes the remaining windows.

To close a window using keys:

1. Choose the Window Close command.
2. Type the number of the window you want to close.
3. Press Enter or click the command name.
   If you've changed the document in the window, Word asks you if you want to save the changes before closing the window.

To close a window using the mouse:

1. Point to the top border or to the right border of the window you want to close.
2. Click both mouse buttons simultaneously.
   If you've changed the document in the window, Word asks you if you want to save the changes before closing the window.

Saving Changes in All Windows at Once

You can use one command to save all of the changes in all of your open documents at once.
   To save changes in all open documents:

• Choose the Transfer Allsave command.

USING REVISION MARKS AND ANNOTATIONS

This Chapter Contains the Following:

Using Revision Marks
  Turning on Revision Marking
  Turning off Revision Marking
  Approving Revisions One by One
  Making All Marked Changes and Removing Revision Marks
  Rejecting All Marked Changes and Removing Revision Marks
Using Annotations
  Moving Between Annotation Marks and Annotation Text
  Using an Annotation Window
  Opening the Footnote/Annotation Window
  Closing the Footnote/Annotation Window
  Editing and Formatting Annotations
  Editing Annotation Text
  Editing an Annotation Mark
  Formatting Annotation Text
  Formatting Annotation Marks
  Controlling Where the Annotation Text Prints
  Moving Annotations
  Deleting Annotations
  Consolidating Annotations
  Using annot_merge.mac to Merge Annotations into One Copy
  Using annot_collect.mac to Create a Separate Annotations Document

If you have to review a document before changes can be made, you can use Word's revision mark features to mark additions and corrections so that they can be approved before the changes are actually made. If you want to add comments, you can insert comments in the text and format them as hidden text, then remove them later; or you can use Word's annotation features to add annotation marks and comments, compile annotations from several copies, and remove all annotations when the corrections are done. This chapter shows you how to mark revisions and use the annotation features.

USING REVISION MARKS

When you need to keep track of several versions of a document, you can use revision marks to mark changes on a document before the actual corrections are made. When you turn on revision marking, Word does the following:

- Marks any new text you insert with a format you specify (such as an underline).
- Marks text you delete with the strikethrough format (for example, ~~strikethrough~~) but does not delete it from the document.
- Inserts revision bars in the margin next to each line you change if requested.

Figure 5-1 shows an example of revision marks in a Word document.

Turning on Revision Marking

To turn on revision marking:

1. Choose the Format revision-Marks Options command. Word displays the command fields shown in Figure 5-2.
2. In the "add revision marks" field, choose Yes.
3. In the "inserted text" field, choose the format you want Word to use for any text you add to the document. For example, if you choose Uppercase, Word formats all inserted text as uppercase.

```
1═0·········1·········2·········3·········4·······5···════════
   Dear·Boss:¶
   ¶
   We,·the·employeesyour·staff,·would·like·you·to·consider·our·
   requests,·which·are·as·follows:¶
   ¶
        →    better·paycompensation¶
        →    shorter·working·hours¶
        →    more·vacation·time¶
        →    better·benefits¶
        →    more·office·parties¶
   ¶
   If·you·don't·meet·our·demandsrequests,·we'll·have·to·
   consider·what·to·do·next.¶
   ¶                                    ▶
   Sincerely,¶
   ¶
   ¶
   ¶
   ¶
                                                    ═MEMO.DOC═
COMMAND: Copy Delete Format Gallery Help Insert Jump Library
         Options Print Quit Replace Search Transfer Undo Window
Edit document or press Esc to use menu
Pg1 Li6 Co33        {pay}              ?              MR    Microsoft Word
```

Figure 5-1.   **Revision marks.**

4. In the "revision bar position" field, choose one of the following options:

Option	Description
None	Does not add revision bars.
Left	Inserts revision bars in the left margin next to every line you change.
Right	Inserts revision bars in the right margin next to every line you change.
Outside	Inserts revision bars in the right margin on odd-numbered pages and in the left margin on even-numbered pages, next to every line you change.

    If your document has multiple columns, Word inserts revision marks beside the column containing the edited line.

5. Press Enter or click the command name. Word displays the letters "MR" (Mark Revisions) in the status line to remind you that revision marking is turned on.

    After turning on revision marking, edit the document. Word marks the revisions according to your instructions. When you're finished editing, you (or someone else) will want to review the changes, approve the chan-

```
┌───────────────────────────────────────────────────────────────┐
│┃ Dear Boss:                                                    ┃│
│┃                                                               ┃│
│┃ We, the employees, would like you to consider our requests,   ┃│
│┃ which are as follows:                                         ┃│
│┃                                                               ┃│
│┃         —    better pay                                       ┃│
│┃         —    shorter working hours                            ┃│
│┃         —    more vacation time                               ┃│
│┃         —    better benefits                                  ┃│
│┃         —    more office parties                              ┃│
│┃                                                               ┃│
│┃ If you don't meet our demands, we'll have to consider what    ┃│
│┃ to do next.                                                   ┃│
│┃                                                               ┃│
│┃ Sincerely,█                                                   ┃│
│┃                                                               ┃│
└───────────────────────────────────────────────────────────────┘
FORMAT REVISION-MARK OPTIONS
      add revision marks: Yes No
      inserted text: Normal Bold(Underlined)Uppercase Double-underlined
      revision bar position: None(Left)Right Outside
Select option                                                    █
Pg1 Co11          {requests}          ?            MR   Microsoft Word
```

Figure 5-2.　　**The Format revision-Marks Options command fields.**

ges individually or all at once, or reject the changes and delete all the
revision marks. If you want to accept some changes and reject others,
you'll search for the portions of text that have been revised, as described
in the following section.

Turning off Revision Marking

After you turn on revision marking, Word will continue to mark revisions
until you turn it off or quit Word.

　　To turn off revision marking:

1.　Choose the Format revision-Marks Options command.
2.　In the "add revision marks" field, choose No.
3.　Press Enter or click the command name.

　　After you've turned off revision marking, you can still use the Format
revision-Marks commands to accept or reject revisions, as described in
the following sections.

Approving Revisions One by One

To review revisions that have been made to a document while revision marking is turned on, you can use the following procedure. After considering a revision, you can choose to accept the revision as marked and make the change, reject the revision and remove the revision marks, skip over the revision and leave it marked for later action, or make a different correction of your own.

Before you review a revised document, you'll probably want to do the following:

• Move the cursor to the beginning of the document (Word searches from the cursor position to the end of the document).
• Turn off revision marking as described in the preceding section.

To approve revisions one by one:

1. Choose the Format revision-Marks Search command. Word selects the first revised line.
2. Do one of the following:
   • To make the change as marked, choose the Accept-Revisions command.
   • To reject the change and remove the revision marks from the selected text, choose the Undo-Revisions command.
   • To leave the selected text alone and move to the next revision, press S.
   • To escape from the Format Revision-Marks menu, press Esc.

Making All Marked Changes and Removing Revision Marks

When you have reviewed and accepted the changes, you can make the changes in part or all of the document.

To make the marked changes and remove the revision marks:

1. Select the part of your document where you want to make the changes and remove the marks. If you want to change the entire document, press Shift+F10.
2. Choose the Format Revision-Marks Accept-Revisions command. Word does the following:

   • Deletes text marked with the strikethrough character format.

- Removes the special format (uppercase, for example) you specified from inserted text to blend it in with the other text in your document.
- Removes revision bars from the margins.

Rejecting All Marked Changes and Removing Revision Marks

To reject the marked changes and remove the revision marks:

1. Select the part of your document where you want to remove the marks. If you want to remove marks from the entire document, press Shift+F10.
2. Choose the Format Revision-Marks Undo-Revisions command. Word does the following:
   - Deletes text inserted while revision marking was turned on.
   - Removes the strikethrough format from all text.
   - Removes revision bars from the margins.

USING ANNOTATIONS

If you want to insert marks and comments into a Word document that was created by another person, you can use a special form of footnotes called annotations. This feature is one way to review or edit a document on the screen.

Like footnotes, annotations are indicated by reference marks at specific locations in the document text. The reference marks—frequently the commentator's initials or unusual characters, such as an asterisk—tell the reader to look for a comment at the end of the document.

To enter annotations:

1. Move the cursor to where you want to enter an annotation.
2. Choose the Format Annotation command. The command's fields are shown in Figure 5-3.
3. In the "mark" field, type the character(s) you want to use as the annotation mark. For example, you might want to use your initials, or a special mark like an asterisk.

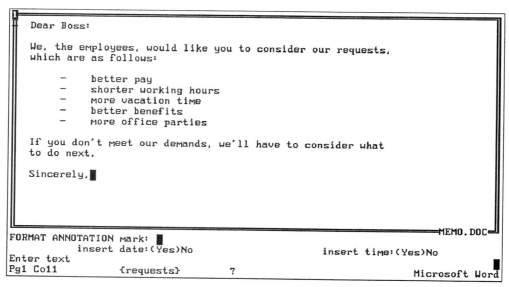

Figure 5-3.   **The Format Annotation command fields.**

4. In the "insert date" field, choose Yes if you want Word to insert the date after the mark.

    Word puts a comma between the mark and the date. Word gets the current date from your computer system. The format of the date is controlled by the "date format" field of the Options command.

5. In the "insert time" field, choose Yes if you want Word to include the time in the annotation mark.

    Word uses a comma to separate the time from the rest of the mark, as shown in Figure 5-4. Word gets the current time from your computer's clock. The format of the time is controlled by the "time format" field of the Options command.

6. Press Enter or click the command name.

    Word inserts the annotation mark, preceded by a number, and moves the cursor to the end of the document so you can type the annotation text.

7. Type the annotation text. The text can be any length you want.

8. To insert more annotations move the cursor to the next place you want to insert a comment, then repeat steps 2 through 7.

    Word automatically numbers all annotations sequentially, and adjusts the numbers when you add or rearrange annotations.

```
which are as follows:

        -     better pay
        -     shorter working hours1PSB
        -     more vacation time
        -     better benefits
        -     more office parties

If you don't meet our demands, we'll have to consider what
to do next.

Sincerely,



◆
1PSB, 11/5/88, 10:58 AM  You hardly work now!█
◆
                                                   ═MEMO.DOC═
COMMAND: Copy Delete Format Gallery Help Insert Jump Library
        Options Print Quit Replace Search Transfer Undo Window
Edit document or press Esc to use menu
Co46              {requests}        ?              Microsoft Word
```

Figure 5-4.   **Inserting an annotation with date and time fields.**

Moving Between Annotation Marks and Annotation Text

The Jump Annotation command quickly moves the cursor to the next annotation mark, or back and forth between annotation marks and their associated text.

Here's how the command works:

To Jump to	Do This
The next annotation mark	Move the cursor into the document text. Choose the Jump Annotation command.
The annotation text associated with an annotation mark	Select the annotation mark. Choose the Jump Annotation command.
The annotation mark associated with annotation text	Move the cursor into the annotation text. Choose the Jump Annotation command.

Using an Annotation Window

If you'd like to see your document text at the same time you view your annotations, you can use the Window Split Footnote command to open a window that displays footnotes and annotations at the bottom of the screen, as shown in Figure 5-5. You can open a footnote-annotation window with keys or with a mouse.

Opening a Footnote/Annotation Window

To open a footnote window using keys:

1. Choose the Window Split Footnote command.
2. In the "at line" field, type a line number at which you want to split the Word window, or press F1 to display a highlight in the selection bar, then use the Down or Up arrow keys to move the highlight to where you want to split the window.
3. Press Enter or click the command name. Word draws the window at the bottom of the screen.

Figure 5-5.   **Using an annotation window allows you to view your text and your annotations at the same time.**

```
┌─────────────────────────────────────────────────────────────────┐
│ Dear Boss:                                                        │
│                                                                   │
│ We, the employees, would like you to consider our requests,       │
│ which are as follows:                                             │
│                                                                   │
│        –      better pay                                          │
│        –      shorter working hours1PSB                           │
│        –      more vacation time                                  │
│        –      better benefits2PSB                                 │
│        –      more office parties3PSB                             │
│                                                                   │
│ If you don't meet our demands, we'll have to consider what        │
│ to do next.                                                       │
│2──────────────────────────────────────────────────────────────── │
│ 1PSB, 11/5/88, 10:58 AM  You hardly work now!                     │
│ 2PSB, 11/5/88, 11:00 AM  OK, I'll give you dental coverage.       │
│ 3PSB, 11/5/88, 11:00 AM  OK, OK, we'll celebrate Halloween.       │
│ ◆                                                                 │
│                                                        MEMO.DOC    │
│COMMAND: Copy Delete Format Gallery Help Insert Jump Library        │
│         Options Print Quit Replace Search Transfer Undo Window     │
│Edit document or press Esc to use menu                             │
│Pg1 Co1             {requests}         ?              Microsoft Word│
└─────────────────────────────────────────────────────────────────┘
```

To open a footnote-annotation window using the mouse:
1. Point to the right border of the document window where you want to split the window.
2. Hold down the Shift key and click either mouse button to open the window.

Closing the Footnote/Annotation Window
When you close a footnote window, Word expands the document window to its previous size. You can use either the keyboard or the mouse to close the window.
To close a footnote-annotation window with keys:

1. Move the cursor to the footnote-annotation window.
2. Choose the Window Close command.
3. Press Enter or click the command name.

To close a footnote-annotation window with the mouse:

1. Point to the right border of the footnote-annotation window.
2. Click both mouse buttons simultaneously.

Editing and Formatting Annotations

You can edit and format the text of annotations just as you would any other text in your document.

Editing Annotation Text
Don't delete or change the annotation mark preceding the annotation text.
To edit the text of an annotation:

1. If you want to display annotations in a window at the bottom of the screen, choose the Window Split Footnote command as described in "Using an Annotation Window" earlier in this chapter.
2. Select the annotation mark of the annotation whose text you want to edit.
3. Choose the Jump Annotation command to move the cursor to the annotation text.
4. Edit the text.

Editing an Annotation Mark

You can change an annotation mark. For example, you might want to change an ampersand to an asterisk, or add or remove the time or date from the annotation mark. Don't delete or change the number preceding the mark, because Word automatically numbers all annotations and footnotes.

To edit an annotation mark:

1. Select the annotation mark in your document.
2. Choose the Format Annotation command .
3. If you want to specify a new character, type the new character in the "mark" field.
4. Choose Yes or No in the "date" and "time" fields as necessary.
5. Press Enter or click the command name.

Formatting Annotation Text

You can use all of Word's formatting commands to format the text of annotations. For example, you might want to use a smaller point size, different font, indent annotations, or format the annotation text as hidden text. You can use the Format Character command to apply character formats or use the Format Paragraph command to apply paragraph formats. You can also change the Annotation style supplied with Word to change the format of all annotations automatically.

See Chapters 7 and 8 for more information about formatting characters and paragraphs. See "Changing Styles" in Chapter 11 for instructions on how to change Word's automatic styles, such as the Annotation style.

Formatting Annotation Marks

You may want to change the format of annotation marks. For example, you might want to make the marks into superscripts, make them bold or italic, or make them hidden text. Figure 5-6 shows annotation marks formatted as superscripts and as hidden text, and annotation text formatted as hidden text. You can use the Format Character command to change each annotation mark individually. You can change the Annotation ref. style in NORMAL.STY to change the format of all annotation marks at the same time.

See Chapter 7 for more information about formatting characters. See "Changing Style" in Chapter 11 for instructions on how to change Word's automatic styles, such as the Annotation ref. style.

```
1 L [ · · · · · · · · 1 · · · · · · · · 2 · · · · · · · · 3 · · · · · · · · 4 · · · · · · · · 5 · · · · · [ · · · · ] · · · · · · · · 7 · · · · ·
         →    better·pay¶
         →    shorter·working·hours¹ᴾˢᴮ¶
         →    more·vacation·time¶
         →    better·benefits²ᴾˢᴮ¶
         →    more·office·parties³ᴾˢᴮ¶
      ¶
      If·you·don't·meet·our·demands,·we'll·have·to·consider·what·
      to·do·next.¶
      ¶
      Sincerely,¶
      ¶
      ¶
      ◘
      1PSB,·11/5/88,·10:58·AM··You·hardly·work·now!¶
      2PSB,·11/5/88,·11:00·AM··OK,·I'll·give·you·dental·coverage.¶
      3PSB,·11/5/88,·11:00·AM··OK,·OK,·we'll·celebrate·Halloween.¶
      ◆
                                                                =MEMO.BAK=
COMMAND: Copy Delete Format Gallery Help Insert Jump Library
         Options Print Quit Replace Search Transfer Undo Window
Edit document or press Esc to use menu
Pg1 Li18 Co1      {¶}                  ?               Microsoft Word
```

Figure 5-6.   **Annotation marks and annotation text after formatting changes.**

Figure 5-7.   **Printed annotations.**

```
Dear Boss:

We, the employees, would like you to consider our requests,
which are as follows:

      -     better pay
      -     shorter working hours1PSB
      -     more vacation time
      -     better benefits2PSB
      -     more office parties3PSB

If you don't meet our demands, we'll have to consider what
to do next.

Sincerely,
```

```
1PSB, 11/5/88, 10:58 AM  You hardly work now!
2PSB, 11/5/88, 11:00 AM  OK, I'll give you dental coverage.
3PSB, 11/5/88, 11:00 AM  OK, OK, we'll celebrate Halloween.
```

Controlling Where the Annotation Text Prints

Although the text for annotations is stored at the end of the document, it won't necessarily appear there when you print your document. By default, Word prints annotations at the bottom of the pages on which their annotation marks appear, as shown in Figure 5-7. If there's not enough room to print all the annotations at the bottom of the page, Word prints the rest on the next page. If you don't like this arrangement, you can tell Word to print the annotations at the end of each division, or, if your document is not divided into divisions, at the end of the document. The "footnotes" field of the Format Division Layout command controls the printed position of both footnotes and annotations.

To control the position of annotation text in your document:

1. Choose the Format Division Layout command.
2. In the "footnotes" field choose one of the following options:

Option	Positions Annotations
Same-page	At the bottom of the page on which the annotation references appear.
End	At the end of the division containing the cursor. If you have not divided your document into divisions, Word prints the annotation text at the end of the document.

3. Press Enter or click the command name.

Moving Annotations

To move an annotation:

1. Select the annotation mark.
2. Press the Del key.
3. Move the cursor to the new position.
4. Press the Ins key.

Deleting Annotations

You can delete annotations individually, or use one of Word's macros (small programs that perform sets of instructions) to delete all annotations from a document.

To delete annotations individually:

1. Select the annotation mark.
2. Press the Del key.
   Word automatically deletes the annotation text .

To delete all annotations from a document using the *annot_remove.mac* macro:

1. Use the Transfer Load command to load the document containing the annotations you want to delete.
2. Use the Transfer Glossary Load command to load the MACRO.GLY file, which contains the macros.
3. Press Ctrl+A, then release those keys and press R to run the *annot_remove.mac* macro.
   When the macro finishes removing all annotation marks and text, it displays a message asking you to save the document with a new name so that the copy containing annotations will also be saved in case you need it.
4. Type a new name for the document.
5. Press Enter.

Consolidating Annotations

To make it easier to respond to annotations on several copies of a Word document, you can use one of Word's macros to gather the annotations together in one place. Word has two macros that consolidate annotations:

Macro Name	Description
annot_merge.mac	Gathers annotations from several copies of the document and merges them into one copy of the document. Using this macro, you end up with both the marked-up document and all the annotations in one place.
annot_collect.mac	Gathers annotations from several copies of the document and lists them in separate document, along with the page numbers on which the anno-

tation marks occur in the original document. Using this macro, you end up with a document containing only a list of annotations. You can then print this document or save it for your records.

To use these macros efficiently, the copies of the document must be identical except for annotation marks throughout the document and annotation text at the end of the documents.

Using annot_merge.mac to Merge Annotations into One Copy
To merge annotations from several copies of a Word document:

1. If you have more than one window open, choose the Transfer Clear All command. Otherwise, choose Transfer Clear Window.
2. Use the Transfer Glossary Load command to load the glossary file MACRO.GLY, which contains the macro files.
3. Press Ctrl+A, then release those keys and press M to run the *annot_merge.mac* macro.
    The macro displays a message asking you for the name of the destination document.
4. Type the name of the document to which you want all the annotations to be copied, then press Enter.
    For example, if you want all of the annotations to be merged into the file named MYCOPY.DOC, type *MYCOPY.DOC*. The macro loads the document, then splits the screen into two windows and displays a message asking you for the name of the first source document.
5. Type the name of the copy of the document from which you want to merge the annotations, then press Enter.
    For example, if you're merging annotations from files named LEES-COPY.DOC, ANNSCOPY.DOC, and BOSSCOPY.DOC, type *LEES-COPY.DOC*.
    The macro loads the source document into the second window, jumps to the first annotation mark, and highlights the preceding sentence. Then the macro searches the destination document to find the matching sentence. If it finds the the matching sentence in the destination document, it copies the annotation mark and the annotation text from the source document to the destination document, and moves on to the next annotation mark. If the macro doesn't find a matching sentence in the destination document, it pauses and asks you to move the highlight to where you want to insert the annotation mark in the des-

tination document. When the macro reaches the end of the source document, it saves the destination document and displays a message asking you for the next source document.

6. Repeat step 5 for each source file you want to copy annotations from.

Using annot_collect.mac to Create a Separate Annotations Document

To copy annotation text and page numbers from several documents and compile them into a separate file:

1. If you have more than one window open, choose the Transfer Clear All command. Otherwise, choose Transfer Clear Window.

2. Use the Transfer Glossary Load command to load the glossary file MACRO.GLY, which contains the macro files.

3. Press Ctrl+A, then release those keys and press C to run the *annot_collect.mac* macro.
   The macro displays a message asking you for the name of the destination document.

4. Type the name of the document in which you want to save the list of annotations, then press Enter. The macro displays a message asking you if you want to be prompted to enter the name of each source document (a document from which you are copying annotations).

5. Choose Yes or No. If you press Y to choose Yes, the macro will display a message when it needs you to type the name of the next document form which to gather annotations. If you press N to choose No, the macro chooses the Library Document-retrieval Query command so you can create a list of documents from which to gather annotations. (See Chapter 21 for instructions on using the Library Document-retrieval Query command.)

6. The macro compiles the list of annotations from the source documents and saves them in the destination document you specified. Respond to any messages that appear on the screen during the process.

CHAPTER

6

USING THE SPELLING CHECKER, THESAURUS, AND WORD COUNT FEATURES

This Chapter Contains the Following:

After you've revised your document, you'll probably want to check the spelling before you pass it along to someone else. If you find that you use a word frequently, you'll want to substitute some synonyms so your writing won't sound too repetitious. After you have perfected your masterpiece, you may want to find out how many wirds it contains. This chapter shows you how to do these tasks.

CHECKING SPELLING

When you've finished editing your document, you can use Word's spelling checker to check for typing errors and spelling mistakes. Word compares words in your document with words in its own standard dictionary, or in a dictionary you've created. The "speller path" field of the Options command tells Word where to find the spelling checker file.

Word checks all words of two characters or more not only for the arrangement of letters (the spelling), but also for improper punctuation combined with letters, such as *;so*. If you've typed the same word too many times in a sentence, such as *the the*, the spelling checker will tell you that, too. Word checks text formatted as hidden, whether or not it's visible on the screen.

You can check the spelling of:

- The entire document: Word checks the spelling in a document from the cursor to the end of the document, so you probably want to move the cursor to the beginning of the document before you start the checking process.
- Selected text: You can select a single word or a block of text for Word to check. This feature is especially handy if you've just added a small portion of new text to a document in which you've already perfected the spelling.

Checking Spelling with the Standard Dictionary

Unless you use a lot of uncommon words in your documents and you want to take the time to create your own dictionaries, you'll want to check the spelling in your documents with Word's standard dictionary, SPELL-AM.LEX. Because the spelling checker begins at the position of the cursor and moves toward the end of the document, you might want to move the cursor to the beginning of the document before invoking the spelling checker.

To check the spelling in a document using the standard dictionary:

1. If necessary, move the cursor to the beginning of the text , or select the text you want to check in only part of a document.
2. Press Alt+F6 or choose the Library Spell command.
   Word loads the spelling checker file and opens the Spell window at the bottom of the screen, as shown in Figure 6-1. If Word can't find the spelling checker file or doesn't find any errors, it won't open the Spell window. Instead, it will display a message asking you to insert a disk or saying that no errors were found. As soon as Word loads the file, it begins the spelling check. If the spelling checker reaches the end of the document, or the end of the selected text, without finding any mispelled words, it displays a message saying so. When the spelling checker finds a word that doesn't match a word in its dictionary, it displays that word, along with a list of alternative spellings, as shown in Figure 6-1.
3. If you want the spelling checker to check punctuation or ignore words in uppercase letters in your document, choose the Options command,

Figure 6-1.   **The Library Spell command opens another window.**

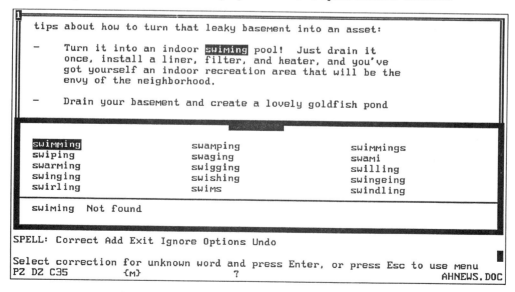

```
┌┬══════════════════════════════════════════════════════════════════┐
│1                                                                    │
│  tips about how to turn that leaky basement into an asset:          │
│                                                                     │
│  —   Turn it into an indoor ▓swiming▓ pool!  Just drain it          │
│      once, install a liner, filter, and heater, and you've          │
│      got yourself an indoor recreation area that will be the        │
│      envy of the neighborhood.                                      │
│                                                                     │
│  —   Drain your basement and create a lovely goldfish pond          │
│                                                                     │
├─────────────────────────────────████████████─────────────────────── │
│                                                                     │
│  ▓swimming▓          swamping            swimmings                  │
│  swiping             swaging             swami                      │
│  swarming            swigging            swilling                   │
│  swinging            swishing            swingeing                  │
│  swirling            swims               swindling                  │
├─────────────────────────────────────────────────────────────────── │
│  swiming   Not found                                                │
└───────────────────────────────────────────────────────────────────┘
SPELL: Correct Add Exit Ignore Options Undo

Select correction for unknown word and press Enter, or press Esc to use menu  ▮
PZ DZ C35           {M}                    ?                        AHNEWS.DOC
```

then choose Yes in the "check punctuation" and/or "ignore all caps" fields, then press Enter. The "ignore all caps" feature is especially useful if your document contains a lot of acronyms, such as NASA, USGS, OMB, etc. Keep in mind, however, that this feature may cause the spelling checker to skip words that are capitalized in titles and headings, too.

4.   To deal with the displayed word, do one of the following:

If You Want to	**Do This**
Type the correct spelling	Choose Correct.
	Type the correct spelling.
	If you want Word to remember the correction you made for future occurrences of the same text, choose Yes in the "remember correction" field.
	Press Enter or point to CORRECT and click the left mouse button. If the word you type doesn't match any words in its dictionary, the spell checker displays a message asking you if you want to try again.
Choose from the list of alternatives	Press F4 if you want to see more alternatives. (If there are no more alternatives, Word will beep.)
	Use the arrow keys to highlight the alternative you want, then press Enter, or point to the alternative and click the right mouse button.
Skip the word	Choose Ignore. Word displays the next unmatched word.
Add the word to a dictionary	Choose Add.
	Choose the dictionary to which you want to add the word: Standard, Document, or User. (See "Using Different Dictionaries" later in this chapter for more information about dictionaries.)
Go back to a previous word	Choose Previous.
Undo the last spelling change.	Choose Undo.
Exit from the spelling checker	Choose Exit.

Using Different Dictionaries

The spelling checker can use three dictionaries to check your documents:

1.   The standard dictionary (the default choice).
2.   A document dictionary you create to go with a specific document.
3.   A user dictionary you create to keep words you use from time to time in a group of documents.

The spelling checker always uses the standard dictionary unless you specify another. You can add and delete words from the standard dictionary, so you may never need to create another dictionary unless you work with complex documents. You can add words that you use frequently to the standard dictionary, such as your name, your town, your company's name, and any special terms you use in documents.

Creating a Dictionary or Adding Words to an Existing Dictionary

Any time the spelling checker finds a word that doesn't match a word in its dictionary, it displays that word for your response. To save the time and frustration of dealing with uncommon words that you use frequently, such as your last name, you can add them to the standard dictionary, or to a dictionary you've created.

To add a word to a dictionary during the spell checking session, choose Add as described under "Checking Spelling with the Standard Dictionary" in the previous section. To add a list of words to a dictionary all at once, use the following procedure. You can use this procedure to create a new dictionary or to add more words to an existing dictionary.

To add a list of words to a dictionary:

1.   Start Word, and type the words you want to add to a dictionary in a new, empty document. You can press Enter between words or just use a space to separate them.
2.   When you're finished typing the words, select the document.
3.   Press Alt+F6 or choose the Library Spell command.
4.   If you're adding words to the standard dictionary or creating or adding to a document dictionary, skip to step 6. If you're creating or adding to a user dictionary, choose the Options command from the Library Spell menu, then accept Word's proposed name of SPECIALS.CMP or type the name of the user dictionary you want to create or add words to and press Enter. Although you can add any extension you want, Word looks for a .CMP extension when it searches

for dictionaries, so it's easiest if you include a .CMP extension when naming a file (such as MATHDICT.CMP), or simply omit the extension (such as MATHDICT) and let Word add the .CMP extension.

5. Choose the Add command from the Library Spell menu.
6. Choose one of the following:

Choose	If You Want to
Add Standard	Add words to the standard dictionary, making them available to all documents.
Add User	Add words to a user dictionary you've created.
Add Document	Add words to or to create a special dictionary for a particular document.

7. Press Enter or click the command name.

Word keeps new terms that you've added to the standard dictionary in a file named UPDAT-AM.CMP. Figure 6.2 illustrates adding words to a dictionary.

Figure 6-2.   Adding words to a dictionary.

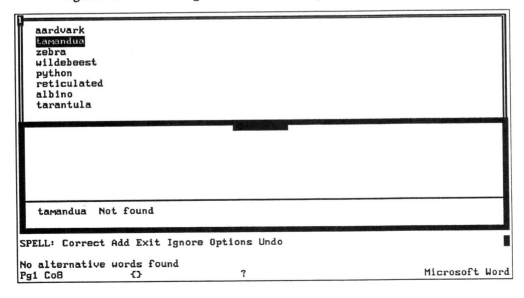

Changing or Deleting a Word from a Dictionary

If you've added a misspelled word to a dictionary, you can change it. You should also occasionally delete obsolete words you've added to dictionaries because the longer the list of words in a dictionary, the longer it takes the spell checker to compare words when checking a document.

You can't delete words from the standard dictionary. But you can delete words that you've added to a user dictionary, a document dictionary, or words that you've added to the standard dictionary, which are stored in the UPDAT-AM.CMP file.

To change or delete a word:

1. Use the Transfer Load command from the main menu to load the dictionary (.CMP) file containing the word you want to change or delete.
2. Change or delete the word.
3. Press Ctrl+F10 or use the Transfer Save command to save the edited file.

Don't add or rearrange words in a dictionary file while you're editing using this procedure. Use the procedure listed in the previous section to add words to a dictionary.

Checking Spelling with a User Dictionary

Word automatically uses the standard dictionary and the document dictionary (if any) to check documents. If you want to use a user dictionary you've created, you have to load the user dictionary file after choosing the Library Spell command.

If you've created a user dictionary and want to use it instead of the standard dictionary to check your document:

1. Move the cursor or select text if necessary.
2. Press Alt+F6 or choose the Library Spell command.
   Word loads the spelling checker file and opens the Spell window. As soon as Word loads the file, it begins the spelling check.
3. When Word pauses to present a word not in its dictionary or when it reaches the end of the document, choose the Options command from the Library Spell menu.
4. Type the name of the dictionary in the "user dictionary" field, or press F1 to display a list of files, then highlight one.

5. Press Enter to load the dictionary file. Word continues the spelling check, using the user dictionary in addition to the standard dictionary.

6. When the spell checker displays a word, do one of the following:

If You Want to	Do This
Type the correct spelling	Choose Correct. Type the correct spelling. Press Enter or point to CORRECT and click the left mouse button. If the word you type doesn't match any words in its dictionary, the spell checker displays a message asking you if you want to try again.
Choose from the list of alternatives	Press F4 if you want to see more alternatives. (If there are no more alternatives, Word will beep.) Use the arrow keys to highlight the alternative you want, then press Enter, or point to the alternative and click the right mouse button.
Skip the word	Choose Ignore. Word displays the next unmatched word.
Add the word to a dictionary	Choose Add. Choose the dictionary you want to add the word to: Standard, Document, or User.
Go back to a previous word	Choose Previous.
Undo the last spelling change.	Choose Undo.
Exit from the spelling checker	Choose Exit.

Using a Foreign-Language Spelling Checker Program

The entire Word package is available in several foreign languages, including a United Kingdom version of English. You can also order a foreign-language spelling checker program and dictionary file to use with the American version of Word. For more information about how to order or about which languages are available, you can contact Microsoft Corporation.

Once you have the foreign-language spelling checker program and the dictionary file on hand, you can use the following procedure to set up Word so that it will use the foreign-language program instead of the American one.

To use a foreign-language spelling checker:

1. Choose the Options command from the main menu.
2. In the "speller path" field, type the pathname of the directory containing the spelling checker file you want to use. You must type the pathname to the directory containing the file: Word won't search the DOS path to find it.
3. Press Enter or click the command name.
    This option remains set, so Word will continue to use this spelling checker in every session, until you change the setting. If more than one spelling checker file is in the directory you specify in the pathname, Word uses the first one it finds.

USING THE THESAURUS

If you use the same word over and over again in your documents, your writing can become monotonous. To introduce variety, you can use Word's thesaurus to look up synonyms for your most commonly used words.

Looking up Synonyms for a Word

You can look up synonyms for a word in your document, or you can type a word for which to look up synonyms.

To look up synonyms for a word in your document:

1. Select the word for which you want to find synonyms.
2. Press Ctrl+F6 or choose the Library thEsaurus command (Esc, L, E).
    Word displays the thesaurus window, which contains a list of synonyms for the selected word as shown in Figure 6-3. Word draws the window in a location that won't cover up the selected word. If the selected word is not in the thesaurus but Word recognizes the root of the word, the window displays a list of words that are synonyms for the root of the word. For example, if you selected the word "heavier,"

Word would display a list of synonyms of "heavy." If Word doesn't recognize a root, it displays a list of words that are closest to the spelling of the selected word, as well as a message, as shown in Figure 6-4. Make sure you've spelled the selected word correctly. If the list of synonyms is long, press PgDn or PgUp or click the right or left mouse button on the left border of the thesaurus window to scroll the list.

3.   Choose one of the following actions:

If You Want to	Do This
Replace the selected word with a synonym	Use the arrow keys to highlight the synonym you want in the thesaurus window, then press Enter or click the right mouse button on the synonym you want in the thesaurus window.
Look up synonyms of a word in the thesaurus window	Use the arrow keys or the left mouse button to highlight the word in the thesaurus window, then press Ctrl+F6 or click the left mouse button on "CTRL-F6: look up" at the bottom of the window.
Display the previous list of synonyms	Press Ctrl+PgUp or click the left mouse button on "CTRL-PgUp: last word" at the bottom of the thesaurus window.
Close the thesaurus window	Press Esc or click in the document window.

Finding a Synonym for a Word You Type

You can use the thesaurus even if you don't select a word:

1.   Press Ctrl+F6 or choose the Library thEsaurus command (Esc, L, E).
2.   In the thesaurus window, type the word for which you want to see synonyms. (Yes, just start typing! Your word will appear in the thesaurus window, as shown in Figure 6-5.)
3.   Press Enter.

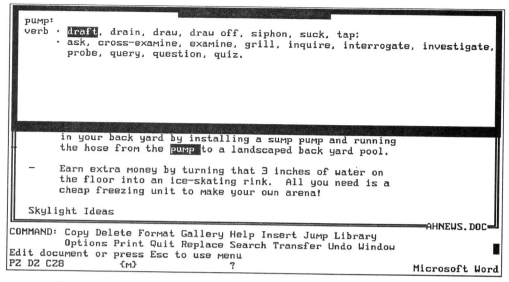

Figure 6-3.   **The thesaurus window lists synonyms of the selected word.**

Figure 6-4.   **If the selected word is not in the thesaurus, Word lists a group of words that are closest to the word's spelling.**

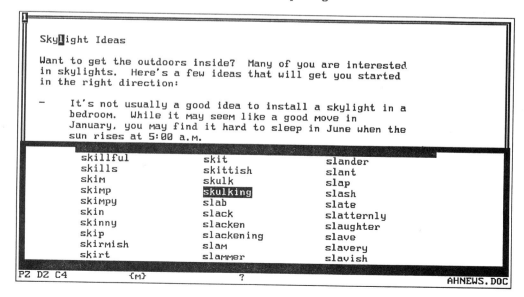

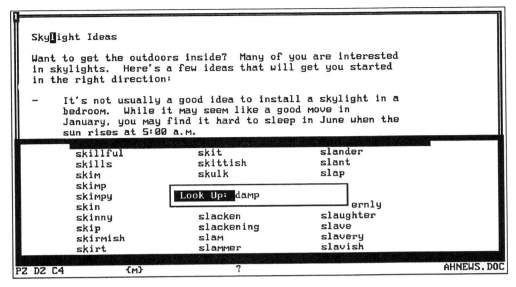

Figure 6-5.   **Typing a word in the thesaurus window.**

COUNTING WORDS IN YOUR DOCUMENTS

Word comes with two small programs that help you count or find words in your documents:

Program Name	Description
Word Count	Counts the number of words in a document.
Word Frequency	Counts the number of words in a document, the number of times the words were used, and makes a list of words sorted by order of frequency.

You can use these programs from the operating system prompt or with the Library Run command in Word. If you want to count the number of words in the document on which you're currently working, save the document before using either of these programs.

Using the Word Count Program

To use the Word Count program to count the number of words in a document:

1. If you're using Word, choose the Library Run command.
2. Type *wc* then a space, then the name of the file you want to count words in. For example, to count the words in the file named NOVEL.DOC, you'd type:

    wc novel.doc

3. Press Enter. Word displays a message like that shown in Figure 6-6.

Using the Word Frequency Program

To use the Word Frequency program to count the number of words in a document:

Figure 6-6.   **The results of the Word Count program.**

```
WORD COUNT+  Version 2.1:LB for M.S. WORD
Copyright (c) Software Heaven, Inc. 1984
Portions Copyright (c) Wayne Holder 1981, 1982.  All rights reserved

There are 589 words in the file
Press a key to resume Word_
```

```
WORDFREQ+  Version 2.1:CP for Microsoft WORD
Copyright (c) Software Heaven, Inc. 1984
Portions Copyright (c) Wayne Holder 1981, 1982.  All rights reserved


593      Total words
299      Unique words
203      Words appearing once
Press a key to resume Word_
```

Figure 6-7.   **The results of the Word Frequency program.**

Figure 6-8.   **A frequency list created by the Word Frequency program.**

```
1  L[•••••••1•••••••••2•••••••••3••••••••••4•••••••••5•••••••••]•••••••••7••••
   33→   THE¶
   22→   A¶
   21→   OF¶
   17→   AND¶
   16→   TO¶
   14→   YOU¶
   11→   IN¶
   8→    YOUR¶
   8→    THAT¶
   7→    IT¶
   5→    ARE¶
   5→    ON¶                                   ▌
   5→    BLOCKS¶
   5→    SHOULD¶
   5→    IS¶
   5→    BUILDING¶
   4→    FOUNDATION¶
   4→    FOR¶
   4→    LOG¶
                                                         ═AHNEWS.FRQ═
COMMAND: Copy Delete Format Gallery Help Insert Jump Library
         Options Print Quit Replace Search Transfer Undo Window
Edit document or press Esc to use menu
Pg1 Li1 Co1        {}                 ?                  Microsoft Word
```

1. If you're using Word, choose the Library Run command.
2. Type *wordfreq*, then a space, then the name of the file in which you want to count words. For example, to count the words in the file named NOVEL.DOC, you'd type:

    wordfreq novel.doc

3. Press Enter. Word displays a message like that shown in **Figure 6-7**.

The Word Frequency program creates a list of the words in a document and stores them in a file with the same name as the original document but with a .FRQ extension. (For example, if you used the Word Frequency program to check the NOVEL.DOC file, it would create a list of words in a file called NOVEL.FRQ.)

To see the frequency list created by the Word Frequency program:

1. In Word, choose the Transfer Load command.
2. Type the name of the .FRQ file (*novel.frq*, for example).
3. Press Enter. Word displays a list similar to that shown in **Figure 6-8**.

You can use a frequency list to check how, often you repeat words. If you find that you use one word too often, try using the thesaurus to find one or more alternatives for that word.

PART III

Changing the Appearance of Text

When you want to change the way text looks on a page, you'll format that text. Word's basic formatting falls into three general categories:

Category	Affects the Appearance of
Character formatting	Individual characters.
Paragraph formatting	Paragraphs.
Division formatting	The entire document, or specific parts of a document when that document is separated into divisions.

Word's formatting is controlled by the following commands:

Command	Controls
Format Character	Bold, italic, underlines, and other styles of type; font types and sizes; colors of formats on the screen; superscripts and subscripts.
Format Paragraph	Indents, alignments, tabs, line spacing, space between paragraphs.
Format Tab	Setting and clearing tabs.
Format Border	Lines and boxes around a paragraph, and shading behind a paragraph
Format Division commands	Columns, margins, page numbers, and the size of the page.
Format Stylesheet commands	Attaching style sheets, and creating and modifying styles in the attached style sheet.
Gallery commands	Loading, modifying, and saving style sheets.

You'll learn more about these commands and types of formatting in this part of the book.

CHARACTER FORMATTING

This Chapter Contains the Following:

Character formatting affects the individual letters, numbers, and symbols that you type. You can format one character or every character in your document at one time. You can:

- Give characters the following formats: **bold,** *italic,* underline, ~~strikethrough~~, UPPERCASE, SMALL CAPS, <u>DOUBLE UNDERLINE</u>, or "hidden."
- Make characters into ^{super}scripts and $_{sub}$scripts, and control the amount by which text is raised or lowered from the baseline. The baseline is the invisible line on which the letters in a sentence "sit:" the bottoms of all characters that don't have descending parts (such as a *p* or a *g)* are on the baseline.
- Change *fonts* and sizes. Fonts are families of characters that share a style—characters that are very straight and simple, for example, as in a Helvetica font, or very curvy and ornate, as in an Old English font. Fonts come in different sizes, which are measured in points. A point is roughly 1/72 of an inch. Word's default point size is 12 points.

Keep in mind that what you see on the screen is not necessarily what you'll get when you print your document. What you see on the screen depends on the capabilities of your display hardware. For example, your display hardware may not be able to display small caps, but will substitute regular-size capitals instead. What you see on a printed page depends on the capabilities of your printer. For example, if you've formatted text as italic but your printer cannot print in italic, you'll probably get underlined text instead. Word lets you choose any format for your characters. If the display device or your printer can't produce that format, Word substitutes the closest format that can be produced. You'll just have to experiment until you're familiar with what your equipment can do.

To see what your text will look like when printed, you can use Word's print preview feature (explained in Chapter 14).

APPLYING CHARACTER FORMATS

The Format Character command controls the way characters look in your document.

To format characters:

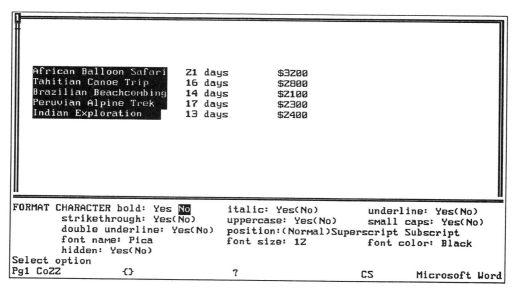

Figure 7-1.   **The Format Character command fields.**

1. Select the characters you want to change.
2. Choose the Format Character command. Word displays the command fields shown in Figure 7-1.
3. Choose the options you want, keeping in mind the following guidelines:
    •   You can format only lowercase letters as uppercase or small caps.
    •   Text formatted as hidden will be invisible unless you've set the "show hidden text" field of the Options command to Yes.
    •   In the "font name," "font size," and "font color" fields, you can press F1 to display a list of fonts, sizes, and colors available for your printer, then highlight the one you want; or you can type a response.
4. Press Enter or click the command name to apply the format.

What You See on the Screen

What you see on the screen as character formatting depends on the type of monitor you have and on the display mode you're using.

Example

ATTENTION!
This store will be closed on **Monday**.

To format text like this, you would:

1. Select "Attention!"
2. Choose the Format Character command.
3. Choose Yes in the "bold," "italic," and "underline" command fields.
4. Press Enter or click the command name to format the word.
5. Select "Monday."
6. Choose the Format Character command.
7. Choose Yes in the Bold command field.
8. Press Enter or click the command name to format the word.

If You're Using	**You'll See Character Formatting as**
Graphics mode	Underlines, italic, bold, and so forth.
Text (character) mode	Different shades of text on a monochrome monitor and different colors of text on a color monitor.

For example, if you're using text mode on a color monitor, italic words may be displayed in blue, bold in red, underlined in green, and so forth. (You can control the colors assigned to character formats—explained in "Changing Colors Assigned to Character Formats" later in this section.) If you're using graphics mode on either a monochrome or a color monitor, you'll see the formats for which you asked —bold, italic, double underlines, and so forth—instead of text in different shades or colors.

Switching Display Modes
Depending on your computer setup, you may be able to switch between several display modes to control how many lines of text are shown on the screen, and to control how Word displays formatting.

To switch modes, you should do one of the following:

- Press Alt+F9 or
- Choose the Options command, press F1 in the "display mode" field, highlight the mode you want, then press Enter.

You may have more choices if you use the Options-command method. If Word beeps and tells you it can't switch modes, make sure you have a graphics card installed. You can't use the graphics mode without one.

Keyboard Shortcuts

You can quickly apply character formats to selected text using the key combinations shown in the following table:

Bold	Alt+B
Italic	Alt+I
Underline	Alt+U
Double underline	Alt+D
Strikethrough	Alt+S
Small caps	Alt+K (affects only lowercase letters)
Hidden text	Alt+E
Superscript	Alt+ + (plus)[1]
Subscript	Alt+ - (hyphen or minus)[1]
Change case	Ctrl+F4 (keep pressing until you see what you want—uppercase, lowercase, or only first letter capitalized)
Back to plain text	Alt+Spacebar

[1] Use the key in the top row, not the key on the numeric keypad at the right of the keyboard.

Note: If you have a style sheet attached to your document, press X between the Alt key and the format letter key listed above. For example, if you have a style sheet attached to your document and you want to make selected text bold, press Alt+XB. (You'll find out more about style sheets in Chapter 11.)

Changing Colors Assigned to Character Formats on Color Monitors
To change a color assigned to a character format on a color monitor:

1. Make sure you're using text (character) mode. (Press F1 in the "display mode" field of the Options command if you're not sure.)
2. Choose the Options command.
3. Move the cursor to the "color" field in the "General Options" group.
4. Press F1. Your screen should now look like Figure 7-2.
5. Use the arrow keys or the mouse to move the cursor to the field you want to change ("italic," for example).
6. Do one of the following:

   • Press PgUp or PgDn until you see the color you want or
   • Press the letter at the top of the screen that has the color you want. For example, if the letter B is displayed in bright blue, that means you can press B to pick bright blue.

7. Repeat steps 5 and 6 to change any other fields you want.
8. Press F1 to set the colors and return to the "colors" field.

Figure 7-2.   **Changing colors assigned to character formats.**

```
                    B C D E F G H   J K L M N O P  × (ignore)
┌──────────────────────────────────────────────────────────────────────┐
│ background for window 1:                          border: sample text  │
│              menus: sample text                 messages: sample text  │
│       menu options: sample text               status line: sample text │
│ font 8.5 pts or less: sample text               uppercase: sample text │
│         9.0 to 10 pts: sample text              small caps: sample text │
│        10.5 to 12 pts: sample text               subscript: sample text │
│        12.5 to 14 pts: sample text             superscript: sample text │
│       more than 14 pts: sample text            hidden text: sample text │
│                bold: sample text             strikethrough: sample text │
│              italic: sample text            bold and italic: sample text │
│           underline: sample text          bold and underline: sample text │
│      double underline: sample text        italic and underline: sample text │
│                                                                        │
│         measure:(In)Cm P10 P12 Pt          display mode: 1             │
│         paginate:(Auto)Manual                    colors: ▮             │
│         autosave:                         autosave confirm: Yes(No)     │
│         show menu:(Yes)No                   show borders:(Yes)No        │
│         date format:(MDY)DMY             decimal character:(.),         │
│         time format:(12)24               default tab width: 0.5"       │
│         line numbers:(Yes)No             count blank space: Yes(No)     │
│         cursor speed: 3                   linedraw character: (|)       │
│         speller path: C:\WORD5\SPELL-AM.LEX                        ▮    │
│ Press F1 and select item. Press letter or use PgUp, PgDn to set color  │
│ Pg1 Li1 Co1      {}                 ?                   Microsoft Word  │
└──────────────────────────────────────────────────────────────────────┘
```

9. Press Enter or click the command name to carry out the Options command.

Formatting One Character at a Time

Word normally assumes that you want to select and format more than one character at a time, except when you're creating superscripts and subscripts. If you want to apply another type of character format (bold, italic, and so forth) to just one character, do this:

1. Place the cursor on top of the character to highlight it.
2. Press the shortcut key combination twice. For example, if you wanted to apply bold to the character, you'd press Alt+B twice (or press Alt+XB twice, if you have a style sheet other than NORMAL.STY attached). For a list of shortcut keys, see the "Keyboard Shortcuts" box earlier in this chapter.

About Fonts, Sizes, and Colors

The fonts, font sizes, and font colors from which you have to choose in the Format Character command fields depend on what type of printer you're using. Look up your printer in Chapter 2 of the *Printer Information for Microsoft Word* manual to see a list of the fonts and sizes your printer can produce. There are two types of fonts: *fixed-pitch fonts*, in which each character occupies the same amount of space, and *proportional fonts*, in which the width of characters is variable (an I will occupy less space than an M, for example). If you're typing a computer program listing or drawing lines around text where you need characters to line up in columns, you'll probably want to use a fixed-pitch font. If you use a proportional font, you may want to set the "show line breaks" field of the Options command to Yes, which makes Word display the line breaks where they will be when printed.

Word always displays text on the screen as 10-point, fixed-pitch type, so if you change fonts or font sizes, you won't see the change on the screen in document view. You will see the different fonts and sizes when you print.

Different fonts come in different sizes, so be sure to choose a font before displaying a list of font sizes; for example, the Pica font may be

---

Helpful Hint

You can specify character formats before you type by choosing the format options with no text selected—this feature applies the format to the insertion point, and any text typed afterward will have that format. For example, a speed typist might enter

>   **fast** is *better*

by pressing Alt+B (for bold), typing "fast," pressing Alt+Spacebar (for plain text), typing "is," pressing Alt+I (for italic), then typing "better."

You can apply any number of character formats at the same time to the selected text: for example, to make text bold and italic, hold down the Alt key and press B, then I.

Note: If you have a style sheet other than NORMAL.STY attached to your document, press X between the Alt key and the letter for the format you want. For example, if you want to make new text bold, press Alt+XB before typing. Using this "X" method always works, so if you have any doubt about the style sheet business, you can always press X in between Alt and the format letter.

Figure 7-3.   **A document with hidden text.**

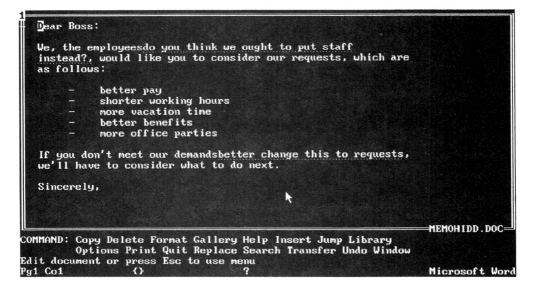

available in 8-, 10-, 12-, and 14-point sizes, but the LinePrinter font may be available only in the 8-point size.

Like fonts and sizes, the font colors available with the Format Character command depend on whether or not your printer can print colors. Word doesn't display the font colors you choose on the screen—you'll have to wait until you print to see them.

Using Hidden Text

Hidden text is so called because you can hide it when you want. Hidden text is generally used to add annotations or codes to a document. Figure 7-3 shows a document that contains hidden text.

Displaying or Hiding Hidden Text

To display or hide hidden text:

1. Choose the Options command.
2. In the "show hidden text" field choose Yes to display the hidden text, or choose No to hide it.
3. Press Enter or click the command name to carry out the command.

If you use Word in the graphics mode, Word draws a dotted underline under displayed hidden text. If you don't use graphics mode, Word displays hidden text in a different color or with a normal underline. No matter whether it's displayed or not, hidden text won't print unless you choose the Print Options command and choose Yes in the "hidden text" field.

When hidden text is displayed, Word counts it to calculate page breaks. Therefore, if you want accurate pagination that doesn't include hidden text, hide text formatted as hidden before choosing any command that causes Word to repaginate, such as the Print commands.

Marking the Location of Hidden Text

You can also mark the location of hidden text even if you don't want to display the text itself.

To insert hidden-text markers into your document:

```
┌──────────────────────────────────────────────────────────────────────────┐
│ Dear·Boss:¶                                                                │
│ ¶                                                                          │
│ We,·the·employees↔·would·like·you·to·consider·our·requests,·              │
│ which·are·as·follows:¶                                                     │
│ ¶                                                                          │
│     →    better·pay¶                                                       │
│     →    shorter·working·hours¶                                            │
│     →    more·vacation·time¶                                               │
│     →    better·benefits¶                                                  │
│     →    more·office·parties¶                                              │
│ ¶                                                                          │
│ If·you·don't·meet·our·demands↔,·we'll·have·to·consider·what·              │
│ to·do·next.¶                                                               │
│ ¶                                                                          │
│ Sincerely,¶                                                                │
│ ¶                                                                          │
│ ¶                                                                          │
│ ¶                                                                          │
│ ■                                                    ═MEMOHIDD.DOC═        │
├──────────────────────────────────────────────────────────────────────────┤
│ COMMAND: Copy Delete Format Gallery Help Insert Jump Library               │
│          Options Print Quit Replace Search Transfer Undo Window      ■     │
│ Edit document or press Esc to use menu                                     │
│ Pg1 Co1          {◆PSB¶...now!¶}    ?                   Microsoft Word     │
└──────────────────────────────────────────────────────────────────────────┘
```

Figure 7-4.   **Hidden-text markers in a document.**

1. Choose the Options command.
2. In the "show hidden text" field, choose No. (You can't display hidden-text markers and the text itself at the same time.)
3. In the "show non-printing symbols" field, choose Partial or All. Word puts a two-headed arrow at each location of invisible hidden text, as shown in Figure 7-4. You can select this arrow to delete or format the hidden text.

REMOVING CHARACTER FORMATS

No matter how many character formats you've applied to text, you can remove all of them with a simple key combination. (This procedure won't, however, remove any character formats controlled by styles; you can find out more about that in Chapter 11.)

To remove all character formats (except those controlled by styles) from text:

1. Select the text.
2. Press Alt+Spacebar.

If you've applied several different character formats to your text (bold, italic, and uppercase, for example), and you want to remove just one (bold, for example) use the following procedure:

To remove a specific character format:

1.   Select the text you want to change.
2.   Choose the Format Character command.
3.   Choose No in the appropriate field.
4.   Press Enter.

REPEATING AND COPYING CHARACTER FORMATTING

If you have a certain combination of character formats you like (such as bold italic Helvetica 14), you can use that combination over and over without choosing all those character formatting commands again.

Copying Formatting with the Mouse

Once you have formatted some text the way you want, you can copy that format to new text using a mouse:

1.   Select the text you want to format.
2.   Point to a character that has the format you want to copy.
3.   Hold down the Alt key.
4.   Click the left mouse button to apply the copied format. This copies all formats attached to the character to which you've pointed.

Repeating the Last Formatting Action

You can use keys to repeat the last formatting action. For example, if you selected text and changed the font, made the text italic, and then made it bold, and then used this procedure to format new text, the new text would be formatted as bold (the last formatting action).

To repeat the last character formatting action:

1.   Format a piece of text.
2.   Select the next piece of text you want to format in the same way.
3.   Press F4 or click the word COMMAND at the left of the menu.

You can repeat steps 2 and 3 to format many pieces of text in the same way.

Saving Character Formats as Styles

You can save character formats as styles, which are named sets of instructions. A style can contain any type of formatting you can do with the Format Character command: bold, italic, small caps, different fonts and sizes, superscripts, and so forth. Once you've defined a certain format as a style, you can select new text and apply that format, no matter how complicated, with just a few keystrokes.

You can learn how to create and apply styles in Chapter 11.

PARAGRAPH FORMATTING

This Chapter Contains the Following:

Displaying Paragraph Marks
Selecting Paragraphs
Applying Paragraph Formats
   Displaying or Hiding the Ruler
Indenting Paragraphs
   Indenting Paragraphs with Keys
   Indenting Paragraphs with the Mouse
Aligning Paragraphs
Changing Line Spacing Within And Between Paragraphs
Positioning Paragraphs Anywhere On A Page
Adding Lines, Boxes, Or Shading To Paragraphs
   Changing or Removing Lines, Boxes, or Shading from a Paragraph
Arranging Paragraphs Side By Side
   Putting Paragraphs Side-by-Side with the Format Paragraph Command
   Putting Paragraphs Side-by-Side with the SIDEBY.STY Style sheet
Searching For Paragraph Formatting
Copying Paragraph Formatting
   Using the Mouse to Copy Paragraph Formatting
   Using the Scrap to Copy Paragraph Formatting
   Saving Paragraph Formatting in a Glossary
   Saving Paragraph Formatting as a Style

Paragraph formatting includes:

• Indenting paragraphs, including left, right, and first line indents.
• Aligning paragraphs horizontally.
• Positioning paragraphs anywhere on a page.
• Changing line spacing within and between paragraphs.
• Putting borders around paragraphs.
• Controlling how page breaks affect paragraphs.
• Setting tabs.

This chapter covers all these types of paragraph formatting except for setting tabs,which is discussed in Chapter 9.

In Word, a paragraph is anything (even a blank line) that ends with a paragraph mark (¶). You insert a paragraph mark into your document every time you press the Enter key. Paragraph marks are always present, but you can choose when to see them.

You've probably noticed that when you press Enter to start a new paragraph, the new paragraph takes on the characteristics of the preceding paragraph. But you can change the format of any paragraph whenever you like. You can format a few paragraphs at a time, or format every paragraph in your document simultaneously.

Word stores a paragraph's format in the paragraph mark, so if you delete a paragraph mark, you'll lose the formatting attached to it, and the text of that paragraph will take on the format of the following paragraph.

DISPLAYING PARAGRAPH MARKS

To display paragraph marks:

1. Choose the Options command. This command can display not only paragraph marks, but also marks for tabs, spaces, newline characters, optional hyphens, and hidden text markers.
2. In the "Visible" field choose one of the following options:

Choose	To Display
Partial	Paragraph marks (¶), newline characters (↵) , optional hyphens (-), and hidden text markers (↔).
Complete	All of the above, plus tab characters (→) and space characters (·).

SELECTING PARAGRAPHS

The general topic of selecting is explained in Chapter 4, "Editing Your Document." Here are a few reminders to make selecting paragraphs easier:

- If you want to format only one paragraph, you don't have to select it—just move the highlight into the paragraph. But, if you want, you can select the paragraph by pressing F10 or clicking the right mouse button in the selection bar next to any line in the paragraph.
- To select several paragraphs press F6, then press F10 until all the paragraphs you want are selected, or hold down the left mouse button and drag the mouse pointer in the selection bar. Figure 8-1 shows the selection bar.
- To select every paragraph in the document press Shift-F10 or point to the selection bar and click both mouse buttons.

Figure 8-1.   **Using the selection bar to select paragraphs with the mouse.**

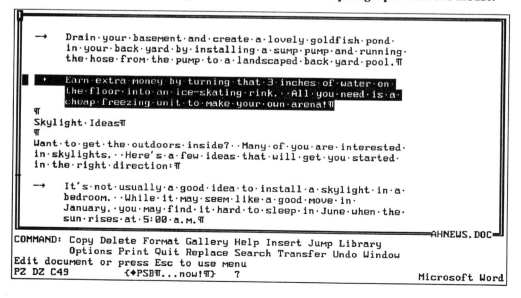

APPLYING PARAGRAPH FORMATS

To format paragraphs, you'll use the Format Paragraph command, and the ruler whose command fields are shown in Figure 8-2. The ruler is a graphic device that allows you to measure distances easily to set indents and tabs in paragraphs. You can display the ruler any time you like.

Displaying or Hiding the Ruler

To display or hide the ruler with keys:

1. Choose the Options command.
2. In the "ruler" field choose Yes to display the ruler, or choose No to hide it.

   To display or hide the ruler with a mouse:

1. Point to the upper right corner of the window. In graphics mode, the mouse pointer changes to three short vertical lines. In text mode, the mouse pointer remains a rectangle.

Figure 8-2.   **The Format Paragraph command fields and the ruler.**

```
⌐ L[·········1·········2·········3·········4·········5·········]·········7····
  →    Drain·your·basement·and·create·a·lovely·goldfish·pond·
       in·your·back·yard·by·installing·a·sump·pump·and·running·
       the·hose·from·the·pump·to·a·landscaped·back·yard·pool.¶

  →    Earn·extra·money·by·turning·that·3·inches·of·water·on·
       the·floor·into·an·ice-skating·rink.··All·you·need·is·a·
       cheap·freezing·unit·to·make·your·own·arena!¶
  ¶
  Skylight·Ideas¶
  ¶
  Want·to·get·the·outdoors·inside?··Many·of·you·are·interested·
  ▓n·skylights.··Here's·a·few·ideas·that·will·get·you·started·
  in·the·right·direction:¶

  →    It's·not·usually·a·good·idea·to·install·a·skylight·in·a·
       bedroom.··While·it·may·seem·like·a·good·move·in·

FORMAT PARAGRAPH alignment: ▓Left▓ Centered Right Justified
     left indent: 0"          first line: 0"          right indent: 0"
     line spacing: 1 li       space before: 0 li       space after: 0 li
     keep together: Yes(No)   keep follow: Yes(No)     side by side: Yes(No)   ▓
Select option
PZ DZ C1          {♦PSB¶...now!¶}    ?                      Microsoft Word
```

2. Click the left mouse button to display the ruler, or click both mouse buttons simultaneously to hide it.

INDENTING PARAGRAPHS

When you indent paragraphs, you set the spacing between the paragraph and the margin, as shown in Figure 8-3. You can specify a left indent, a right indent, and a first line indent.

Word assumes measurements are in inches unless you changed the default unit of measurement in the "measure" field of the Options command. To specify a measurement in units other than the default units, you simply type one of these abbreviations after the measurement number:

Type	To Indicate a Measurement in
in or "	inches
cm	centimeters
p10	10-pitch font (10 characters per inch)
p12	12-pitch font (12 characters per inch)
pt	points (72 points per inch)

Figure 8-3.   **You can specify three indents.**

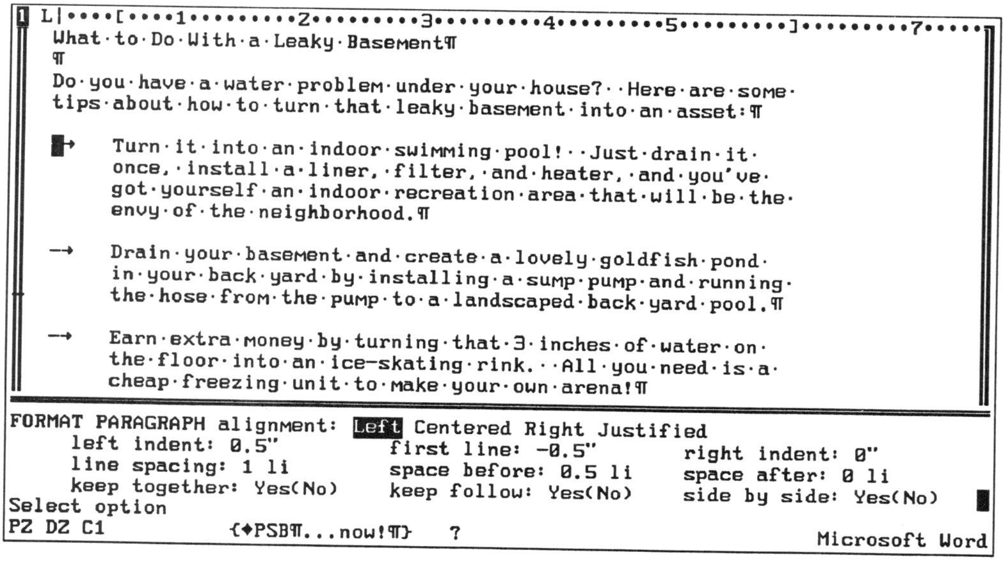

When you use one of these abbreviations, Word converts the measurement you type to its equivalent in the default unit of measurement. In other words, if the default unit of measurement is inches, and you type 40 pt in the "left indent" field, Word converts your 40 points to .56 inches.

Indents are most often measured in hundredths of an inch. For example, to indent a paragraph 3/4 of an inch, you type .75 in the "left indent" field.

Indenting Paragraphs with Keys

To indent paragraphs with keys:

1. Select the paragraphs.
2. Choose the Format Paragraph command.
3. Set the indents you want:

To Indent	Type
Left	A measurement in the "left indent" field. The left indent is measured from the left margin, so if you type *.5* here, the lines in your paragraph will begin 1/2 inch from the left margin.
First line	A measurement in the "first line." field. Word measures the first line measurement from the left indent, not the left margin. For example, if you type *.5* here and you also have a left indent of .5, the first line of the paragraph will begin 1 inch (.5+.5) from the left margin. To create a hanging indent, set a left indent, then type a negative measurement in this field. For example, to indent the text of a numbered paragraph 3/10 of an inch but position the number at the left margin, type *.3* in the "left indent" field, then type *-.3* in the *first line* field.
Right	A measurement in the "right indent" field. Word measures the right indent from the right margin of the document, so if you type *.5* here, the lines in your paragraph will end 1/2 inch from the right margin.

Indenting Paragraphs with the Mouse

To indent paragraphs using the mouse:

1. Select the paragraphs.
2. If the ruler is not displayed, point to the upper right corner of the window and click the right mouse button. Word displays the ruler at the top of the window.
3. Point to the marker in the ruler that represents the indent you want to

---

Example

Instructions for the Jump:¶

   1.→Strap on your parachute, checking all straps and buckles to make sure they are secure.¶
   2.→Jump out of the plane when the pilot informs you that you are over the landing area.¶
   3.→Count to 10.¶
   4.→Pull the ripcord.¶

To duplicate these instructions, you would:

1. Type all text at the left margin—don't try to put spaces before the numbers. Press the Tab key where you see the tab character (→.). Press Enter only where you see paragraph marks(¶).
2. Select the four numbered paragraphs.
3. Choose the Format Paragraph command.
4. In the "left indent" field, type .5.
5. In the "first line field, type −.3
6. Press Enter or click the command name to format the paragraphs.

```
 L|••••[••••1•••••••••2•••••••••3•••••••••4•••••••••5•••••••••]•••••••••7•••••
 ¶
 Skylight·Ideas¶
 ¶
 Want·to·get·the·outdoors·inside?··Many·of·you·are·interested·
 in·skylights.··Here's·a·few·ideas·that·will·get·you·started·
 in·the·right·direction:¶

 →   It's·not·usually·a·good·idea·to·install·a·skylight·in·a·
     bedroom.··While·it·may·seem·like·a·good·move·in·
     January,·you·may·find·it·hard·to·sleep·in·June·when·the·
     sun·rises·at·5:00·a.m.¶

 ▐▶  A·skylight·with·no·cover·can·make·a·room·very·hot·in·
     the·summertime.··We·recommend·that·you·install·a·
     moveable·cover·on·every·skylight,·and·that·you·install·
     the·covers·inside·(climbing·up·on·the·roof·to·cover·
     skylights·gets·very·tedious!).¶
 :::::::::::::::::::::::::::::::::::::::::::::::::::::::::::::::::::::::::
 ◆                                                    ═AHNEWS.DOC═
┌─────────────────────────────────────────────────────────────────────────┐
 COMMAND: Copy Delete Format Gallery Help Insert Jump Library
         Options Print Quit Replace Search Transfer Undo Window
 Edit document or press Esc to use menu
 PZ DZ C1          {◆PSB¶...now!¶}   ?              Microsoft Word
```

Figure 8-4.   **Indent markers in the ruler.**

change. Figure 8-4 shows indent markers in the ruler:

[Left indent
] Right indent
| First line indent

Note: Indent markers may be covered by tab markers (L,C,R,D, or vertical line). If the first line indent and the left indent are the same, the first line marker may be covered by the left indent marker. If the marker you want to move is covered by another marker, drag the top marker off, move the bottom marker to the new position, then drag the top marker back to the original position.

4.   Hold down the right button and drag the indent marker to the new position. (Only the highlight moves.)

5.   Release the mouse button.
     Word moves the indent marker to the new position.

6. Press Enter or click the command name to set the indents.

You'll learn more about using tabs in "Setting Tabs" in Chapter 9.

Keyboard Shortcuts

You can indent paragraphs by default amounts just by pressing keys. Just select the paragraphs to indent, then use the key combinations shown below:

Press	To
Alt+N	Indent whole paragraph from the left margin to the next tab position (usually 1/2 inch)
Alt+F	Indent only the first line to the next tab position (usually 1/2 inch)
Alt+T	Indent all lines except the first line to the next tab position, creating a hanging indent
Alt+M	Decrease left indent back to the previous tab position (usually 1/2 inch)
Alt+Q	Indent paragraph from both left and right margins to the closest tab position (usually 1/2 inch)

You can press all these key combinations several times to set the indent you want.

If you're using a style sheet other than NORMAL.STY, press X between the Alt key and the format letter. For example, to indent the paragraph to the next tab position, press Alt+XN.

ALIGNING PARAGRAPHS

Word aligns paragraphs horizontally between indents (or between margins if you haven't indented your paragraphs). You can choose from four paragraph alignments: left (the default choice), centered, right, and justified.

Here's an example of how these different alignments work. The vertical lines represent the left and right paragraph indents.

> The text in this paragraph is aligned with the left indent (left-aligned).
>
> The text in this paragraph is centered between left and right indents.
>
> The text in this paragraph is aligned with the right indent (right-aligned).
>
> The text in this paragraph is justified— aligned with both left and right indents, and padded with spaces to make line lengths even. (Note that Word does not justify the last line of a paragraph.)

To align paragraphs:

1. Select the paragraphs.
2. Choose the Format Paragraph command.

Keyboard Shortcuts

You can quickly align paragraphs without choosing a command. Just select the paragraphs, then use the key combinations shown below.

Press	To
Alt+L	Align text with left indent
Alt+C	Center text
Alt+R	Align text with right indent
Alt+J	Justify text

Note: If you are using a style sheet other than NORMAL.STY, press an X between the Alt key and the letter above. For example, to center a paragraph when using a style sheet, you'd press Alt+XC. You can learn more about style sheets in Chapter 11.

3. In the "alignment" field choose Left, Centered, Right, or Justified.
4. Press Enter or click the command name to format the selected paragraphs.

CHANGING LINE SPACING WITHIN AND BETWEEN PARAGRAPHS

You may want to change the line spacing in all or part of your document. Word allows you to specify not only the line spacing within a paragraph, but also the space before and after a paragraph.

To determine the amount of space between paragraphs, Word adds the space after a paragraph to the space before the next paragraph. For example, if you add 5 points of space after one paragraph and add 5 points of space before the following paragraph, Word puts 10 points of space between the two paragraphs.

Word assumes measurements you type in the "line spacing," "space before," and "space after" fields are in lines (one line = 12 points or 1/6 inch) unless you type one of these abbreviations after the measurement number:

Type	To Indicate a Measurement in
in or "	inches
cm	centimeters
p10	10-pitch font (10 characters per inch)
p12	12-pitch font (12 characters per inch)
pt	points (72 points per inch)

To change line spacing in paragraphs:

1. Select the paragraphs.
2. Choose the Format Paragraph command.
3. Set the spacing you want.

To Set the Spacing	Type a Measurement in This Field
Within paragraphs	"Line spacing"
Before paragraphs	"Space before"
After paragraphs	"Space after"

4. Press Enter or click the command name to format the paragraphs.

Keyboard Shortcuts

You can also set line spacing without choosing a command. Just select the paragraphs, then use the key combinations below:

Press	To
Alt+2	Double-space text.
Alt+1	Single-space text.
Alt+O (letter "O")	To "open" spacing (insert one blank line) before paragraphs.

Note: If you are using a style sheet other than NORMAL.STY, press an X between the Alt key and the formatting character. For example, to double-space a paragraph, you'd press Alt+X2. You can learn more about style sheets in Chapter 11.

POSITIONING PARAGRAPHS ANYWHERE ON A PAGE

As well as using indent and alignment options to position paragraphs horizontally on a page, you can use the Format pOsition command to place paragraphs anywhere on a page by specifying both the vertical and the horizontal position. When a paragraph is positioned with the Format pOsition command, surrounding text "flows" around it, the same way text in a magazine article flows around a photograph. You can use this Word feature to create imaginative page layouts. For example, you might choose to center a boxed paragraph on a page or to move a paragraph into the left or right margin, creating a "sidebar" paragraph.

To learn more about using the Format pOsition command to position paragraphs, see "Positioning Objects Anywhere on a Page" in Chapter 14, "Perfecting Your Pages."

ADDING LINES, BOXES, OR SHADING TO PARAGRAPHS

You can draw lines above, below, or beside a paragraph, or enclose a paragraph in a box to make it stand out from the rest of your text. You can also add shading to the background of a paragraph. Figure 8-5 shows some examples of what you can do with the border options.

Word determines the length of border lines by calculating the size of the paragraph and adding some white space around it to form a paragraph "block." You can adjust the width of the paragraph and the surrounding lines or shading by indenting the paragraph. Just like any paragraph, you can align the text within boxes and lines by choosing alignment options as described in "Aligning Paragraphs" earlier in this chapter. When adding shading, Word fills the paragraph block with the intensity of shading you specify.

Shading does not appear on the screen, but you can choose the Print preView command to see it, and it will show up in your printed document. Depending on your printer, there may be other differences between what you see on your screen and what you'll see in your printed document. If your printer can print IBM graphics characters, borders and shading will print exactly as they appear on the screen. However, if your printer doesn't support the IBM graphics characters, you won't be able to print bold, double, or thick lines. You can check the *Printer Information for Microsoft Word* manual to see what your printer can do.

Figure 8-5.   **Paragraphs with borders and shading options.**

```
+===============================+
| This paragraph has a          |
| double-lined box around       |
| it.                           |
+===============================+
```

```
+-------------------------------+
| This paragraph has a          |
| single-lined box around       |
| it.                           |
+-------------------------------+
```

```
This paragraph has normal
lines above and below and a
medium shading
(intensity=40).
```

```
━━━━━━━━━━━━━━━━━━━━━━━━━━━━━━━━━
This paragraph has thick
lines on the top and
bottom.
━━━━━━━━━━━━━━━━━━━━━━━━━━━━━━━━━
```

```
‖ This paragraph has double    ‖
‖ lines on the right and       ‖
‖ left.                        ‖
```

```
+-------------------------------+
| This paragraph has a bold     |
| box and a light shading       |
| (intensity=10).               |
+-------------------------------+
```

Word keeps all the text in a boxed paragraph on the same page, so if a page break would naturally occur within the boxed text, Word will shift the entire paragraph to the next page.

To add lines, a box, or shading to a paragraph:

1. Select the paragraph.
2. Choose the Format Border command.
3. In the "type" field, choose Box if you want to completely enclose the paragraph, or choose Lines if you want to add lines on one or more sides of the paragraph.
4. In the "line style" field, leave the proposed setting as Normal (a thin single line), or press F1 and highlight Bold, Double, or Thick.
5. Choose from the following options:

If	Do This
You can print in color and to choose a different color	Press F1 in the "color" field and select a color to print the lines in
You chose Lines in the "type" field	Choose Yes or No in the "left," "right", "above," and "below" fields to tell Word where to draw lines
You want to add back-ground shading	Press F1 in the "background shading" field, then highlight a number to specify how dark you want the shading, or type a number between 1 and 100. The higher the number, the darker the shading

6. Press Enter or click the command name to carry out the command.

Figure 8-6 illustrates drawing lines around a paragraph. If you draw lines or boxes around consecutive paragraphs, the paragraphs may share a common line. To put space between the lines or boxes, you insert a blank line between them, or add space between paragraphs by selecting them then specifying measurements in the "space before" and "space after" fields of the Format Paragraph command.

```
┌─────────────────────────────────────────────────────────────────────────┐
│▌L0··········1····[····2·········3··········4···]····5·········6··········7····▐│
│                          ¶                                                │
│                          ¶                                                │
│                  This·paragraph·will·have·                                │
│                  double·lines·at·top·and·bottom·                          │
│                  when·I'm·through·with·it.¶                               │
│           ◆                                                               │
│                                                                           │
│                                                                           │
│                                                                           │
│                                                                           │
│                                                                           │
│                                                                           │
│                                                                           │
│                                                                           │
│                                                                           │
│                                                                           │
├───────────────────────────────────────────────────────────────────────────┤
│FORMAT BORDER type:  None Box(Lines)        line style: Double    color:  Black  │
│   left: Yes(No)        right:(Yes)No       above: Yes(No)        below: ▓Yes▓ No│
│   background shading: 0                     shading color: Black           ▮│
│Select option                                                              │
│Pg1 Co19              {¶}                ?               Microsoft Word     │
└───────────────────────────────────────────────────────────────────────────┘
```

Figure 8-6.   **Adding lines to a paragraph with the Format Border command.**

┌───┐
│   **Helpful Hint**   │
├───┤
│   │
│ If you want to put more than one paragraph in the same box, press   │
│ Shift+Enter at the end of all paragraphs except for the last paragraph you│
│ want to box. Pressing Shift+Enter inserts a newline character, which   │
│ breaks the line without creating a new paragraph. To end the last   │
│ "paragraph," press Enter.   │
│   Your text will look as if it were broken into separate paragraphs, but│
│ Word will consider it to be one paragraph, and will draw a box around all │
│ the text between one paragraph mark and the next.   │
│   │
└───┘

Changing or Removing Lines, Boxes, or Shading from a Paragraph

To change or remove lines or boxes:

1. Select the paragraph you want to change.
2. Choose the Format Border command.

3. Change the command fields to match the options you want. To remove lines choose No in the "left," "right," "above," and "below" fields.

4. Press Enter or click the command name to change the paragraph.

ARRANGING PARAGRAPHS SIDE BY SIDE

Word has several ways in which you can arrange paragraphs side by side, like those shown in Figure 8-7. In this section, we'll cover two ways: one method that formats paragraphs with the Format Paragraph command, and one method that uses a style sheet to format the paragraphs.

Paragraphs formatted as side-by-side paragraphs don't appear that way in document view, as shown in Figure 8-8. To see paragraphs side by side as shown in Figure 8-9, you'll have to turn on the "show layout" option of the Options command or switch to print preview. (You'll learn more about print preview in Chapter 14).

Putting Paragraphs Side-by-Side with the Format Paragraph Command

To create side-by-side paragraphs using the Format Paragraph command:

1. Determine the width of the text area at the location where you want to insert the paragraphs. The formula is:

Width of text area = (width of paper - left and right margins).

2. Write down the width of the paragraphs. Be sure that the width of both paragraphs plus the width of the space between paragraphs adds up to the width of the text area. For example, your figures might look something like the following for side-by-side paragraphs in a 6-inch wide text area:

- left paragraph width   2.0 inch
- right paragraph width   3.5 inch
- space between paragraphs   .5 inch
                              ─────────
                              6.0 inch

```
L0••••••••••1•••••••••2•••••••••3••••[••••4•••••••••5•••••••••]•••••••••7••••
       Conversational·Spanish↓
         MWF·10—11:30·AM↓
       Valdez·Hall·Rm.·106¶
                                    Did·you·know·the·United·
                                    States·has·the·third·
                                    largest·Spanish·speaking·
                                    population·in·the·world?··
                                    Come·learn·the·second·
                                    language·of·your·own·
                                    country,·so·you·can·
                                    travel·comfortably·in·
                                    California,·Texas,·
                                    Florida,·New·Mexico,·and·
                                    other·exotic·locations.¶



                                                            ═SBSPARAS.DOC═
COMMAND: Copy Delete Format Gallery Help Insert Jump Library
         Options Print Quit Replace Search Transfer Undo Window
310 characters
Pg1 Co36           {¶}                    ?              Microsoft Word
```

Figure 8-7.   **Side-by-side paragraphs in document view.**

Figure 8-8.   **Side-by-side paragraphs in "show layout" view.**

```
L]•••••••••1•••••••••2•••••••••═
       Conversational·Spanish          Did·you·know·the·United·
         MWF·10—11:30·AM↓              States·has·the·third·
       Valdez·Hall·Rm.·106¶            largest·Spanish·speaking·
                                       population·in·the·world?··
                                       Come·learn·the·second·
                                       language·of·your·own·
                                       country,·so·you·can·
                                       travel·comfortably·in·
                                       California,·Texas,·
                                       Florida,·New·Mexico,·and·
                                       other·exotic·locations.¶
                                       ◆



                                                            ═SBSPARAS.DOC═
COMMAND: Copy Delete Format Gallery Help Insert Jump Library
         Options Print Quit Replace Search Transfer Undo Window
Edit document or press Esc to use menu
Pg1 Co28           {¶}                    ?              Microsoft Word
```

3. Write down the indents you need to set up the paragraphs. Remember to measure the left indents (for both paragraphs) from the left document margin and the right indents from the right margin. For example, to format a 2-inch wide left -hand paragraph in a 6-inch wide text area, you'd set a left indent of 0 and a right indent of 4 inches. To format a 3.5-inch wide right-hand paragraph in the same text area with .5 inch of space between the paragraphs, you'd set a left indent of 2.5 inches and a right indent of 0 for the right-hand paragraph. Figure 8-9 shows how this is done.

   Note: The left indents of the paragraphs control their positions. If the left indent for the right-hand paragraph is not larger than the left indent for the left-hand paragraph, the paragraphs may not end up side by side.

4. To switch to show layout view so you can see the paragraphs side by side as you type them, press Alt+F4 or choose the Options command and choose Yes in the "show layout" field.

5. Type the left-hand paragraph, then select it.

Figure 8-9.   **The indent settings control the position of side-by-side paragraphs.**

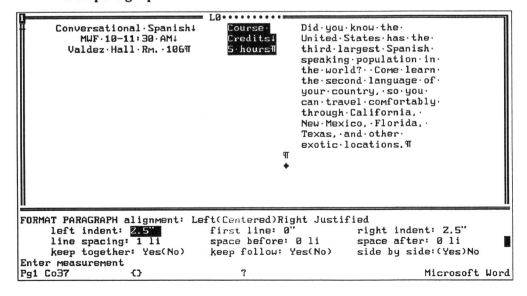

6. Choose the Format Paragraph command, fill in the "left indent" and "right indent" fields, choose Yes in the "side-by-side" field, choose any other options you want, then press Enter.

7. Type the right-hand paragraph, then select it.

8. Choose the Format Paragraph command, fill in the "left indent" and "right indent" fields, choose Yes in the "side-by-side" field, choose any other options you want, then press Enter.

Once you've formatted side-by-side paragraphs in this way, you can save that format as a style so you can use it later, or you can copy and save the paragraph marks as glossary entries. See Chapter 11 for more information about styles, or see "Saving Text and Graphics for Later Use: Using Glossaries" in Chapter 4 for, more information about glossary entries.

Putting Paragraphs Side-by-Side with the SIDEBY.STY Style Sheet

You can also put paragraphs side by side by using styles from the SIDEBY.STY style sheet which comes with Word. (You can learn more about style sheets in Chapter 11.) Don't type the paragraphs before beginning the following procedure. You're going to attach the style sheet, change to "show layout" mode to see the paragraphs more easily, then type and format the paragraphs. To use the following procedure, your document must have Word's default settings of 8.5-inch paper and left and right margins of 1.25 inches.

To use the SIDEBY.STY style sheet to create side-by-side paragraphs:

1. If necessary, copy the SIDEBY.STY file onto the disk and into the directory containing your document. The SIDEBY.STY file is included with Word on the Utilities disk.

2. Choose the Format Stylesheet Attach command.

3. Press F1 and highlight SIDEBY.STY in the list of stylesheets.

4. Press Enter or click the command name to attach the stylesheet to your document.

5. Choose the Options command.

6. In the "show layout" field, choose Yes, then press Enter. This step allows you to see your paragraphs side by side as you create them.

7. Type the text for the left-hand paragraph.

8. Press Alt+2L to apply the left-hand paragraph style.

9. Type the text for the right-hand paragraph.
10. Press Alt+2R to apply the right-hand paragraph style.
11. Repeat steps 7 through 10 to create up to 32 sets of side-by-side paragraphs.

If you want to create more than 32 sets of side-by-side paragraphs, put a blank line after the 32nd set, then type and apply styles to 32 more.

At times you may want to have two or more paragraphs in the right column, as shown in Figure 8-10. To put more than one paragraph in the right column:

1. Follow steps 1 through 10 in the procedure above.
2. Type the text for the next right-hand paragraph.
3. Press Alt+2R to apply the right-hand style to the paragraph.
4. Repeat steps 2 and 3 to add more paragraphs if necessary.

If you'd like to add space between the paragraphs in the right column, select the second (and third and fourth, etc.) paragraphs, then press Alt+XO to add space before the paragraphs.

Figure 8-10.   **Side-by-side paragraphs with more than one paragraph in the right column.**

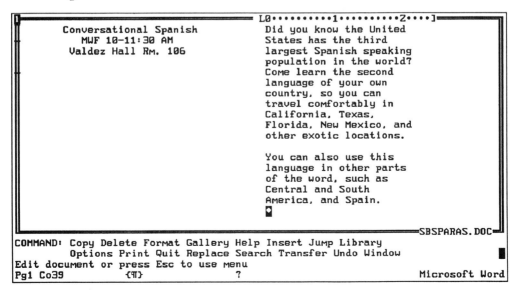

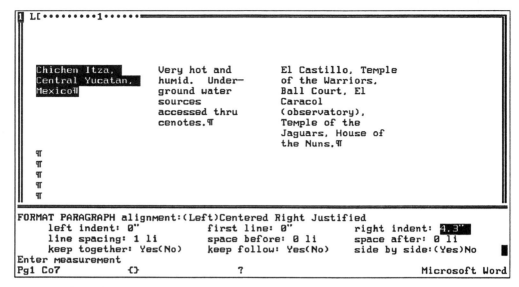

Figure 8-11.   **Three side-by-side paragraphs.**

You can also create three side-by-side paragraphs like those in Figure 8-11. Use the same basic procedure as described above, except press Alt+3L to format the left paragraph, press Alt+3C to format the center paragraph, and press Alt+3R to format the right paragraph.

SEARCHING FOR PARAGRAPH FORMATTING

To search for paragraph formatting, Word uses the Format sEarch Paragraph command. This command searches only for formats applied with the Format Paragraph command or with the formatting key combinations. To search for styles attached to paragraphs, use the Format sEarch Style command (refer to "Searching for and Replacing Styles" in Chapter 11 for instructions).

To search for paragraph formatting:

1. Choose the Format sEarch Paragraph command.
    Word displays the command fields for the Format Paragraph command.

Helpful Hint

You can copy characters along with a formatted paragraph mark to a glossary for later use.

For example, you might want to copy a bullet character (Alt+254 [type numbers on the numeric keypad] makes a nice one) followed by a tab character and a formatted paragraph mark (→.¶) containing the indent and the tab settings you use for a bulleted list. Then, when you want to start a bulleted list, just use the Insert command to insert that glossary entry, then type the new text in front of the paragraph mark.

---

2. Choose options in the fields to specify the formats for which you want to search. For example, if you want to search for a centered paragraph, choose Center in the "alignment" field.
3. Press Enter to begin searching. Word highlights the first paragraph it finds with the same format.
4. Press Shift+F4 if you want to search again for the next paragraph with that format.

COPYING PARAGRAPH FORMATTING

You can copy paragraph formatting using four different methods. The first two of these methods are for use during one editing session with Word. The last two methods save paragraph formatting for later use.

Using the Mouse to Copy Paragraph Formatting

To use the mouse to quickly copy a paragraph format from one place to another:

1. Select the paragraphs you want to format.
2. Move the mouse pointer to the selection bar next to a paragraph that has the format you want to copy.
3. Hold down the Alt key and click the right mouse button.

Using the Scrap to Copy Paragraph Formatting

You can use the Copy and Insert commands to quickly copy paragraph formatting:

1. Select the paragraph mark (¶) of the paragraph whose format you want to copy. (Choose the Options command, then choose the Partial option to see paragraph marks if necessary.)
2. Choose the Copy command to copy the paragraph mark to the scrap.
3. If you're changing the format of an existing paragraph, select the paragraph mark of the paragraph you want to affect, then press Shift+Ins. If you want to insert the paragraph mark, then type new text, move the cursor to the new location, then press Ins. If you selected an existing paragraph mark, the copied formatting will replace the old formatting. If you want to type new text, move the cursor in front of the copied paragraph mark, then type.

Saving Paragraph Formatting in a Glossary

If you want to use a certain paragraph format over and over again, you can save the paragraph mark as a glossary entry. Then you can insert it any time you want to replace the format of an existing paragraph or type new text in front of it.

To save a paragraph format in a glossary, then use it to format new text:

1. Select the paragraph mark (¶) of the paragraph whose format you want to copy.
2. Use the Copy command to define the format as a glossary item. (See "Saving Text and Graphics for Repeated Use: Using Glossaries" in Chapter 4 for more information about defining glossary items.)
3. When you want to use that format for new text, use the Insert command to insert the glossary item.

Saving Paragraph Formatting as a Style

You can save both paragraph formatting and character formatting as a style in Word. Then you can use that style over and over again to format new paragraphs. (See Chapter 11 for more information about creating and using styles.)

TABS AND TABLES

This contains the following:

Adding New Columns
Adding Lines and Borders to Tables

When everyone used typewriters or primitive word processing software, you had to use tabs to position all text that you didn't want to start at the left margin. With Word, this task is no longer necessary. You have several options at your disposal to accomplish the tasks you used to do with tabs:

To	Use
Indent a paragraph	The Format Paragraph command (discussed in "Indenting Paragraphs" in Chapter 8).
Arrange text in flowing columns (like a newspaper article)	The Format Division Layout command (discussed in Chapter 10, "Division Formatting").
Put paragraphs side-by-side	The Format Paragraph command or styles (discussed in "Arranging Paragraphs Side by Side" in Chapter 8).

However, you'll still want to use tabs in the following situations:

- To put data in tables:
  Aardvarks $99 each
  Opossums $75 each
- To align columns of text in special ways:

Decimal Alignment	Centered	Right Alignment
43.221	Kim	11
91.50	Rebecca	90
8.2	Erika	46
966.8	Manuel Jose	1,322

- To do a simple indent:
  All I have to say to you, my son, is:
  Don't do that again!
- To create bulleted or numbered lists (often in combination with indents, as explained in "Indenting Paragraphs" in Chapter 8):

  1. Type the letters.   • desks
  2. Make copies.   • chairs
  3. Mail the originals.   • telephones
  4. File the copies.   • notepads

SETTING TABS

You can use the Format Tab Set command and/or the ruler to set tabs and draw vertical lines in paragraphs. The following sections show you how.

Displaying Tab Characters

You insert a tab character every time you press the Tab key. Tab characters are small arrows that point right (→). Tab characters are invisible unless you choose to display them.

To see tab characters (and all other special formatting characters):

1. Choose the Options command.
2. In the "show nonprinting symbols" field, choose All.

To hide tab characters (and all other special formatting characters):

1. Choose the Options command.
2. In the "show nonprinting symbols" field, choose None.

Word has four types of tabs that align text in certain ways: left, right, center, and decimal tabs. Figure 9-1 illustrates how text aligned at these tabs would look. Word also has a special tab type that draws a vertical line in paragraphs at the tab position—that's what creates the vertical line you see in Figure 9-1. The vertical-line tab type is normally used to draw lines between columns in tables.

Setting Individual Tabs

You can set tabs for a paragraph before you type the text by placing the cursor before the paragraph mark on a blank line. However, it's usually easier to type your text first and press the Tab key wherever you want a tab. Don't worry if your text doesn't line up; it will be taken care of when you set tabs using one of the following procedures.

To set tabs, you'll use Word's Format Tab Set command and the ruler. The ruler allows you to measure distances easily and see the position and type of tabs in your paragraphs. If you're using a mouse, you can also use the ruler to set, move, and delete tabs without choosing a command.

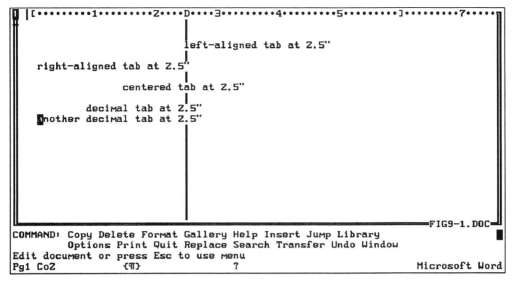

Figure 9-1.   **Text aligned at different types of tabs.**

When you choose the Format Tab Set command, Word automatically displays the ruler. However, you can choose to display or hide the ruler whenever you want by choosing Yes in the "ruler" field of the Window Options command or by clicking the right mouse button while pointing to the upper right corner of the window.

Setting Tabs with the Format Tab Set Command

To set tabs with the Format Tab Set command:

1. Select the paragraphs containing the text and tab characters.
2. Press Alt+F1 to choose the Format Tab Set command and put a highlight in the ruler, as shown in Figure 9-2.
3. Press the right and left arrow keys to move the highlight on the ruler to the position where you want the tab. Word displays the measurement for the position in the "position" field.

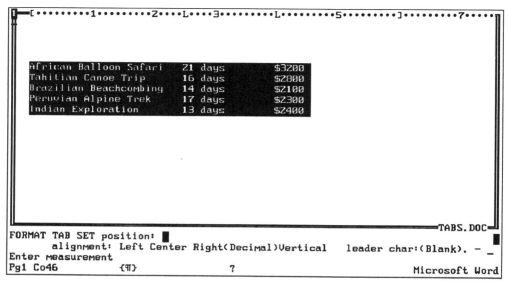

Figure 9-2.   **Setting tabs with the Format Tab Set command and the ruler.**

4. Press a letter to choose the type of tab you want:

Press	To Choose	Description
L	Left	Aligns left edge of text with the tab position.
C	Center	Centers text on the tab position.
R	Right	Aligns right edge of text with the tab position.
D	Decimal	Aligns decimal points in numbers with the tab position.
V	Vertical	Draws a vertical line at the tab position.

5. Repeat steps 3 and 4 to set all the tabs you want in the paragraphs.
6. Press Enter or click the command name to carry out the command.

Figure 9.2 illustrates setting tabs with Format Tab Set command.

Setting Tabs with the Mouse and the Ruler

To set tabs with the ruler:

1. Select the paragraphs containing the tab characters.
2. If the ruler is not displayed, point to the upper right corner of the window and click the right mouse button.
3. If you want to set a different type of tab (centered, right, decimal, or vertical line), point to the L just to the left of the ruler (as shown in Figure 9-3) and click the left mouse button until you see the first letter of the alignment you want (L, C, R, D for Left, Center, Right, or Decimal, respectively) or a vertical line symbol (|).
4. Point to the position on to where you want to insert the tab on the ruler and click the left mouse button.
5. Repeat steps 3 and 4 for each tab you want to set in the selected paragraphs.

Example

Bananas $7.80
Extra Large Cage $175.50

To create this very simple table, you would:

1. Type the text, pressing the Tab key where you want a tab. The text might look something like the following (assuming you chose All in the "show nonprinting symbols" field of the Options command to see the tab characters):
   Bananas→ $7.80
   Extra Large Cage→ $175.50
2. Select both paragraphs.
3. Press Alt+F1 to choose the Format Tab Set command and display a highlight in the ruler.
4. Use the right and left arrow keys to move the highlight in the ruler to an appropriate position for the decimal point in the second column.
5. Press D to choose a decimal tab.
6. Press Enter

```
D[· · · · · · · · ·1· · · · · · · · ·2· · · · ·L· · ·3· · · · · · · · ·L· · · · ·D· · ·5· · · · · · · · · · ·]· · · · · · · · ·7· · · ·
  ¶
  ¶
  ¶
  ¶
  ¶
  African·Balloon·Safari ›    21·days→        $3200.25¶
  Tahitian·Canoe·Trip ›      16·days→        $2800.92¶
  Brazilian·Beachcombing ›   14·days→        $2100.63¶
  Peruvian·Alpine·Trek→      17·days→        $2300.49¶
  Indian·Exploration ›       13·days→        $2400.95¶
  Everglades·Adventure ›      4·days→        $·495.95¶
  ¶
  ¶
  ¶
  ¶
  ¶
  ¶
  ¶
  ¶
                                                              ═TABS.DOC═
COMMAND: Copy Delete Format Gallery Help Insert Jump Library
         Options Print Quit Replace Search Transfer Undo Window
Edit document or press Esc to use menu
Pg1 Co49              {c}              ?                    Microsoft Word
```

Figure 9-3.   **Setting tabs on the ruler.**

Changing the Default Tab Spacing

Word sets default tab spacing at 1/2 inch, which is why the cursor jumps to the next inch or 1/2-inch position when you press the Tab key. As you saw in the previous section, you can set individual tabs wherever you like. You can also change the default tab spacing to a new measurement.

To change the default tab spacing:

1. Choose the Options command. Word displays the command fields shown in Figure 9-4.
2. In the "default tab width" field, type a new measurement. For example, if you wanted to set default tab stops every 3/4 inch, type *.75* and Word would put tabs at .75, 1.5, 2.25 inches, etc. Word assumes the measurements you type are in inches unless you've changed the default unit of measurement in the "measure" field or you type a unit an abbreviation after the number, such as *cm* for centimeters or *pt* for points. For example, to specify tabs every 50 points, you could type *50 pt.*
3. Press Enter or click the command name.

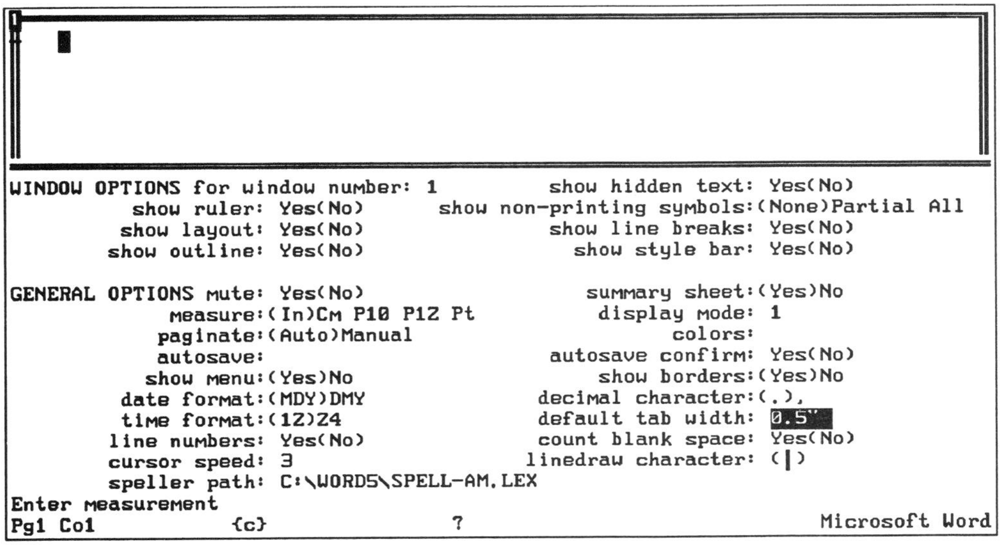

```
┌─────────────────────────────────────────────────────────────────┐
│▐                                                                 │
│ ▐                                                               ║║
│                                                                 ║║
│                                                                 ║║
│                                                                 ║║
│                                                                 ║║
└─────────────────────────────────────────────────────────────────┘
```

```
WINDOW OPTIONS for window number: 1         show hidden text: Yes(No)
         show ruler: Yes(No)      show non-printing symbols:(None)Partial All
        show layout: Yes(No)              show line breaks: Yes(No)
       show outline: Yes(No)               show style bar: Yes(No)

GENERAL OPTIONS mute: Yes(No)                summary sheet:(Yes)No
            measure:(In)Cm P10 P12 Pt        display mode: 1
           paginate:(Auto)Manual                   colors:
           autosave:                    autosave confirm: Yes(No)
          show menu:(Yes)No                 show borders:(Yes)No
        date format:(MDY)DMY            decimal character:(.),
        time format:(12)24             default tab width: ▓0.5"▓▓
       line numbers: Yes(No)           count blank space: Yes(No)
       cursor speed: 3                 linedraw character: (│)
       speller path: C:\WORD5\SPELL-AM.LEX
Enter measurement
Pg1 Co1            {c}                  ?              Microsoft Word
```

Figure 9-4. ,   **The Options command controls default tab spacing.**

Moving, Deleting, and Changing the Types of Tabs

Moving and deleting tabs is just as easy as setting them. You can use either the ruler or the Format Tab Set command to change and rearrange your tabs.

Changing Tabs with the Format Tab Set Command

To use the Format Tab Set command to delete a tab or change the type of tab:

1. Select the paragraphs you want to affect.
2. Press Alt+F1 to choose the Format Tab Set command and display a highlight in the ruler.
3. Use the Down arrow key to move the highlight to the first tab you want to change.
4. Do one of the following:

- If you want to change the tab type, press a letter to choose the new tab type:

  L   Left
  C   Centered
  R   Right
  D   Decimal
  V   Vertical line

  or

- If you want to delete the tab, press Del.

5. Press Enter or click the command name.
    To move a tab with the keys:

    1. Select the paragraphs you want to affect.
    2. Press Alt+F1 to choose the Format Tab Set command and put a highlight in the ruler.
    3. Use the Down and Up arrow keys to highlight to the tab you want to move.
    4. Move the tab to a new position as follows:

    PressTo
    Ctrl+Left Move tab to left
    Ctrl+Right Move tab to right

5. Repeat steps 3 and 4 to move all the tabs you want.
6. When all tabs are where you want them, press Enter or click the command name.

Changing Tabs with Mouse and the Ruler

To change a tab type or delete a tab using the mouse and the ruler:

1. Select the paragraphs you want to affect.
2. If the ruler is not displayed, point to the upper right corner of the window and click the right mouse button.
3. To change the type of a tab, point to the L just left of the ruler, then click the left mouse button until the first letter of the alignment you want is visible, then point to where you want to insert a tab on the ruler and click the left mouse button.
    To delete a tab, point to the tab in the ruler and click both mouse buttons simultaneously.

To move a tab with the mouse:

1. Select the paragraphs you want to affect.
2. If the ruler is not displayed, point to the upper right corner of the window and click the right mouse button.
3. Point to the tab in the ruler that you want to move.
4. Hold down the right mouse button and drag the highlight to a new position.
    Only the highlight moves at this point.
5. Release the mouse button. The tab marker moves.

Setting All Tabs Back to the Default Positions
To set all tabs in a paragraph back to their default positions (as specified by the "default tab width" field of the Options command):

1. Select the paragraph.
2. Choose the Format Tab Reset-All command.

Filling Tab Spaces with Leader Characters

If you don't want empty space to appear before a tab, you can fill in the tab space with leader characters. For example, you might want leader characters in an index, like these periods:

The Beginning 1
The Middle 99
The End 250

Word has three types of leader characters you can use: periods (.), hyphens (-), and underscores (_). To see leader characters on the screen, you should make sure the "show nonprinting symbols" field of the Options command is set to None or Partial; if it's set to All, you'll see just the tab character (an arrow).

To fill a tab space with leader characters using the keys:

1. Select the paragraphs to be affected.
2. Press Alt+F1 to choose the Format Tab Set command and put a highlight in the ruler.
3. If you're setting a new tab, use the Right or Left arrow key to move the highlight on the ruler to where you want to insert the tab. If you're adding leader characters to an existing tab, use the Down or Up arrow key to move the highlight to the tab you want to affect.

4. If you're setting a new tab, type the leader character you want (a period, a hyphen, or an underscore), then press a letter for the tab type you want (L for left, C for centered, R for right, D for decimal, V for vertical line). If you're adding leader characters to an existing tab, type the leader character you want (a period, a hyphen, or an underscore).

5. Repeat steps 3 and 4 if necessary to add leader characters to other tabs in the selected paragraphs.

6. Press Enter or click the command name.

To fill a tab space with leader characters using the mouse:

1. Select the paragraphs you want to affect.
2. If the ruler is not displayed, point to the upper right corner of the window and click the right mouse button.
3. To choose a new leader character, point to the space between the window number and the tab type letter, as shown in Figure 9-5.
4. Click the left mouse button until you see the leader character you want (., -, or _).

Figure 9-5.   **Adding leader characters with a mouse and the ruler.**

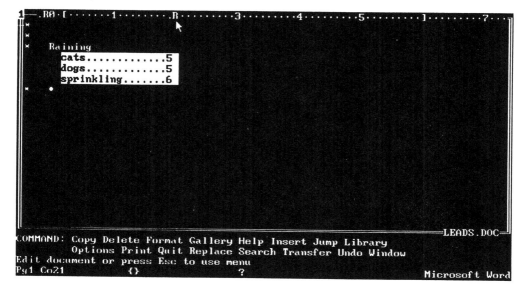

5. If you want to change the tab type, as well as adding leader characters, point to the left of the ruler and click until you see the letter for the tab type you want (L for Left, C for centered, R for right, D for decimal, I for vertical line).

6. Point to the tab you want to change on the ruler or to the position where you want to add a new tab and click the left mouse button.

7. Repeat steps 3 through 6 to add leader characters to more tabs in the selected paragraphs.

8. Press Enter or click the command name.

CREATING TABLES

Tables contain information arranged in rows and columns. Figures 9-6 and 9-7 show examples of different types of tables you can create with Word.

You'll use tabs to control the position of columns in Word tables. (If you want to put paragraphs, each containing several lines of information, in a table format, you'll use the "side-by-side" option of the Format Paragraph command, as explained in Chapter 8).

Figure 9-6.   **Side-by-side text in a table.**

```
┌─────────────────────────────────────────────────────────────────────┐
│                                                                       │
│  Save the Whales Banner       $50.00    Start your own protest group with │
│                                          this beautiful 5' x 7' silk banner │
│                                          stretched between two 6-foot poles. │
│                                          Black, white, and gray-toned whales │
│                                          on a blue-green background with     │
│                                          bright red letters.                 │
│                                                                       │
│  We Need Forests Poster       $12.00    Did you know that many people don't │
│                                          realize that the oxygen we breathe  │
│                                          comes from green plants?  This      │
│                                          attractive poster explains how our  │
│                                          ecology works.                      │
│                                                                       │
│  Plastic is Forever Poster    $12.00    Most people never think about what  │
│                                          happens to the plastic that goes    │
│                                          into their trash cans.  This poster │
│                                          graphically depicts the tons of     │
│                                          plastic that we bury every year in  │
│                                          landfills.                          │
│                                                             CATALOG.DOC│
│COMMAND: Copy Delete Format Gallery Help Insert Jump Library           │
│         Options Print Quit Replace Search Transfer Undo Window        │
│Edit document or press Esc to use menu                                 │
│Pg1 Co48         {·}                 7              Microsoft Word      │
└─────────────────────────────────────────────────────────────────────┘
```

```
                         First Quarter Sales

              Foils    Epees    Sabers   Helmets   Jackets   Gloves
  January     259.75   125.00   190.50    79.99    152.25    92.50
  February    225.95   205.25   102.99   105.99     99.75   103.00
  March       195.25   180.00   125.75    80.95     59.00    79.00
```

```
                                                      SPREDSHT. DOC
COMMAND: Copy Delete Format Gallery Help Insert Jump Library
         Options Print Quit Replace Search Transfer Undo Window
Edit document or press Esc to use menu
Pg1 Col              {→}                  ?          Microsoft Word
```

Figure 9-7.   **A spreadsheet in a table.**

Guidelines for Tables

The preceding sections in this chapter showed you how to insert and change tabs in paragraphs, so you already know the basics of creating tables. Because your screen may not display text as it will appear when printed, here are some general rules that you should follow when creating tables:

- It's usually easier to type the text first, and press the Tab key between the columns, not attempting to align the columns. That way, you can easily see where to set the tabs to accommodate the longest piece of text in a column, and you can tell if all the text for a row will fit on one line. (You may need to adjust the margins or shorten the text if it won't.)
- Always use tabs to align text in tables—not spaces. If you use spaces or a mixture of tabs and spaces, your columns may not be aligned when printed, even if they look perfectly straight on your monitor screen. If you need to move columns, move the tabs instead of adding spaces.
- To align numbers with decimal points in columns, be sure to use decimal tabs to position those columns.

- To check a table before you print choose the Options command, set the "show nonprinting symbols" field to All to see space characters and tab characters, and set the "show line breaks" field to Yes to see where each line breaks. Because more text can sometimes fit on a printed line than on your screen, you may need to scroll horizontally to see the line break characters at the end of each line. When you want to turn off the line break characters and speed up Word, press Alt+F7 to hide line breaks.
- Display the ruler when checking a table. (Choose the Options command, then choose Yes in the "show ruler" field, if necessary, to display the ruler.)

When you press Alt+F7 or choose Yes in the "show line breaks" field of the Options command, Word adjusts the ruler to match the font and size of the text as it will be when printed—an inch on the ruler measures an inch of printed text. (You may need to scroll right to see the right edge of your table.)

Creating a Table with the Format Tab Set Command

This section contains general instructions and examples for creating tables by setting tabs.

Here are the general instructions for creating a table by setting tabs:

1. Type the text you want to put in the table, pressing the Tab key between columns. At the end of the table rows, press Shift+Enter to insert newline characters or Enter to insert paragraph marks. (Don't try to align columns yet.)

   Using Shift+Enter to break the line at the end of the table rows has the advantage of keeping the whole table in one paragraph. This allows you to put borders around it or position it more easily.
2. Select the lines or paragraphs that make up the table.
3. Set the tabs to position the columns. For example, you might want to set a decimal tab for the second column at 1.5 inches, and set a right-aligned tab for the third column at 3 inches, etc.

See the following examples to guide you in setting up tables.

If you want to create a table containing side-by-side paragraphs, you'll have to use the "side-by-side" option of the Format Paragraph command, as explained in "Arranging Paragraphs Side by Side" in Chapter 8.

However, if you want to create a table that contains text wrapping only in the last column, you can use a combination of paragraph indents and tabs, as shown in the next Example box.

Example: Creating a Spreadsheet-type Table

Barrels of Oil Sold This Quarter

(All figures are in millions)

Region→	January→	February→	March
North→	11.72→	12.325→	11.88
East →	14.9→	16.52→	19.02
South →	13 →	12.76→	12.31
West →	10.5→	10.755→	10.1

To create this table, you would:

1. Type all the text, pressing the tab key where you see the arrow tab characters (→).
2. Select the column heading line (Region, January, etc) and set centered tabs at 1.5, 2.5, and 3.5 inches.
3. Select the next four lines (North, East, South, West) and set decimal tabs at 1.5, 2.5, and 3.5 inches. Using decimal tabs ensures that the numbers will be aligned on the decimal points. (If you were using numbers without decimal points, you might want to use right-aligned tabs; or if you were using text, you might want to use left-aligned or centered tabs instead.)

Creating Tables with Macros

Macros are brief programs that perform a series of Word tasks. You can create your own macros to automate your word processing (that's covered in Chapter 22). You can also use the macros that are supplied with Word in a MACRO.GLY file on the Word Utilities 2 disk . Three of these supplied macros can help you set up tables:

Macro Name	Description
table.mac	Asks you for the first tab position and for the distance between all following tabs.
tabs.mac	Asks you to specify the positions and alignment for each tab.
tabs2.mac	Asks you to specify the number of columns in the table, the first tab position, and the alignment for the first tab, then sets all the following tabs.

Example: Creating a Table with Wrapping Text in the Last Column

Class→	Time→	Cost→	Description
Japanese I →	MW 6-7pm→	$15.00→	Students learn Japanese for daily situations and travel. Emphasis on pronunciation and vocabulary.
Swimming I→	MWF 1-2pm →	$45.00→	For beginning swimmers. Students learn basic breaststroke, crawl, and floating techniques.

To create this table, you would:

1. Type all the text, pressing the Tab key wherever you see a tab character (→). Let the text wrap at the end of the lines, press Enter to end the paragraphs, and don't try to align the columns.
2. Select all the paragraphs.
3. Set left-aligned tabs at 1.5, 2.5, and 3.5 inches. This example uses left-aligned tabs for simplicity, but you may need different types of tabs in your columns, depending on how you want text in the column to be aligned.
4. Set the left paragraph indent at 3.5, and the first line indent at -3.5. This setting makes the text wrap even with the last tab position.

Don't be afraid to try the macros. You can always change tab positions and alignments later if you don't like the ones the macros create for you.

Loading the Table Macro Files

Word's macros come with Word in the MACRO.GLY file on the Utilities 2 disk. If you have a hard disk, you probably copied this file to the Word program directory when you ran the SETUP program. If you have a floppy-disk system, you'll have to load this file from a disk drive.

To load one of the table macros:

1. Start Word and choose the Transfer Glossary Load command. (You can also use the Transfer Glossary Merge command if you want to merge the macro glossary entries with other glossary entries (See Chapter 4 for more information about using glossaries.)
2. Type *macro*, or press F1 and highlight MACRO.GLY in the list. If the MACRO.GLY file is in another directory or on another disk drive, type the pathname and/or drive name before pressing F1 to see a list of files. For example, if the file is in a directory called STUFF, you could type \STUFF, then press F1; if the file is on drive B, you could type *B:*, then press F1.
3. Press Enter or click the command name to load the file. If you've made changes to the glossary you're using, Word will ask you if you want to save these changes before loading the MACRO.GLY file. When you've loaded the MACRO.GLY file, you're ready to run the table macros.

Running the table.mac Macro

The table.mac macro asks you for the position (in inches) of the first tab, then asks you how far apart you want all following tabs to be. For example, you could specify that the first tab be positioned at .75 inch, and specify 1.5 inches between all following tabs.

You can either type the text you want in the table, then select it and set the tabs, or select a blank paragraph mark, set up the tabs, then type the text.

To run the table.mac macro:

1. If desired, type the text you want in the table, press the Tab key between columns, then select the table text.
2. Choose the Insert command.
3. Press F1 to display the list of macros in MACRO.GLY.
4. Highlight table.mac in the list.

5. Press Enter to begin running the macro.
6. Following the instructions that appear in the message line.

Running the tabs.mac Macro

The tabs.mac macro asks you for the position (in number of characters) and alignment for a tab, then asks you for the next, and continues until you stop the macro. For example, you could tell Word to position a centered tab at 7 characters, a right-aligned tab at 20 characters, and a decimal tab at 35 characters, then stop the macro.

You can either type the text you want in the table, then select it and set the tabs, or select a blank paragraph mark, set up the tabs, then type the text.

To run the tabs.mac macro:

1. If desired, type the text you want in the table, press the Tab key between columns, then select the table text.
2. Choose the Insert command.
3. Press F1 to display the list of macros in MACRO.GLY.
4. Highlight tabs.mac in the list.
5. Press Enter to begin running the macro.
6. Follow the instructions that appear in the the message line, specifying first a position for a tab, then an alignment. Type a zero (0) when you want to stop the macro.

Running the tabs2.mac Macro

The tabs2.mac macro asks you for the number of columns in the table, the position (in inches) of the first tab, and the alignment to use for all tabs (the macro uses the same alignment for all tabs), then it sets the tabs for you. For example, you could specify 4 columns, specify that the first tab be positioned at .75 inch, and specify decimal tabs.

You can either type the text you want in the table, then select it and set the tabs, or select a blank paragraph mark, set the tabs, then type the text.

To run the *tabs2.mac* macro:

1. If desired, type the text you want in the table, press the Tab key between columns, then select the table text.
2. Choose the Insert command.
3. Press F1 to display the list of macros in MACRO.GLY.
4. Highlight tabs2.mac in the list.
5. Press Enter to begin running the macro.
6. Follow the instructions that appear in the message line.

Editing and Formatting Tables

Editing text and formatting characters and paragraphs in tables is just like editing and formatting text anywhere else in a Word document. You just have to keep in mind that the columns are controlled by tabs, so in most cases you probably won't want to delete or change the type of tabs in a table. This section gives you some tips on common editing and formatting you'll want to do in tables.

Selecting Columns

To select one or more columns in a table, you select the rectangular area containing the columns:

1. Move the cursor to one corner of the rectangular area you want to select.
2. Press Shift+F6 to turn on column selection mode. You'll see the letters "CS" appear in the status line.
3. Use the arrow keys or point and click with the mouse to move the cursor to the other corner of the rectangle and highlight the column(s).

Deleting Columns

To delete one or more columns in a table:

1. Select the rectangular area that contains the column text and the following tab characters. (If necessary, choose the Options command, then choose All in the "show non-printing symbols" field to display tab characters.)
2. Press the Del key. Word deletes the selected columns and shifts any following columns to the left.

Moving Columns

If you want to move the last column in a table, you must insert tab characters at the end of each row, then select the text and the tab characters.

To move one or more columns in a table:

1. Select the rectangular area that contains the column text and the following tab characters. (If necessary, choose the Options command, then choose All in the "show nonprinting symbols" field to display tab characters.)
2. Press the Del key. Word deletes the selected columns and shifts any following columns to the left. You'll see a block in the scrap area at

the bottom of the screen, as shown in Figure 9-8. The block reminds you that there are columns in the scrap.

3. Select the first character of the column before which you want to insert the deleted columns.

4. Press the Ins key. Word inserts the columns from the scrap and shifts any following columns right.

Copying Columns

If you want to copy the last column in a table, you must insert tab characters at the end of each row, then select the text and the tab characters.

To copy one or more columns in a table:

1. Select the rectangular area that contains the column text and the following tab characters. (If necessary, choose the Options command, then choose All in the "show nonprinting symbols" field to display tab characters.)

Figure 9-8.   **Word displays a block in the scrap area to remind you there are columns in the scrap.**

```
.................................................................
                         APPENDIX A
  ⋈
  ⋈
  ⋈    The following table summarizes the cost of overtime due to
       printer breakdowns in the past year.
  ⋈
  ⋈
       Date of               ▌uration of          Cost of
       Breakdown             Breakdown            Overtime
       January 15            6 hours              $250.00
       January 22-23         8 hours              $510.00
       February 13           4 hours              $190.00
       April 4-6             20 hours             $1300.00
       July 9                2 hours              $80.00
       September 23-24       10 hours             $720.00
       October 16            5 hours              $220.00
       November 3            6 hours              $350.00

                                                      ═FBSTUDY.DOC═
COMMAND: Copy Delete Format Gallery Help Insert Jump Library
         Options Print Quit Replace Search Transfer Undo Window     ▊
Saving C:\WORD5\FBSTUDY.SVD
Pg19 Co24         {Durati...urs→■}   ?              Microsoft Word
```

2. Use the Copy command or press Alt+F3. Word puts a copy of the selected columns in the scrap. You'll see a block in the scrap area at the bottom of the screen, as shown in Figure 9-8. The block reminds you that there are columns in the scrap.

3. Select the first character of the column before which you want to insert the copied columns.

4. Press the Ins key. Word inserts the columns from the scrap and shifts any following columns right.

Adjusting the Width of Columns in Tables

If you need to make columns wider or narrower, you move the tabs that determine the positions and alignment of the columns. If each row in your table is a paragraph, be sure to select all the rows you want to affect before you move the tab. If your table is one paragraph (the rows end with a line break character rather than with paragraph marks), just move the cursor into the table before changing the tab setting. See "Moving, Deleting, and Changing the Types of Tabs" earlier in this chapter for instructions on changing the position of tabs.

Adding New Columns

If you want to add a new column to the right side of a table, you'll just set a new tab position and type the text for the new column.

If you want to add a column inside of an existing table, follow this procedure:

1. Select the column before which you want to insert the new column.

2. Press the Tab key. Word inserts a new column of tab characters and shifts the following columns right.

3. Move the cursor to the top row of the new column and type your text there.

4. Press the Down arrow key to move the cursor down to the next row in the same column, then type the text for that row. Repeat this step to fill in all rows in the new column.

Adding Lines and Borders to Tables

Tables are paragraphs, so you can use the same Word features to add lines or borders to tables as you would use to add lines and borders to paragraphs. If your table is one paragraph, you can draw lines or a box around the entire paragraph. If each row in your table is a separate paragraph, you can draw lines between the rows or box each row separately. To draw lines between columns, you can position and draw vertical

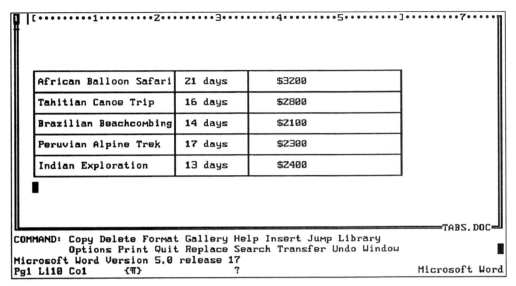

Figure 9-9.   A table with vertical lines and borders.

lines in the same way you set a tab for the paragraph. Figure 9-9 shows some formatting you can add to tables.

For more information about adding borders to paragraphs, see "Adding Lines, Boxes, or Shading to Paragraphs" in Chapter 8. For more information about drawing vertical lines in paragraphs, see "Setting Individual Tabs" earlier in this chapter.

10

DIVISION FORMATTING

This Chapter Contains the Following:

In previous chapters, you learned how to format characters and paragraphs. In this chapter, you'll learn how to divide your document into divisions and how to format those divisions.

WHAT'S A DIVISION?

In Word, the term *division* can refer to the format of the entire document or just part of a document. If you want part of your document to have a different page layout from the rest, you separate that part into a different division, then you format that division. If you don't separate your text into divisions, Word considers your document to be one division, and the options you choose will apply to your entire document. In Word, the Format Division commands control the format of a division as follows:

Command	Controls
Format Division Layout	Number and width of columns.
Format Division Margins	Width of margins and page size, position of running heads and running feet, and the size of the page.
Format Division Line Numbers	Line numbering.
Format Division Page Numbers	Position and format of page numbers.

The options you choose in any of the Format Division command fields affect only selected divisions. You can select just one division by moving the cursor into it, or select several divisions at a time by highlighting them. If you have separated your text into divisions and you want a Format Division command to affect the entire document, press Shift+F10 or use the mouse to select the entire document before you choose the command. Figure 10-1 shows an example of a document divided into several divisions.

Starting a New Division

When you want one division to end and another to begin, you insert a division mark. For example, if you wanted part of your document to have two columns and part to have one column, you'd insert a division mark between the two parts to divide the document into two divisions.

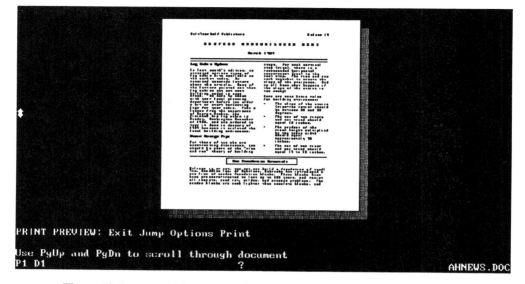

Figure 10-1.   **A document divided into divisions.**

A division mark indicates the end of a division, just like a paragraph mark indicates the end of a paragraph. And just like a paragraph mark, all of the division's formatting is stored in the division mark, so if you delete it, you'll lose the division's formatting and the text that preceded the division mark will become part of the following division.

Word normally begins new divisions on the next page. If you want the new division to begin somewhere else, you'll tell Word where to begin it with the Format Division Layout command.

Inserting a Division Mark

To insert a division mark:

1. Place the cursor where you want to insert a division mark.
2. Press Ctrl+Enter. A division mark (a double dotted line) appears just above the cursor to mark the ending of the previous division. Figure 10-2 shows a division mark. Word changes the page number in the status area to reflect the division. For example, the lower left corner

```
┌─────────────────────────────────────────────────────────────────┐
│█ L[•••••••1•••••••2•••••••3•••••••4•••••••5•••••••]•••••••7••••█│
│█                                                                █│
│                 AMATEUR HOMEBUILDERS NEWS                        │
│                                                                  │
│                      March 1989                                  │
│                                                                  │
│ ::::::::::::::::::::::::::::::::::::::::::::::::::::::::::::::::::: │
│ █og Cabin Update                                                 │
│                                                                  │
│ In last month's edition, we surveyed various types of log        │
│ cabin kits available on the market today.  We received           │
│ numerous letters about the article.  Many of the letters         │
│ pointed out that log cabins may not meet building codes in       │
│ some areas.  Be sure to check with your local planning           │
│ department before you order a kit or start harvesting logs       │
│ for your cabin.  Take a lesson from the experience of George     │
│ Bushes, who finished his log cabin in Woodsy, Washington         │
│ December of 1988, and was ordered to tear it down in January     │
│ of 1989 because it violated the local building ordinances.       │
│                                                    ═AHNEWS.DOC═  │
│ COMMAND: Copy Delete Format Gallery Help Insert Jump Library     │
│           Options Print Quit Replace Search Transfer Undo Window │
│ Edit document or press Esc to use menu                       █   │
│ P1 D2 C1              {}                 ?          Microsoft Word│
└─────────────────────────────────────────────────────────────────┘
```

Figure 10-2.   **Pressing Ctrl+Enter inserts a division mark.**

of the screen displays something like *"P1 D2"*, to indicate that the cursor is in Page 1 of Division 2.

Remember that a division mark indicates the end of a division, so if you want to format the text that comes before a division mark, be sure to move the cursor in front of the division mark before you choose a Format Division command.

Specifying Where the New Division Will Print

By default, Word begins new divisions on the same page. If you want your new division to begin somewhere else, follow the procedure below (Figure 10-3).

1. Make sure the cursor is in the division you want to affect.
2. Choose the Format Division Layout command.
3. In the "division break" field, choose one of the following options.

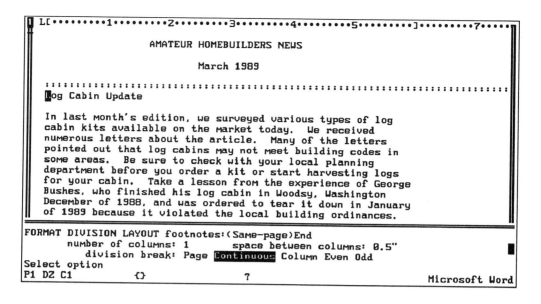

Figure 10-3.   **Specifying where the division containing the cursor will print.**

Option	Begins the Division
Page	At the top of the next page.
Continuous	On the same page as the preceding division (this choice is the default).
Column	At the top of a new column. This option works only when the preceding division has the same number of columns as the selected division. If it doesn't, Word starts the new division at the top of the next page.
Even	At the top of the next even-numbered page.
Odd	At the top of the next odd-numbered page.

Reuniting Divisions by Deleting Division Marks

You can always delete a division mark and unite divisions again. Just like a paragraph mark, a division mark contains the formatting for a division. So when you delete a division mark, you remove all the formatting associated with it, and the text becomes part of the following division.

To delete a division mark and unite divisions:

1. Select the division mark.
2. Press the Del key.

SETTING THE PAGE SIZE

By default, when calculating how much text can fit on a page, Word assumes that you're using 8.5 x 11-inch paper. If you're using a different paper size, use the following procedure to notify Word.

1. Choose the Format Division Margins command.
2. In the "page length" and "width" fields, type your paper's dimensions in inches.
3. Press Enter or click the command name.

CREATING MULTIPLE COLUMNS

Word allows you to create columns in two different ways:

To Create	Use
Columns of equal width in which the text "flows" from the bottom of one column to the top of the next, as in a newspaper	The Format Division Layout command.
Items arranged in rows and columns	The Format Tab Set command.

This section shows you how to create flowing columns of text. See Chapter 9 to learn how to create rows and columns with the Format Tab Set command.

To create flowing, newspaperlike columns of text, use the Format Division Layout command. Although you can set the number of columns before you type the text, you'll generally find it easier to type all your information, then put it into columns.

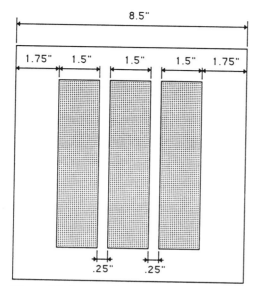

Figure 10-4.   **Laying out columns.**

When you're planning for columns, keep in mind that you're working with a limited amount of space—the width of your page. As illustrated in Figure 10-4, be sure to calculate spacing for:

• left, right, and gutter margins
• all columns
• space between columns.

To create multiple columns:

1. Select the division you want to affect. If your document is not divided into divisions, the entire document will be affected.
2. Choose the Format Division Layout command.
3. In the "number of columns" field, type the number of columns you want.
4. If you want to change the default 1/2-inch space between columns, type a measurement for the amount of space you want between columns in the "space between columns" field.
5. Press Enter or click the command name.

Don't worry if you only see one column of text on the screen after you've specified two or more. You can't see multiple columns on the

```
┌─────────────────────────────────────────────────────────────┐
│ █                                                             │
│     Stair Design Tips                                         │
│                                                               │
│     Those of you who are                                      │
│     constructing staircases                                   │
│     should be aware of the "rise                              │
│     and run" theory of building                               │
│     steps.  For each vertical                                 │
│     step (rise), there is a                                   │
│     recommended horizontal                                    │
│     measurement (run) to the                                  │
│     next step.  The rise and run                              │
│     work together to create the                               │
│     slope of the staircase.  And                              │
│     we all know what happens if                               │
│     the slope of the stairs is                                │
│     too steep!                                                │
│                                                               │
│     ..........................                                │
│     █ere are some basic rules                       AHNEWS.DOC│
├─────────────────────────────────────────────────────────────┤
│ COMMAND: Copy Delete Format Gallery Help Insert Jump Library  │
│          Options Print Quit Replace Search Transfer Undo Window│
│ Saving C:\WORD5\AHNEWS.SVD                                    █│
│ PZ DZ C1            {}              ?          Microsoft Word  │
└─────────────────────────────────────────────────────────────┘
```

Figure 10-5.   **A two-column division displayed in document view.**

Figure 10-6.   **A two-column division displayed in show layout view.**

```
┌─────────────────────────────────────────────────────────────┐
│ █                                                             │
│     Stair Design Tips            Here are some basic rules    │
│ █                                for building staircases:     │
│     Those of you who are                                      │
│     constructing staircases      —  The slope of the stairs   │
│     should be aware of the "rise    (rise-run ratio) should   │
│     and run" theory of building     be between 30 and 35      │
│     steps.  For each vertical       degrees.                  │
│     step (rise), there is a                                   │
│     recommended horizontal       —  The sum of two risers     │
│     measurement (run) to the        and one tread should      │
│     next step.  The rise and run    equal 25 inches.          │
│     work together to create the                               │
│     slope of the staircase.  And —  The product of the        │
│     we all know what happens if     riser height multiplied   │
│     the slope of the stairs is      by the treat width        │
│     too steep!                      should equal              │
│                                     approximately 75 inches.  │
│     ..........................                                │
│                                  —  The sum of one riser      │
│                                                     AHNEWS.DOC│
├─────────────────────────────────────────────────────────────┤
│ COMMAND: Copy Delete Format Gallery Help Insert Jump Library  │
│          Options Print Quit Replace Search Transfer Undo Window│
│ Edit document or press Esc to use menu                        █│
│ PZ DZ C1            {¶}             ?          Microsoft Word  │
└─────────────────────────────────────────────────────────────┘
```

screen unless you use Word's show layout view. You can see the difference in Figures 10-5 and 10-6.

Working with Columns in Show Layout View

To see your multiple columns in show layout view:

• Press Alt+F4.

  or

1. Choose the Options command.
2. In the "show layout" field, choose Yes.
3. Press Enter or click the command name.

You can use key combinations to jump from column to column in show layout view:

To Jump to	Press
The next column	Ctrl+5 (on numeric keypad)+Right arrow key
The previous column	Ctrl+5 (on numeric keypad)+Left arrow key

The ruler shows the settings for the column that contains the cursor, as shown in Figure 10-6, thus making it easier to indent paragraphs and set tabs within columns.

You can also switch to print preview to see a miniature version of pages with multiple columns. You can learn more about perfecting your pages in show layout view and in print preview in Chapter 14.

No matter whether you see multiple columns on your screen, Word prints the document in multiple columns if the division is formatted that way.

Adding Lines Beside and Between Columns

To add lines beside or between columns, you use the Format Border command to insert a vertical line beside all the paragraphs in a column, as shown in Figure 10-7.

If you want to insert lines between columns, do this first:

1. Choose the Format Division Layout command.
2. In the "space between columns" field, type a zero (0).
3. Press Enter or click the command name.

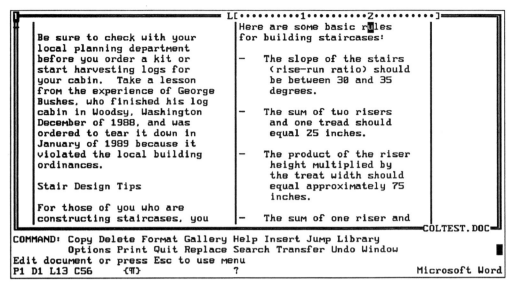

Figure 10-7.   **Lines beside columns.**

To add lines beside or between columns:
1. Press F6 to turn on selection mode.
2. Use the mouse or the arrow keys to select all the paragraphs in the column you want to add a line beside.
3. Choose the Format Border command.
4. In the "type" field, choose Lines.
5. In the "left" and "right" fields, choose Yes if you want to add a line on that side of the column.
6. Press Enter or click the command name to draw the lines.

Changing Column Breaks

Word automatically breaks a column when the text reaches the bottom margin on the page, and starts it again at the top margin. If Word's column breaks don't meet your needs, you can insert a column break wherever you want in document view or in "show layout" view.

To insert a column break:

1. Place the cursor where you want the column break.

```
slope of the staircase.  And
we all know what happens if
the slope of the stairs is
too steep!

..........................
Here are some basic rules
for building staircases:

    -   The slope of the stairs
        (rise-run ratio) should
        be between 30 and 35
        degrees.

    -   The sum of two risers
        and one tread should
        equal 25 inches.

    -   The product of the
                                            AHNEWS.DOC
COMMAND: Copy Delete Format Gallery Help Insert Jump Library
        Options Print Quit Replace Search Transfer Undo Window
Edit document or press Esc to use menu
PZ DZ C1              {}                   ?          Microsoft Word
```

Figure 10-8.   **Pressing Alt+Ctrl+Enter (on the numeric keypad) inserts a column break line.**

2. Press Alt+Ctrl+Enter (use the Enter key on the numeric keypad). Word inserts a dotted line, as shown in Figure 10-8.
3. Choose the Format Division Layout command.
4. In the "division break" field, choose Column.
5. Press Enter.

To delete a column break:

1. Select the column break line.
2. Press the Del key.

ADDING OTHER DIVISION FORMATS

Although the position of running heads, running feet, and page numbers are controlled by the Format Division commands, they can also be affected by other commands, so they deserve chapters of their own. You'll find more information about these subjects in the following sections:

To Set	See
Running heads and feet	"Adding Running Heads or Running Feet" in Chapter 13
Page numbers	"Adding Page Numbers" in Chapter 13
Line numbering	"Numbering Lines" in Chapter 17

COPYING DIVISION FORMATS

Just like a paragraph mark, a division mark contains the formatting for a division. You can copy the division mark and its associated formatting to another location by using the Copy and Insert commands, or you can copy and save it as a glossary entry for later use. You could even save an entire document—such as a memo or invoice form—as a glossary entry, then insert it and fill in the blank spots whenever you need it. See Chapter 4 for more information about moving text and using glossaries.

You can also save a division format as a style, then apply it to other divisions whenever you want. See Chapter 11 for more information about using styles.

CHAPTER

11

SAVING CHARACTER, PARAGRAPH, AND DIVISION FORMATTING: USING STYLES

This Chapter Contains the Following:

Attaching a Style Sheet from the Gallery
Changing Styles
  Changing a Style 's Format by Copying a Format from the Document
  Changing a Style in the Gallery
    Changing a Style's Key Code, Name, or Remark
    Changing a Style's Formatting Instructions
  Changing Word's Automatic Styles
Searching For and Replacing Styles
Removing Styles From Document Text
Deleting Styles
Merging Style Sheets
Moving and Copying Styles Between Style Sheets
Printing a Style Sheet
How Style Sheets Affect Formatting Keys and Help
Changing Styles Into Direct Formatting

Word offers you a very powerful way to apply quickly character, paragraph, and division formats to your documents by recording these formats as styles. Using styles has these advantages:

- You can apply both character and paragraph formatting to paragraphs in one step to save time.
- You can press one key combination to apply formats that might otherwise involve choosing several commands from a menu.
- You can use a style over and over again to give your documents a consistent format.
- If you change a style, Word automatically reformats all text with that style.

WHAT'S A STYLE?

A style is a format (a "look") that you save to use again. Here are Word's three types of styles and the types of formatting they can contain:

Style Type	Can Contain
Character	Any formats you can apply with the Format Character command.
Paragraph	Any formats you can apply with the Format Character, Format Paragraph, Format Tab Set, Format Border, or Format pOsition commands.
Division	Any formats you can apply with the Format Division Layout, Format Division Margins, Format Division line-Numbers, Format Running-head, and Format Division Page-number commands.

Once you've saved formats as styles, you can apply them to your documents whenever you want. You could, for example, select your text, then apply a character style that changes your text to 10-point Helvetica, a paragraph style that changes the line spacing to 1-1/2 and indents the first line of paragraphs, and a division style that changes the margins and formats the text into two columns. Because you use key combinations to apply styles, you could do all this formatting by pressing only three key combinations!

Probably the most useful and commonly used styles are paragraph styles, because when you create a paragraph style, you can use any combination of character and paragraph format options. For example, you can create a paragraph that's in bold Courier 14-point font, centered, and double-spaced. Paragraph formats can include tabs and borders, too.

Using a style is simple. Say you've formatted a paragraph to look like this:

```
┌─────────────────────────────────┐
│          CHAPTER 1              │
└─────────────────────────────────┘
```

The text is bold, the font is Times, the font size is 14 points, and the paragraph is centered and boxed. To use this format for all chapter headings, you could record this format as a paragraph style, then use a key combination to apply this style to all of your chapter heading paragraphs to make them look alike.

Styles are saved in special files called *style sheets*. Word comes with a default style sheet named NORMAL.STY, to which it automatically attaches to all new documents. The styles in NORMAL.STY are called *automatic styles*, because Word automatically applies them to text unless you specify another style. You can change Word's automatic styles to change the default format Word adds to your documents. You'll learn more about that in "Changing Word's Automatic Styles" later in this chapter.

Most of the time, you'll want to create new styles of your own and add them to NORMAL.STY so that your styles will always be available to use with every document. You can also keep styles in specialized style sheet files that you load only when you need them. For example, you might want to create a special INVOICE.STY file containing styles for invoices, or a special BOOK.STY file containing styles to use in your novels.

INTRODUCTION TO STYLE COMMANDS

In typical Word fashion, there are many commands and methods you can use to work with styles. You use two sets of commands when you work with styles:

Commands	Description
Format Stylesheet commands	Let you create new styles and attach different style sheets to your document. These commands allow you to

Gallery commands   work with styles contained in the style sheet that is attached to your document. Let you view, save, merge and rename style sheets, insert, modify, copy, or delete styles. These commands allow you to work with styles in any style sheet.

It's not really as complicated as it may at first sound. In this chapter, you'll learn the easiest ways to create, save, and apply styles to your document.

CREATING A STYLE

To create a style, you'll follow two steps:
1. Record the format you want to use in the style.
2. Save the style in a style sheet.

The easiest way to record the format for a style is to use formatted text as a model, so that's the method used in the procedure below.
To create a style:

1. Format some characters, a paragraph, or a division, using the format options you want to save as a style. For example, you might want to change the point size or the font for a few characters, make a paragraph bold and centered, or create a three-column division. When formatting a paragraph to create a style, you can add character formats, tabs, and borders, as well as indents, alignments, line spacing, and other paragraph formats. The only rule for paragraph styles is that all characters in the paragraph must have the same character format. You can't format part of a paragraph one way and part another; for example you can't use half bold and half italic, or different fonts in different words.
2. Select the characters, the paragraph, or the division mark.

Helpful Hint

If you like working with glossary entries but you'd really rather not get into styles, you can store paragraph and division formats in glossaries, then insert the glossary entries wherever you want that format. Here's how this method works:

1. Format a paragraph or a division the way you want it. For example, you could add bold format, borders and indents to paragraphs, change the margins or number of columns in a division, and so forth. You don't need text in your sample paragraph or division.
2. Select the paragraph mark or the division mark after the sample.
3. Use the Copy command to name the entry and add it to the glossary.
4. When you want to use that format, just use the Insert command to insert the paragraph mark or division mark.

See Chapter 4 for more information about working with glossaries.

Figure 11-1.   **The Format Stylesheet Record command fields.**

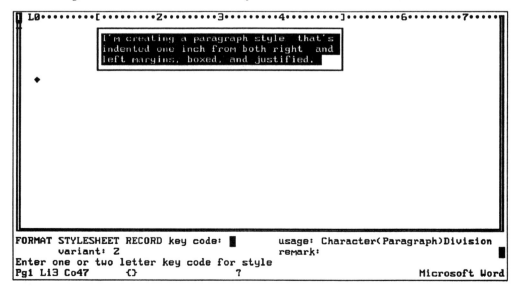

3.   Choose the Format Stylesheet Record command. Word displays the command fields shown in Figure 11-1.

4.   In the "key code" field, type a one or two-character code that you want to use to apply the style. Pick a combination you'll be able to remember later. Don't begin a key code with the letter X—(that makes applying the style difficult—use any other letters or numbers. For example, as a key code for a chapter heading style, you might type *ch*.

5.   In the "usage" field, choose the kind of formatting you want the style to do: Character, Paragraph, or Division.

6.   In the "remark" field, type a short note to remind yourself what the style does. For example, for a paragraph style that formats chapter headings, you might type *chapter heading*.

7.   Press Enter or click the command name to create the style and apply the style to the selected text.

Word adds the styles you create to the style sheet attached to the document, which is normally Word's default style sheet, NORMAL.STY. Styles in NORMAL.STY are automatically available to all documents. To save those styles in another style sheet to use only on special occasions, see "Saving Styles" later in this chapter.

Basing a New Style on an Existing Style

If you want to use the basic format of one style but not modify the original style, you can base a new style on an existing style.

To base a new style on an existing one:

1.   Select text that has the style you want to use as a base for your new style.

2.   Make any changes to the text that you want to be included in the new style.

3.   Choose the Format Stylesheet Record command.

4.   In the "key code" and "remark" fields type a new key code and type a short remark for the new style.

5.   Press Enter or click the command name to record the new style.

Example: Creating a Paragraph Style

Let's say you want to create a paragraph style for a course catalog. You want the text to be small to fit in the catalog, so the style will specify 8-point type. The style will also contain tabs to set the position of the time information and course description, and the description part of the paragraph will "wrap," like this:

Spanish I→   MWF 10-11 a.m.→   Introduction to the Spanish language. Students will learn the basics of grammar and pronunciation. No prerequisites.

To create this style, you'd perform the following steps. This example assumes that you haven't changed Word's standard margins and that you're using inches as the default measurement.

1. Type the sample paragraph shown above, pressing the Tab key where the arrows (→) are shown. Let the lines wrap naturally—don't try to make anything line up and don't press the Enter key until you reach the end of the paragraph. Your text should look something like this:

   Spanish I→ MWF 10-11 a.m.→ Introduction to the Spanish language. Students will learn the basics of grammar and pronunciation. No prerequisites.

2. Select the paragraph.
3. Choose the Format Character command, type *8* in the "font size" field, then press Enter. This command changes the font size to 8 points.
4. Choose the Format Paragraph command, type *4* in the "left indent" field, and type *-4* in the "first line indent" field, then press Enter. This command creates the hanging indent, which wraps the text in the last "column."
5. Press Alt+F1 to choose the Format Tab Set command and put a highlight in the ruler, then move the highlight to the 2-inch mark and press L, then move the highlight to the 4-inch mark and press Enter. This command sets the tabs at 2 and 4 inches.
6. Choose the Format Stylesheet Record command.

7. Type *cc* in the "key code" field, type *course catalog* in the "remark" field, then press Enter.
Word has already determined that this is a Paragraph style, so you're leaving the "usage" field alone. You're also leaving the "variant" field alone, accepting the number Word suggests.

You've created the style and applied it to the paragraph. To see your new style, follow the instructions in "Viewing Style Descriptions" later in this chapter

Example: Creating a Division Style

Let's say you want to create a division style for a document that will be printed double-sided and bound. You want to make the left and right margins one inch wide, add a 1/2-inch gutter margin to allow room for binding, and make the margins "mirror" each other, so that inside and outside margins will match on facing pages.

To create this style, you'd perform the following steps. This example assumes that you're using inches as the default measurement.

1. Choose the Format Division Margins command.
2. In the "left" and "right" fields, type *1*.
3. In the "gutter" field type, *.5*.
4. In the "mirror margins" field, choose Yes.
5. Press Enter to set the division.
6. Choose the Format Stylesheet Record command.
7. In the "key code" field, type *fp* (for "facing pages").
8. In the "usage" field, choose Division.
9. In the "remark" field, type *facing pages*.
10. Press Enter to record the style.

If you have the style bar displayed, you'll see the letters "FP" appear beside the division mark (the double dotted line) at the end of the division.

VIEWING STYLE DESCRIPTIONS

When you want to see the styles from which you have to choose, you'll go to Word's Gallery screen. The Gallery contains a whole menu of commands just for working with styles.

To see styles in the attached style sheet:

• Choose the Gallery command.

If you have only NORMAL.STY attached to your document, the Gallery screen may have only a few styles in it, or it may even be completely blank. Figure 11-2 shows the Gallery screen with only one style displayed, the "course catalog" style created in the preceding example.

For some reason known only to Word programmers, Word displays only those styles you've added or modified in the NORMAL.STY file, although there are actually many styles contained in the file. For more information about viewing or changing the styles contained in NORMAL.STY, see "Changing Word's Automatic Styles" later in this chapter.

Figure 11-2.   **The Gallery screen with NORMAL.STY loaded.**

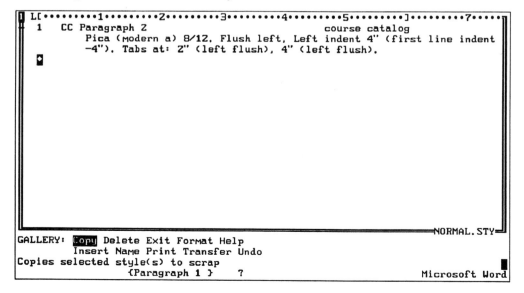

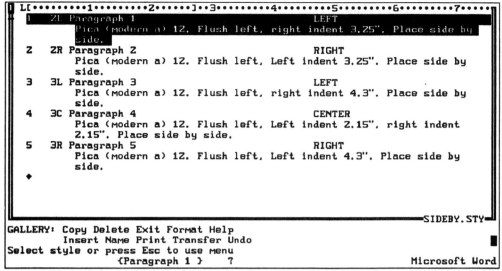

Figure 11-3.   The Gallery screen with SIDEBY.STY loaded.

If you have a style sheet other than NORMAL.STY attached to your document, you may see a screen similar to the one shown in Figure 11-3, which shows the styles included in the SIDEBY.STY file (included with Word).

You can view the styles any time you need to remind yourself of which styles are included in a style sheet, or to see the key codes assigned to styles. You'll notice that the Gallery command brings up a whole new menu, the Gallery menu. You can use Gallery commands to view and modify any style sheet, whether it's attached to your document or not.

Loading Style Sheets into the Gallery Window

Sometimes you may want to load another style sheet to see what it contains, or to change it without attaching it to your document. Loading a style sheet into the Gallery window doesn't change the styles in your document because the style sheet is not attached until you say so. For example, when you're looking for a specific style, you might want to load a style sheet to see if it contains the style you're seeking.

To load style sheets into the Gallery window:

1.   Choose the Transfer Load command from the Gallery menu.

2. Type the name of the style sheet you want, or press F1 to display a list of style sheet names, then select the one you want.

3. Press Enter or click the command name to load the file.

Exiting from the Gallery Menu

To exit from the Gallery menu:

• Choose the Exit command.

If you loaded a new style sheet file, Word displays the following message: *Enter Y to attach new style sheet, N to keep old one, or Esc to cancel*

Press Y if you want to replace the attached style sheet with the one you loaded; press N if you want to keep the same style sheet attached; or press Esc if you don't really want to exit from the Gallery.

DISPLAYING KEY CODES IN THE DOCUMENT WINDOW

To see which styles are attached to your text, you can display the key codes in a part of the Word window called the *style bar*. If only Word's automatic styles are attached to a paragraph, Word displays an asterisk (*) in the style bar. Figure 11-4 shows the key codes for the styles used in a course catalog.

To display key codes in the document window:

1. Choose the Options command.
2. In the "style bar" field choose Yes.
3. Press Enter or click the command name to display the style bar in the window.

USING STYLES

Once you've saved a format as a style, you can use that style to apply that format to a paragraph you've already typed, or you can apply it to the cursor before you type the text.

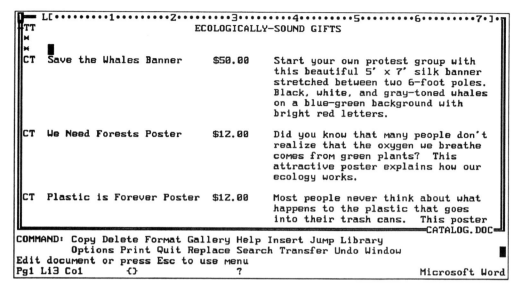

Figure 11-4.   **You can display the style bar to see key codes for styles applied to text in your document.**

If you want to repeat a paragraph style in subsequent paragraphs, you can just move the cursor to the paragraph mark containing the style, then press Enter to begin a new paragraph with the same style.

A paragraph style is saved in a paragraph's mark, and a division style is saved in a division's mark, so if you delete one of these marks, you'll lose the style attached to the text.

Looking Up a Style's Key Code

The easiest way to apply a style is to use its key code. If you don't know the key code, choose the Gallery command to display the list of styles, look up the key code you need (it's displayed at the left of the style description), then choose Exit.

If you'd like to add a key code to a style you've created, see "Changing a Style in the Gallery" later in this chapter.

Applying a Style

You can apply a style in two different ways: by using a key code or selecting the style's name from a list.

To apply a style using a key code:

1. If the style is contained in a style sheet other than NORMAL.STY, follow the instructions in "Attaching a Stylesheet to a Document" later in this chapter to attach the style sheet to your document. If the style is in NORMAL.STY, it's always available, so you can skip to step 2.
2. Select the text you want to format. If you're going to apply a division format, you don't have to select the entire division—you can just move the cursor into the division you want to affect.
3. Hold down the Alt key and type the key code. For example, if you want to apply the course catalog style and the key code is CC, press Alt+CC.

To apply a style by selecting it from a list:

1. If the style is contained in a style sheet other than NORMAL.STY, follow the instructions in "Attaching a Stylesheet to a Document" later in this chapter to attach the style sheet to your document. If the style is in NORMAL.STY, it's always available, so you can skip to step 2.
2. Select the text you want to format.
3. Choose the Format Stylesheet command, then choose the type of style you want to apply: Character, Paragraph, or Division.
4. Press F1 to display the list of styles of that type.
5. Highlight the name of the style you want.
6. Press Enter to apply the style.

Why Applying Styles Sometimes Yields Surprising Results

When you use Format Character commands or shortcut keys (such as Alt+B) to format text, then you apply a style to that text, and you may not get exactly the formatting specified in the style. For example, if you've used Alt+B to format the characters in a paragraph as bold, and then you apply a style in which the character format is defined as plain text, you'll end up with bold text. This occurs because the formats you apply with the Format Character command or the shortcut keys take precedence over character formats in styles.

To make sure that your text will have only the format specified in a style:

1. Select the text.
2. Press Alt+Spacebar to remove any character formatting not specified in a style.

You can do this either before or after applying a style.

Applying Styles Repeatedly

If you want to apply the same style at several different places in your document, you can use the "repeat command" key, F4, to speed up the process:

1. Apply the style to the first selection.
2. Select the next paragraphs to which to apply the style.
3. Press F4.

Word repeats the last formatting action, applying the same style to the selected paragraphs.

SAVING STYLES

Word has many ways to save styles, depending on where you are in Word's menu system and in the editing process. Pick the method that's right for you from the list below.

If You Want to	Do This
Save changes to style sheets and save changes to Word files at the same time	Choose the Transfer Allsave command. Word will ask you to name your Word file(s) if you haven't already done so.

Save changes to the attached style sheet (from the main menu) or to the style sheet displayed in the Gallery window, using the same file name	1. Choose the Gallery Transfer Save command. 2. Press Enter.
Save changes to the attached style sheet (from the main menu) or to the style sheet displayed in the Gallery window in a different file. For example, you might add new invoice styles to NORMAL.STY, then want to save the changes in a special style sheet called INVOICE.STY.	1. Choose the Gallery Transfer Save command. 2. Type a new file name in the "filename" field. Either type an .STY extension or use no extension and let Word add it—Word uses .STY to find style sheets. 3. Press Enter.

If you forget to save your styles before you choose the Quit command, Word displays a message asking you if you want to save changes to the style sheet. If you press Y for Yes, Word saves your changes in the attached style sheet.

ATTACHING A STYLE SHEET TO A DOCUMENT

You can apply only the styles in the style sheet that's attached to your document. Word automatically attaches NORMAL.STY to all documents, so you don't need to use one of these procedures if you want to use styles you've added to the NORMAL.STY file. Perform one of the following procedures only if you want to attach another style sheet that you've created or that came with Word.

Attaching a Style Sheet from the Main Menu

To attach a style sheet other than NORMAL.STY from the main menu:

1. Choose the Format Stylesheet Attach command.

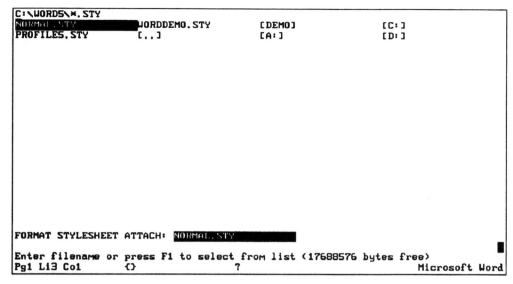

```
C:\WORD5\*.STY
NORMAL.STY                WORDDEMO.STY        [DEMO]              [C:]
PROFILES.STY              [..]                [A:]                [D:]


















FORMAT STYLESHEET ATTACH: NORMAL.STY
Enter filename or press F1 to select from list (17688576 bytes free)
Pg1 Li3 Col          {}                    ?              Microsoft Word
```

Figure 11-5.   **Choosing from a list of style sheet files.**

2. Type the name of the style sheet file you want, or press F1 to select a name from a list of files, as shown in Figure 11-5. You may need to change drives or directories to find the style sheet you want.
3. Press Enter or click the command name to attach the style sheet.

Attaching a Style Sheet from the Gallery

To load a new style sheet into the Gallery, then attach it to your document:

1. Choose the Transfer Load command from the Gallery menu.
2. Type the name of the style sheet you want, or press F1 to display a list of style sheet names, then select the one you want.
3. Press Enter or click the command name to load the file.
4. Choose the Exit command. Word displays the following message: *"Enter Y to attach new style sheet, N to keep old one, or Esc to cancel"*
5. Press Y to replace the attached style sheet with the one you loaded.

CHANGING STYLES

You can change any style, including the styles provided with Word in NORMAL.STY. Whenever you attach a style sheet in which the styles have been changed, Word automatically updates all the "styled" text in your document to match the changes.

There are many ways to change a style. This section deals with two methods that will accomplish everything you want to do: copying a new format from your document, and using the Gallery commands.

Changing a Style's Format by Copying a Format from the Document

To use one of these procedures, you must have already attached the style you want to change to text in your document, or know the key code of the style you want to change.

To change a style when it's already attached to text in your document:

1.   Select text that has the style you want to change.
2.   Use Format commmands or shortcut keys to change the format as you like.
3.   Choose the Format Stylesheet Record command. The command fields should already contain the information for the style.
4.   Press Enter. Word displays this message: *"Style already exists. Enter Y to replace or Esc to cancel."*
5.   Press Y to replace the style's old formatting with the new formatting.

To change a style's format when you know the key code, but haven't applied the style to text in your document:

1.   Select and format some text in your document the way you want the style to be. Be sure to add all the formats you want the style to contain, because Word copies the formatting exactly.
2.   Choose the Format Stylesheet Record command.
3.   In the "key code" field, type the key code of the style you want to change.
4.   Press Enter or click the command name to save the change.
     Word displays this message: *"Style already exists. Enter Y to replace or Esc to cancel."*
5.   Press Y to replace the style's old formatting with the new formatting.

Changing a Style in the Gallery

You can change any aspect of a style, including its key code, format, or remarks, by using the Gallery menu. You can load and change style sheets in the Gallery without attaching them to your document.

The following procedures assume that you've already chosen the Gallery command and loaded the file containing the style you want to change (if necessary).

Changing a Style's Key Code, Name, or Remark
To change a style's key code, name, or remark:

1.   In the Gallery window, select the style you want to change.
2.   Choose the Name command.
3.   Change the text in the "key code," "variant, " or "remark" fields.
4.   Press Enter or click the command name to register the change.

Changing a Style's Formatting Instructions
To change a style's formatting instructions:

1.   In the Gallery window, select the style you want to change.
2.   Choose the Format command from the Gallery menu.
     • If the style is a character style, Word displays the Format Character command fields.
     • If the style is a paragraph or division style, Word displays a menu from which to choose. Choose a command to display the fields you want to change. For example, to change the alignment of a paragraph style, you'd choose Paragraph; if you wanted to change tab settings, you'd choose Tab.
3.   Change the command fields to change the style. For example, to remove bold from a character style, choose No in the "bold" field.
4.   Press Enter or click the command name to change the formatting instructions.

Changing Word's Automatic Styles

As previously mentioned, Word's default style sheet is NORMAL.STY. Although you don't see them in the Gallery window, NORMAL.STY contains many styles that Word automatically applies to text in documents. For example, all paragraphs initially have the Paragraph Standard style, and all divisions have the Division Standard style. Here's a complete list of automatic styles and the formats they control:

Style Name	Automatically Used to Format
Character Annotation ref	Annotation reference marks
Character Footnote ref	Footnote reference marks
Character Page number	Page numbers inserted with the Format Division Page-number command
Character Line number	Line numbers inserted with the Format Division line-Numbers command
Character Summary Info	Summary sheets viewed with the Library Document-retrieval command
Character Line draw	Characters used to draw lines
Paragraph Standard	Paragraph Standards and standard characters
Paragraph Annotation	Text of annotations
Paragraph Footnote	Text of footnotes
Paragraph Running head	Running heads
Paragraph Heading level 1–7	Headings in outlines
Paragraph Table level 1–4	Headings in tables of contents
Paragraph Index level 1–4	Index entries
Division Standard	Divisions.

Example: Changing the Footnote Ref Style

The style Word uses to format footnote reference marks doesn't stand out well from the text. Perhaps you'd like to make it into a superscript (raised from the baseline), and change it to 8-point type to make it smaller than normal text. Here's what you'd do:

1. In the Gallery window choose the Insert command.
2. In the "usage" field choose Character.
3. In the "variant" field press F1, then select Footnote ref from the list.
4. Press Enter to insert the Footnote ref style in the style sheet.
5. Choose the Format command.
6. Type *8* in the "font size" field, then choose Superscript in the "position" field, then press Enter.
7. Use the Transfer Save command to save the file.

Example: Changing the Paragraph Standard Style

The Paragraph Standard style controls the default format of paragraphs and characters in your documents. for example, you might like to change the Paragraph Standard style to have a 1/2 inch first-line indent, 10 points of space before the paragraph, and use the PicaD font. You'd do the following:

1. In the Gallery window choose the Insert command.
2. In the "usage" field choose Paragraph.
3. In the "variant" field, press F1 then select Standard from the list.
4. Press Enter to insert the Paragraph Standard style in the style sheet.
5. Choose the Format Paragraph command.
6. Type .5 in the "first line indent" field, then type 10 pt in the "space before" field, then press Enter.
7. Choose the Format Character command.
8. In the "font" field type *PicaD* or press F1 and select it from the list, then press Enter.
9. Use the Transfer Save command to save the file.

If you want to change the default format Word uses for a piece of text, you can change Word's automatic styles in the NORMAL.STY file. For example, Word's default paragraph format is left-aligned, single-spaced, with no space before or after the paragraph. If you'd like Word to use a different default paragraph style—the first line indented 1/2 inch from the margin, with 10 points of space before the paragraph, for example—you could change Word's Paragraph Standard style. Then Word would automatically use the revised Paragraph Standard style for paragraphs in new documents.

To change the format of an automatic style:

1. If necessary, choose the Gallery command to go to the Gallery.
2. Choose the Insert command from the Gallery menu.
3. In the "usage" field, choose the type of style you would want to change (Character, Paragraph, or Division).
4. In the "variant" field, press F1. You should see a list of all styles of that type in the style sheet. For example, Figure 11-6 shows a list of all paragraph styles in a NORMAL.STY file.

```
Standard             Footnote             Running Head         Heading level 1
Heading level 2      Heading level 3      Heading level 4      Heading level 5
Heading level 6      Heading level 7      Index level 1        Index level 2
Index level 3        Index level 4        Table level 1        Table level 2
Table level 3        Table level 4        Annotation           1  (P1)
2  (CT)              3  (TT)              4                    5
6                    7                    8                    9
10                   11                   12                   13
14                   15                   16                   17
18                   19                   20                   21
22                   23                   24                   25
26                   27                   28                   29
30                   31                   32                   33
34                   35                   36                   37
38                   39                   40                   41
42                   43                   44                   45
46                   47                   48                   49
50                   51                   52                   53
54                   55


INSERT key code: {}                       usage: Character(Paragraph)Division
        variant: Standard                 remark:
Enter variant or press F1 to select from list
                {}                    7                        Microsoft Word
```

Figure 11-6.   **Automatic paragraph styles.**

5. Select the name of the automatic style you want to change. Don't be distracted by all those numbers—they're really just placeholders, numbers Word uses for different "variants" when you create a style.

6. Press Enter or click the command name to insert that style into the style sheet.

7. Choose Format commands from the Gallery menu to change the style the way you want, as described in "Changing a Style's Formatting Instructions" earlier in this chapter.

8. Press Enter or click the command name to change the style.

SEARCHING FOR AND REPLACING STYLES

If your styles have keycodes associated with them, you can easily search for a particular style, or quickly replace all instances of one style with another.

To search for styles:

1. Choose the Format sEarch Style command (Esc, F, E, S).

2. In the "keycode" field, type the letter code associated with the style.

3. In the "direction" field, choose Up to search from the cursor position to the beginning of the document, or choose Down to search to the end.
4. Press Enter or click the command name to begin the search. Word highlights the first paragraph it finds with the specified style.
5. Press Shift+F4 to search for the next occurrence.

To replace styles:

1. Choose the Format repLace Style command (Esc, F, L, S).
2. In the "keycode" field, type the letter code associated with the existing style.
3. In the "with keycode" field, type the letter code of the style with which you want to replace the existing style.
4. In the "confirm" field, choose Yes if you want to approve each replacement before it's made. Choose No if you want Word to make all the replacements automatically.
5. Press Enter to begin the replacements.
   • If you chose Yes in the "confirm" field, Word highlights each occurrence it finds and asks you if you want to replace it. Press Y for Yes or N for No, and Word automatically goes on to the next occurrence. Press Esc if you want to quit the replacement process.
   • If you chose No in the "confirm" field, Word makes all the replacements, then displays the number of replacements in the message line. If this number looks suspiciously high, check your replacements.

REMOVING STYLES FROM DOCUMENT TEXT

To remove any styles you've added to paragraphs and return paragraphs to Word's default style:

1. Select the paragraphs.
2. Press Alt+XP.

Word keeps track of character formatting changes that you make after applying styles. If you apply a style to a paragraph, use the Format Character command or the shortcut keys to make additional changes, then later remove the style, the paragraph will retain the additional character formatting. For example, if you apply a style named Title, then change the font to PicaD, then remove the style, the paragraph will still be displayed in the PicaD font.

DELETING STYLES

If you've created so many styles that the list in the Gallery window is getting too long, you should delete any styles you no longer use.
    To delete a style from a style sheet:

1. Choose the Gallery command, then use the Transfer Load command to load the style sheet if necessary.
2. Select the style you want to delete.
3. Press the Del key.

If the style sheet is attached to your document, Word returns any text with the deleted style to the default style defined in NORMAL.STY.

MERGING STYLE SHEETS

If you want to merge two or more style sheets together, use the Gallery Transfer Merge command:

1. If necessary, use the Gallery Transfer Load command to load the first style sheet you want to use.
2. Choose the Gallery Transfer Merge command.
3. Type the name of the style sheet you want to merge, or press F1, then select the name from the list.
4. Press Enter to merge the styles into one file.

If an incoming style has the same name as a style in the first style sheet, the incoming style will replace the style in the first style sheet.

MOVING AND COPYING STYLES BETWEEN STYLE SHEETS

To move or copy a file to another style sheet:

1. Choose the Gallery command.
2. If necessary, use the Transfer Load command from the Gallery menu to load the style sheet containing the style you want to move or copy.

3. Select the style.

4. If you want to move the style, press the Del key to delete it to the scrap. If you want to copy the style, choose the Copy command from the Gallery menu, then press Enter to put a copy in the scrap.

5. Use the Transfer Load command from the Gallery menu to load the style sheet you want to move or copy to where you want the style. If you deleted a style, Word will ask you if you want to save the changed style sheet before loading another. Answer *Yes*.

6. Move the cursor to the location in the list where you want to insert the style.

7. Press the Ins key.

8. Use the Transfer Save command from the Gallery menu to save the changed style sheet.

PRINTING A STYLE SHEET

To print a style sheet:

1. Choose the Gallery command.

2. If necessary, use the Transfer Load command from the Gallery menu to load the style sheet you want.

3. Choose the Print command from the Gallery menu.

HOW STYLE SHEETS AFFECT FORMATTING KEYS AND HELP

When a style sheet other than NORMAL.STY is attached to your document, you must press the letter X between the Alt key and a format key to use a formatting key combination. This step also applies to the Alt+H key combination used to display a help screen. For example, if you want to make selected text bold when a style sheet is attached, press Alt+XB (instead of the usual Alt+B); if you want to center a paragraph, press Alt+XC. And if you want to see a help screen for a selected command or command field, press Alt+XH.

CHANGING STYLES INTO DIRECT FORMATTING

If you want to convert a Word document into a different type of file for use with another program, you should change the styles in the document into direct formatting. You can do this with the *freeze_style.mac* macro, which replaces the style formatting with the same type of formatting (bold into bold, indents into indents,etc.), but treats the text as though you had applied the formatting with the Format Character, Format Paragraph, or Format Division command, or with the shortcut keys. This conversion may make transferring formatted files easier, because all word processing programs use standard formats such as bold, italic, indents, but only Word uses styles.

All of Word's macros are stored in the MACRO.GLY glossary file, which is part of the Word package.

To change styles into direct formatting using the *freeze_style.mac* macro:

1. Do one of the following:
    *   If you want to replace the current glossary with the MACRO.GLY file, choose the Transfer Glossary Load command.
    *   If you want to merge the entries in the MACRO.GLY file with the entries in the current file, choose the Transfer Glossary Merge command.
2. In the "filename" field, type *macro*, preceded by any drive names or pathnames Word needs to find the file.
3. Press Enter or click the command name to load the MACRO.GLY file. If you chose the Transfer Glossary Load command and you've made any unsaved changes to the glossary you were using, Word asks you if you want to save the current glossary before loading the MACRO.GLY file.
4. Press Shift + F10 to select the entire document.
5. Choose the Insert command.
6. Press F1 to display a list of the glossary entries.
7. Highlight the *freeze_style.mac* macro.
8. Press Enter or click the command name to run the macro and convert the styles to direct formatting.

For more information about working with macros, see Chapter 22.

PART IV

Page Layout and Printing

Microsoft Word can be used as a desktop publishing program as well as a word processing program. You can import graphics from other programs, and change their size or add text to fit your needs. You can make simple line drawings using Word's linedraw feature. You can lay out pages, add headers, footers, footnotes, and position your text and graphics just where you want them. Then you can use Word's print preview and show layout features to make sure everything is just right before you print. This part of the book shows you how to add the finishing touches to your text, how to use the different views of Word to perfect your page layout, and how to use your printer to create the best possible printed document.

INCORPORATING GRAPHICS AND DRAWING LINES

This Chapter Contains the Following:

In this book, the term *graphics* is used to mean drawings, charts, photographs, or any visual element that you can't create with Word. Word makes it easy to incorporate graphics into your documents, as shown in Figure 12–1. You can create a graphic with several popular graphics programs or scan a graphic with a digitizer, then paste the graphic into your Word documents. Word also allows you to change the graphic's size and position, manipulating the page layout to suit your needs.

If you want to do simple, straight line drawings, you can use Word's linedraw feature to draw directly in a Word file. You can choose the character with which you want to draw lines and make it bold or italic. You can also add boxes and bars using Word's paragraph borders, and draw horizontal and vertical lines using tab leader characters and the vertical line tab character. You'll see how to add all these graphic elements to a Word file in this chapter.

PASTING IN GRAPHICS

To paste a graphic from a graphics program into a Word document, you must be able to save the graphic in one of the following formats:

Figure 12-1.   **Graphics in a Word document.**

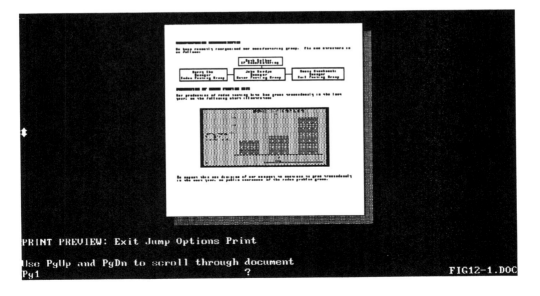

- Microsoft Windows clipboard format.
- Microsoft Pageview picture format.
- Files created with the CAPTURE.COM utility (supplied on the Word Utilities disk 3).
- Microsoft Pageview picture format.
- Print file format (created by printing to a file rather than to a printer).
- Postscript file format (created manually or by printing to a file).
- TIFF B (black and white) and TIFF G (gray scale) file formats (generated by many scanners).
- PC Paintbrush PCX or PCC file formats.
- Lotus PIC file format.
- HPGL plotter files.

The following procedure imports graphics into Word files when running Word on top of DOS or OS/2. If you're using Word with Microsoft Windows and you want to copy a graphic from another Windows program, you can insert the graphic with the Clipboard glossary entry. See the next section, "Importing Graphics from the Clipboard When Running Under Windows," for more information.

To import a graphic into a Word file:

1. Move the cursor to where you want to insert the graphic.
2. Choose the Library Link Graphics command.
3. Do one of the following:
    - Type the filename of the graphic, including any drive letters or pathnames Word needs to find the file; or,
    - Press F1 and select the graphic file from the list, or select Clipboard if you're running Word in Microsoft Windows and you've copied a graphic to the Windows clipboard.
4. If Word is able to detect the file's format, Word displays the format in the "file format" field. If Word can't detect the format, this field will be blank. In that case, move the cursor to the field, then press F1 and select the appropriate format from the list.
5. In the "alignment in frame" field, press F1 and select Left, Right, or Centered.
6. If you want to change the measurement Word displays in the "graphics width" field, press F1 to select from a list of widths or type a measurement . Word assumes this measurement is in inches unless you add a unit abbreviation such as *cm* or *pt*.
7. If you want to change the measurement in the "graphics height" field, press F1 to select from a list of heights, or type a measurement. Word

assumes this measurement is in inches unless you add a unit abbreviation such as *cm* or *pt*.

8. If you want to add white space above and below the graphic, type measurements in the "space before" and "space after" fields. Word assumes this measurement is in inches unless you add a unit abbreviation such as *li*, *cm* , or *pt*.

9. Press Enter or click the command name to import the graphic. Instead of displaying the graphic, Word adds a paragraph of information identifying the graphic file, similar to Figure 12-2. This graphics paragraph always begins with a ".G." code; and the paragraph is formatted as hidden text, so if you want to see it, you'll have to choose Yes in the "show hidden text" field of the Options command. The actual graphic won't be merged until you print or choose the Print pre-View command.

Importing Graphics from the Clipboard When Running Under Windows

If you're running Word under Microsoft Windows and you want to copy a graphic from another Windows program, you can easily insert the

Figure 12-2.   **A paragraph identifying a graphic pasted into a Word document.**

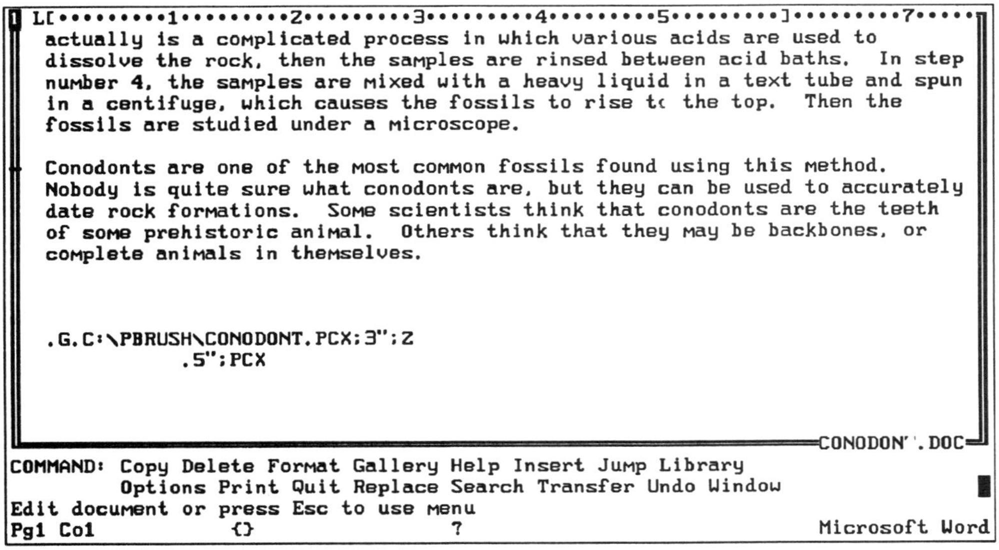

```
▌L[•••••••••1•••••••••2•••••••••3•••••••••4•••••••••5•••••••••]•••••••••7•••••▐
 ▌actually is a complicated process in which various acids are used to         ▐
 ▌dissolve the rock, then the samples are rinsed between acid baths.  In step  ▐
 ▌number 4, the samples are mixed with a heavy liquid in a text tube and spun  ▐
 ▌in a centifuge, which causes the fossils to rise to the top.  Then the       ▐
 ▌fossils are studied under a microscope.                                      ▐
 ▌                                                                             ▐
 ▌Conodonts are one of the most common fossils found using this method.        ▐
 ▌Nobody is quite sure what conodonts are, but they can be used to accurately  ▐
 ▌date rock formations.  Some scientists think that conodonts are the teeth    ▐
 ▌of some prehistoric animal.  Others think that they may be backbones, or     ▐
 ▌complete animals in themselves.                                              ▐
 ▌                                                                             ▐
 ▌                                                                             ▐
 ▌.G.C:\PBRUSH\CONODONT.PCX;3";2                                               ▐
 ▌       .5";PCX                                                               ▐
 ▌                                                                             ▐
 ▌                                                             CONODON'.DOC═▌
COMMAND: Copy Delete Format Gallery Help Insert Jump Library
        Options Print Quit Replace Search Transfer Undo Window          ▮
Edit document or press Esc to use menu
Pg1 Col          {}              ?                        Microsoft Word
```

graphic into a Word document by copying it to the clipboard and using Word's Clipboard glossary entry to insert it.

To use Word's Clipboard glossary entry to insert a graphic:

1. Run the graphics program and copy the graphic to the Windows clipboard.
2. Without quitting Windows, quit the graphics program and start Word.
3. Move the cursor to where you want to insert the graphic.
4. Choose the Insert command.
5. Type *clipboard* , or press F1 to see a list of glossary entries, then use the arrow keys or the mouse to highlight the Clipboard entry.
6. Press Enter to insert the entry in your document.

Importing an Excel Chart When Running Under Microsoft Windows

If you're running Word under Microsoft Windows and you want to use a chart created with the Excel program in your Word document, you can use the following procedure to import the chart as a bitmap. You must be using Windows version 2.0 or later, not the run-time version of Windows.

1. Select the chart in Excel.
2. Hold down the Shift key and select the Edit menu.
3. Choose the Copy Picture command.
4. Hold down the Shift key and choose OK.
5. Without quitting Windows, quit Excel and start Word.
6. Use the procedure listed under "Pasting In Graphics" above to insert the chart into your Word document.

USING THE CAPTURE.COM PROGRAM TO COPY GRAPHICS

If the program in which you've created a graphic can't save the graphic in one of the formats listed under "Pasting in Graphics," you can use the CAPTURE.COM program to copy the graphic so you can use it in a Word document. CAPTURE.COM is included with Word. You need quite a bit of free memory to run CAPTURE.COM, so if your computer doesn't have enough memory, you may see a message telling you that you can't run the program.

If you're running OS/2, you must run CAPTURE.COM and the graphics application you're using in DOS compatibility mode.

If you need to interrupt CAPTURE.COM at any time, press Esc.

To use CAPTURE.COM:

1. If necessary, insert the disk containing the CAPTURE.COM file, or copy the file to your hard disk to run it.
2. Do one of the following:
   - If it's the first time you've used CAPTURE.COM, type *capture /s*, then answer the questions on the screen to describe your system to the program.
   - If you've used CAPTURE.COM before, type *capture* to load the program.

   The operating system loads the program into memory and displays the DOS prompt again.
3. Display the graphic you want to copy.
4. Press Shift+PrintScreen. You'll see a CAPTURE.COM prompt appear at the top of the screen.
5. Do one of the following:
   - Type the name of the file (up to eight characcters) in which you want to save the graphic, then press Enter. CAPTURE.COM adds a .SCR extension to the file.

   or
   - Accept the proposed name CAPTURE.COM gives to the file by pressing Enter. CAPTURE.COM names files with numbers, like CAPT0001.SCR, CAPT0002.SCR, etc.

   If you've enabled clipping (which doesn't work with all programs), CAPTURE.COM adds clipping lines to the boundaries of the screen. You may not be able to see the clipping lines if they're at the edges of the screen. You can use the clipping lines to indicate exactly the portion of the screen you want to copy (this process is called clipping, as in clipping a photograph).
6. Do one of the following:
   - If you have enabled clipping and you want to use the clipping lines to clip the screen, use the Tab key to activate the clipping line you want to move, then use the arrow keys to move the lines to where you want the graphic boundary to be as shown in Figure 12–3. (You

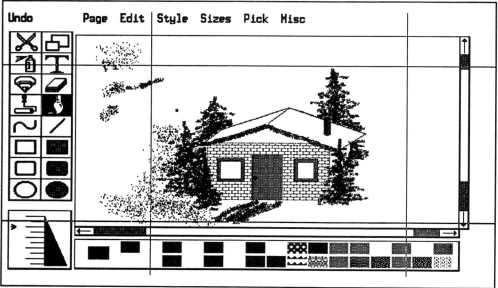

Figure 12-3.   **Capturing a graphic with CAPTURE.COM.**

may not be able to see the clipping lines before you use the arrow keys to move them into the picture.) Only the portion of the graphic within the clipping lines will be copied. When all the lines are where you want them, press Enter.
- If you want to copy the entire screen, press Enter.

Word saves the graphic (it may take a while, so be patient), then beeps when the process is complete.

7.   Repeat steps 3 through 6 to save more graphics if necessary, then quit the graphics program and use the procedure listed under "Inserting Graphics in a Word Document" earlier in this chapter to include the copied graphics in your Word files.

CHANGING THE POSITION OF A GRAPHIC

You can use the Delete and Insert commands to move a graphic to a new location, or use the Format pOsition command to specify an exact location on a page. To move the graphic, you select and move the .G.

paragraph that describes it. The graphic will appear in the new location when you print or choose the Print preView command.

CHANGING THE SIZE OF A GRAPHIC

If you want to change the size of a graphic after you've inserted the graphics paragraph, use the Library Link Graphics command again:

1. Select the .G. paragraph.
2. Choose the Library Link Graphics command.
3. Change the "graphics width" and "graphics height" fields as desired.
4. Press Enter or click the command name to carry out the command.

ADDING A BORDER AND/OR SHADING TO A GRAPHIC

You can add a border and shading to a graphic the same way you add a border to a text paragraph in Word. Figure 12-4 shows a graphic with a border and shading.

1. Select the .G. paragraph that describes the graphic.
2. Choose the Format Border command.
3. Choose the type of border and/or shading intensity you want. See "Adding Lines, Boxes, and Shading to Paragraphs" in Chapter 8 if you need more information.
4. Press Enter or click the command name.

ADDING TEXT TO A GRAPHIC

You can add a caption underneath a graphic, or if you've added a border to a graphic, you can add text within the border, as shown in Figure 12-5.

To add a caption underneath a graphic:

• Type the caption in a paragraph following the .G. paragraph.

Figure 12-4.   **A graphic with an added border and shading.**

Figure 12-5.   **The graphic on the top has a caption underneath it; the graphic on the bottom has text within the border.**

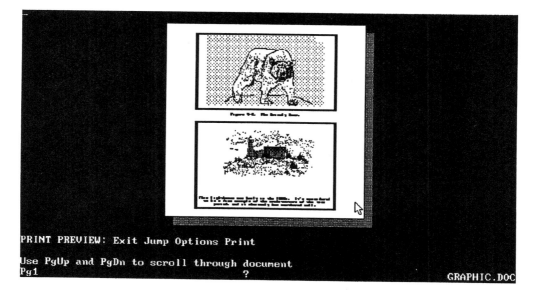

The caption is just like any other text paragraph, so you can use the Format Character and Format Paragraph commands to make it look just the way you want.

To add text within the border of a graphic:

1. If necessary, add a border to the graphic using the procedure in the previous section, "Adding a Border and/or Shading to a Graphic."
2. Place the cursor at the end of the .G. paragraph, just before the paragraph mark.
3. Press Shift+Enter to start a new line in the paragraph. (Shift+Enter inserts a newline character, which breaks the line without beginning a new paragraph.)
4. Type and format the text.

Text entered in this way is part of the graphics paragraph, so it will appear within the paragraph's border. To format the text, you use the Format Character command. If you use the Format Paragraph command, the entire graphics paragraph will be affected.

DELETING A GRAPHIC

A graphic can be easily deleted, just like any other paragraph in Word:

1. Select the .G. paragraph.
2. Press the Del key.

POSITIONING GRAPHICS ANYWHERE ON A PAGE

A graphic is contained in a paragraph, so you can use the Format pOsition command to position it anywhere on a page, just like any other paragraph. When a graphic is positioned with the Format pOsition command, surrounding text "flows" around it, just like the text flows around photographs in a magazine article. See "Positioning Objects Anywhere on a Page" in Chapter 14 for more information about using the Format pOsition command.

DRAWING LINES

You can use three different methods to draw lines with Word:

Method	Description
Format Border command	Draws boxes and lines around paragraphs.
Line draw mode	Allows you to use arrow keys to draw connecting lines and rectangles.
Tabs	Allows you to draw vertical lines with the vertical line tab type and to draw horizontal lines with leader characters before tabs.

Take a look at Figures 12-6 and 12-7 to see what you can do with these line-drawing features.

Using the Format Border Command

If you want to draw lines or boxes around selected paragraphs, using the Format Border command is the easiest way to do it. Lines and boxes inserted with the Format Border command are part of the format of the paragraph they surround. If you copy, move, or add text to the paragraph, the lines and boxes move or adjust accordingly. For more information about using the Format Border command, see "Adding Lines, Boxes, and Shading to Paragraphs" in Chapter 8.

Using Line Draw Mode

When you use line draw mode, you insert line characters directly into your document as text. You can then use the Format Character and Format Paragraph commands to change these line characters.

Your printer may not be able to print lines that you see on your monitor screen. To avoid unpleasant surprises, look up your printer in Chapter 2 of the *Printer Information for Microsoft Word* manual, and get the answers to two questions:

1. Does your printer support the IBM Extended Character Set? If your printer does *not* support the IBM Extended Character Set, use the procedure listed under "Changing the Line Draw Character" to choose the Hyphen/Bar Set of line draw characters before you begin drawing lines.

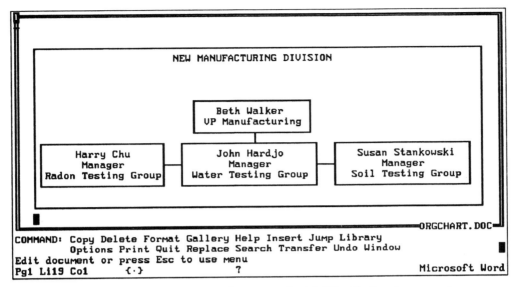

Figure 12-6.   **A line drawing created with Word's line draw mode.**

Figure 12-7.   **A line drawing created with Word's Format Border and Format Tab Set commands.**

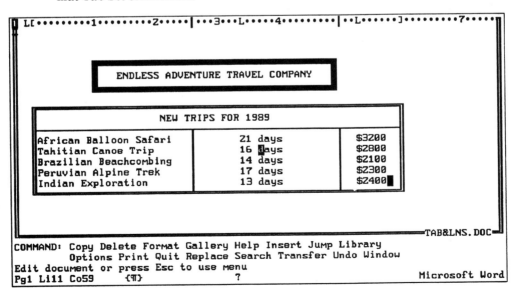

2. Do you need to use a specific font to draw lines? If you can use only one font to draw lines, use the Format Character command to change to that font before you begin drawing lines.
    To use line draw mode:

*   Move the cursor to where you want to begin drawing lines.
*   Press Ctrl+F5 to turn on line draw mode. Word displays "LD" in the status line to remind you that you're using line draw mode.
*   Use the following keys to draw lines:

Key	To Draw
Left and right arrow	Horizontal lines.
Up and down arrow	Vertical lines.
Home	A line from the cursor position to the paragraph's left indent.
End	A line from the cursor position to the paragraph's right indent.

Don't worry if you draw some lines you don't want; you can easily erase them later, using the procedure in the next section, "Erasing Lines."

*   Press Ctrl+F5 when you're ready to exit line draw mode. You'll need to turn off line draw mode when you want to skip over blank space, then use Ctrl+F5 to turn it back on again when the cursor is in the right spot and you're ready to draw lines. The line draw indicator, LD, will disappear from the status line.

Erasing Lines
To erase lines:

1. If necessary, press Ctrl+F5 to turn off line draw mode. The line draw indicator, LD, will disappear from the status line.
2. Do one of the following:
    *   Use the backspace key to erase backwards.
    or
    *   Select the portion of the line you want to delete, then press the Del key to delete it.

Word adjusts the text as you erase line characters, just like when you erase text characters. You may need to insert spaces or tab characters to make lines match up again.

Changing the Line Draw Character

Word normally uses a single line character to draw in line draw mode, but you can draw with any character you like. You could choose to draw with asterisks (*) for example, with equal signs (=) or number signs (#), or with one of the character sets that Word lists for you to choose from.

To change the line draw character:

1. Choose the Options command.
2. In the "linedraw" field, type a character or press F1 to see a list of line-drawing characters. If you press F1, you'll see the following options:

Name	Description
Single Set	Uses characters in the IBM extended character set to draw single lines and corners.
Double Set	Uses characters in the IBM extended character set to draw double lines and corners.
Hyphen/Bar Set	Uses characters available on the keyboard to draw lines, and uses the plus sign (+) to draw corners. Use this set if your printer doesn't use the IBM extended character set.
Various graphics characters	If you select one of these graphics characters, Word draws both horizontal and vertical lines using the same character, and doesn't use any corner characters to connect lines at corners.

If you type a character that Word can't draw lines with, Word displays the message "Not a valid line drawing character."

3. Press Enter or click the command name to change the drawing character.

Note: Your printer may not be able to duplicate all of the characters listed in the "linedraw" field of the Options command. If you choose a character that your printer can't handle, Word substitutes another character when it prints, so the result may not be what you want. Check the *Printer Information for Microsoft Word* manual to see if your printer supports the IBM extended character set, and experiment a little if necessary to see which characters your printer can reproduce.

Mixing Text and Lines

Mixing text with lines can cause problems if not done carefully. Here are some guidelines to help you produce a good document:

- Always use a fixed-pitch font—such as Pica or Prestige—for text that will have lines drawn around it. This selection ensures that the width of the text characters will match the width of the line draw characters.
- Draw the lines first, then use overtype mode (F5) to type text in the appropriate spots.
- When typing text between lines use the Down arrow key rather than the Enter key to move the cursor down.
- Don't use paragraph formats that change the location of a paragraph, such as indents, alignments, or space before and after paragraphs—these may cause lines to move, too.
- If you use a font smaller than 12 points when drawing lines, choose Auto in the "line spacing" field of the Format Paragraph command to ensure that your vertical lines will be solid lines.

Using Tabs to Draw Lines

You can use the vertical line tab type to draw vertical lines in paragraphs, and you can use leader characters to fill in the spaces between tabs with horizontal lines of hyphens, periods, or underscore (solid line) characters. See "Filling Tab Spaces with Leader Characters" in Chapter 9 for complete information about the process if necessary. Figure 12-8 illustrates drawing lines with tab leader characters and vertical-line tab types.

Leader characters won't appear on the screen if you've chosen All in the "show nonprinting symbols" field of the Options command. Instead, you'll see just the tab character. Change the "show nonprinting symbols" field of the Options command to Partial or None if you want to see the leader characters.

To draw vertical lines with tabs:

1. Press Alt+F1 to choose the Format Tab Set command and put a highlight in the ruler.
2. Use the arrow keys to move the highlight in the ruler to where you want to draw a vertical line.
3. Type V to choose a vertical line tab type.

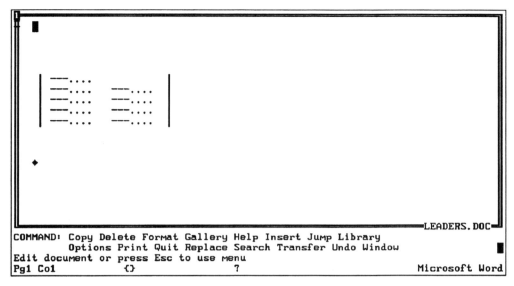

Figure 12-8.   **Drawing lines with underscore tab leader characters and vertical-line tab types.**

4. Repeat steps 2 and 3 until you've positioned the vertical lines you want.
5. Press Enter or click the command name.

To draw horizontal lines with tabs:

1. Press Alt+F1 to choose the Format Tab Set command and put a highlight in the ruler.
2. Do one of the following:
    *   If you're setting a new tab, use the arrow keys to move the highlight on the ruler to where you want to insert the tab. (If you want to draw a line all the way across a page, move the highlight to the right margin.)
    *   If you're adding leader characters to an existing tab, use the arrow keys to move the highlight to the tab you want to affect.
3. Do one of the following:
    *   If you're setting a new tab, type the leader character you want to draw the line with (a period, a hyphen, or an underscore), then press a character for the tab type you want (L for left, C for centered, R for right, D for decimal, V for vertical line). You can draw both

horizontal and vertical lines at the same time by choosing the vertical line tab type and choosing an underscore leader character.

- If you're adding leader characters to an existing tab, type the leader character you want (a period, a hyphen, or an underscore).

4. Repeat steps 2 and 3 if necessary to add leader characters to other tabs.

5. Press Enter or click the command name.

13

ADDING PAGE NUMBERS, RUNNING HEADS AND RUNNING FEET, AND FOOTNOTES

This Chapter Contains the Following:

This chapter shows you how to add the finishing touches to your document: page numbers, running heads and running feet, and footnotes. Figures 13-1 and 13-2 show how these elements might look on a printed page.

ADDING PAGE NUMBERS

Word doesn't add page numbers to your document until you say so. You then specify exactly where and how to you want the page numbers to be printed. Word has two commands that affect page numbers:

Command	Allows You to
Format Division	Turn page numbering on or off in a division;
Page-numbers	choose to mark pages with numbers, Roman numerals, or letters; start a new division at page 1; reposition numbers by typing measurements; specify the starting page number for a division.

Figure 13-1.   **Page with a running head and a running foot.**

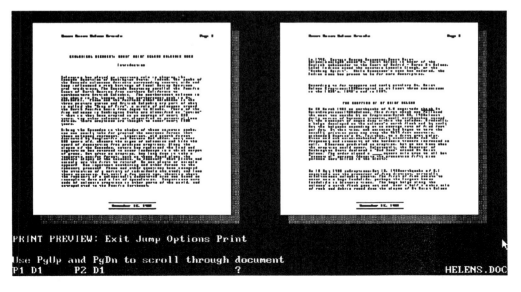

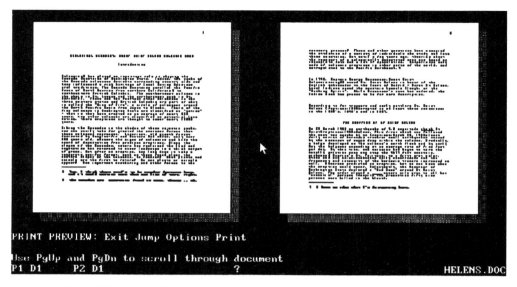

Figure 13-2.   **Page with a page number and footnotes.**

Format Running-head Add text, time, and date as well as page numbers to the top (running head) or bottom (running foot) of each page.

Note: If you use the Format Division Page-numbers command *and* the Format Running-head command to add page numbers, you'll end up with more than one number on each page. However, you can put a page number in a running head or running foot with Format Running-head command, then use the Format Division Page-numbers command to change the type of numbers or to start numbering the division at a specific page number.

Adding and Formatting Page Numbers with the Format Division Page-numbers Command

By default, Word starts every division with the number that page would have if numbered consecutively throughout your document. In other words, if the previous division ends on page 18, Word numbers the pages of the new division starting with 19. However, you can start the page numbers for a new division at 1 or any other number, or you can omit page numbers altogether. You can choose from standard Arabic numerals, Roman numerals, or letters. And you can also specify the position of the numbers on the page.

You can use the Format Division Page-numbers command to add only page numbers to your pages, as shown in Figure 13-3, or to specify the type of page numbers and the starting page number for page numbers included in running heads or feet.

To specify page numbers with the Format Division Page-numbers command :

1.   Move the cursor into the division you want to affect. If you haven't divided your document into divisions, your choices will affect the entire document.
2.   Choose the Format Division Page-numbers command. Word displays the command fields shown in Figure 13-3.
3.   If you want to add page numbers, choose Yes. If you're just specifying the type of page numbers for running heads or running feet, make sure to choose No in this field.

Figure 13-3.   **The Format Division Page-numbers command controls the format of page numbers.**

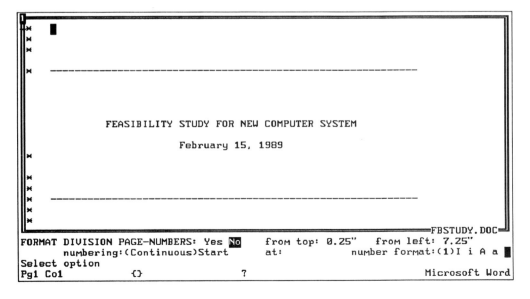

4. If you want to start page numbering for the division at a specific number, choose Start in the "numbering" field, and type the starting page number in the "at" field.

5. Choose the number format you want:

Option	Format Name	Example
1	Arabic numerals	1, 2, 3
1	Uppercase Roman numerals	I, II, III
i	Lowercase Roman numerals	i, ii, iii
A	Uppercase letters	A, B, C
a	Lowercase letters	a, b, c

6. If you want to change Word's default position for page numbers , type measurements in the "from top" and "from left" fields. Word's default position for page numbers is .5 inch from the top edge and 7.25 inches from the left edge of the paper. Some printers cannot print very close to the top or bottom of the page. In general, it's a good idea not to position any text any closer than .25 inches from the edge of the page. To position a page number in the bottom margin, type a large measurement—such as *10.5*—in the "from top" field.

7. Press Enter or click the command name.

You won't see page numbers in document view. You have to switch to print preview, as shown in Figure 13-4. See "Using Print Preview" in Chapter 14 for more information.

ADDING RUNNING HEADS OR RUNNING FEET

When you want to print text at the top of each page, you add a running head (sometimes called a header). When you want to print text at the bottom of each page, you add a running foot (sometimes called a footer). In Word, running heads and running feet belong to divisions, but you can use the same running heads or running feet throughout your document, or create different running heads and running feet for each division. Running heads and running feet can contain any sort of text you want, as well as date, time, and page-number fields that Word fills in when you print the document.

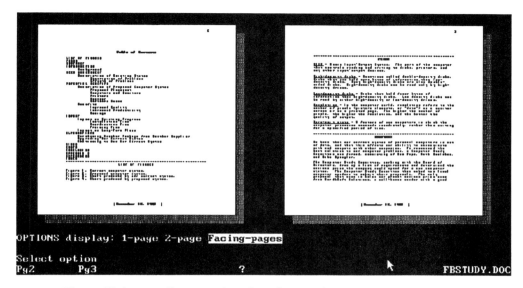

Figure 13-4.   **Page numbers in print preview.**

The Basic Procedure

You use the Format Running-head command to add running heads or running feet to your document. The basic procedure is:

1. Move the cursor to a blank paragraph (just a paragraph mark) at the beginning of a division. If your document isn't separated into divisions, move the cursor to a blank paragraph at the beginning of the document, as shown in Figure 13-5.
2. Choose options in the Format Running-head command fields to determine where the running head or running foot will print.
3. Type and format the text you want to appear in the running head or running foot.

Using the Format Running-head Command

When you use the Format Running-head command, you can choose from several options to create exactly the running head or running foot you want. For example, instead of having the same running head and running

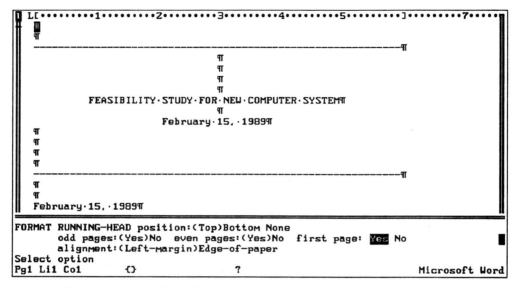

Figure 13-5.   Creating a running-head paragraph at the beginning of a document.

foot on each page, you may want to create different running heads or running feet for even and odd pages in your document, as seen in Figure 13–6.

To create different running heads for odd- and even-numbered pages, you'll use the Format Running-head command once to create the running head for the odd-numbered pages, then use the command again to create the running head for the even-numbered pages. If you want to create different running feet for facing pages, you'll use the Format Running-head command two more times, once to create the running foot for the odd-numbered pages, then again to create the running foot for the even-numbered pages. Figure 13-7 shows the fields in the Format Running-head command.

You can also choose whether you want the running head or foot to appear on the first page of a division, and whether you want the left side of the running head to align with the left document margin, or with the left edge of the paper. Figure 13-8 illustrates the difference between these options.

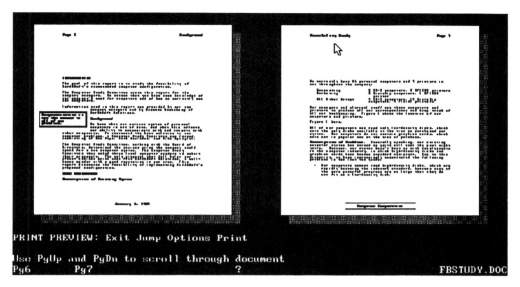

Figure 13-6.   **Word can create different running heads and running feet for even and odd pages.**

Figure 13-7.   **Creating a running foot with the Format Running-head command.**

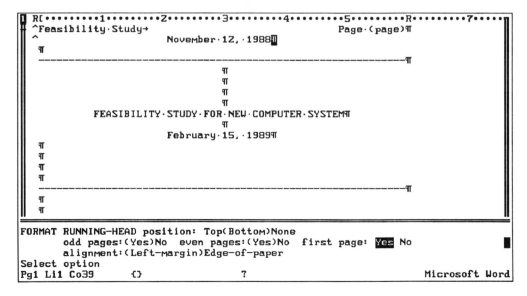

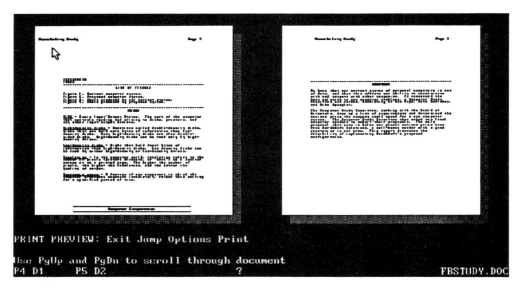

Figure 13-8.   **Different alignments of running heads.**

To add a running head or running foot to a division:

1. Move the cursor to the beginning of the division you want to affect. Running heads and running feet should be the first paragraphs in a division. If your document isn't separated into divisions, you'll move the cursor to the beginning of the document, and Word will add running heads or running feet to the entire document.
2. Press Enter to create a blank paragraph, then move the cursor back up to that paragraph mark.
3. Choose the Format Running-head command.
4. In the "position" field, choose Top if you're creating a running head, or choose Bottom if you're creating a running foot.
5. In the "odd pages" field, choose Yes if you want the running head or running foot to appear on odd pages.
6. In the "even pages" field, choose Yes if you want the running head or running foot to appear on even pages.
7. In the "first page" field, choose Yes if you want the running head or running foot to appear on the first page of the division.
8. In the "alignment" field, choose Left-margin if you want to align the left edge of the running head or running foot with the left margin,

like the rest of the text in your document, or choose Edge-of-paper to align the left edge of the running head or running foot with the left edge of the page.

9. Press Enter or click the command name. Word formats the paragraph as a running head or running foot, as shown in Figure 13-9.

If you have the style bar displayed, you'll see a code for the running head or running foot you've just added. See "Viewing Codes for Running Heads in the Style Bar" later in this chapter for more information about what these codes mean.

Note: If you accidentally format a paragraph as a running head or running foot, choose the Format Running-head command again, then choose None in the "position" field to remove the format and return the paragraph to normal.

Figure 13-9.   **A paragraph formatted with the Format Running-head command. The next step is to enter and format the text.**

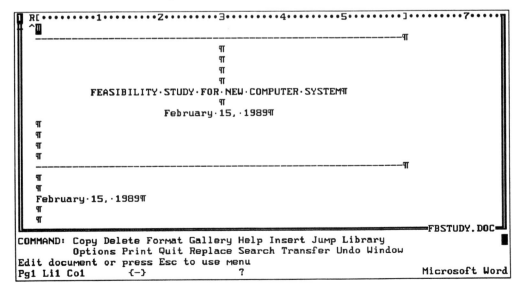

Entering the Text for a Running Head or Running Foot

After you've used the Format Running-head command to set up a paragraph as a running head or running foot, you're ready to type the text you want to appear on the pages. You can include time, date, and page number fields that Word will automatically update when you print the document.

To enter the text for a running head or running foot:

1. Type the text.
2. Choose the following actions as desired:

In Order to Add	Do This
Page number	1. Move the cursor to where you want the page number to appear. Make sure there's blank space (at least one space character) in front of the cursor. 2. Type *page*. 3. Press F3. Word replaces *page* with (page). Word will fill in this field with the actual page number when you print the document.
Date of printing	1. Move the cursor to where you want the date to appear. Make sure there's blank space (at least one space character) in front of the cursor. 2. Type *date*. 3. Press F3. Word replaces *date* with (date). Word will fill in this field with the date from your computer's system when you print the document.
Time of printing	1. Move the cursor to where you want the time to appear. Make sure there's blank space (at least one space character) in front of the cursor. 2. Type *time*. 3. Press F3. Word replaces *time* with (time). Word will fill in this field with the time from your computer's clock when you print the document.

When Word updates the page, date, or time fields, Word prints the text using the format set by these command fields:

Field Name	Uses the Format Currently Chosen In
Page	"number format" field of the Format Division Page-numbers command (default is Arabic numerals—1,2, 3, etc.).
Date	"date format" of the Options command (default is month/day/year—12/25/88, etc.)
Time	"time format" of the Options command (default is 12-hour time—11:30 a.m., etc.).

Figure 13-10 shows running-head and running-feet paragraphs after adding and formatting the text. The first paragraph sets a running head for odd-numbered pages. The second paragraph sets a running head for even-numbered pages. The third paragraph sets a running foot that will appear on all pages.

To see the true position and appearance of running heads and running feet, you use the Print preView command or press Ctrl+F9 to switch to print preview. Figure 13-11 shows running heads and running feet in print preview. For more information about using print preview, see "Using Print Preview" in Chapter 14.

Figure 13-10.   **Paragraphs that create running heads and running feet.**

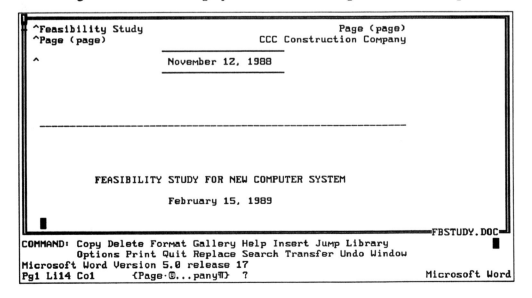

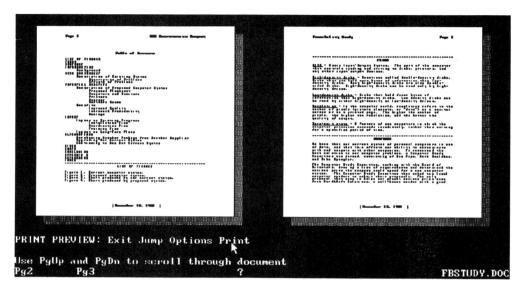

Figure 13-11.   **Running heads and running feet in print preview.**

Keyboard Shortcut

If you want to use Word's default formats for running heads or running feet that appear on both odd and even pages, you can quickly create them this way.

1. Move the cursor to the beginning of the division to which you want to add running heads or running feet.
2. Type and format a paragraph containing the text and fields you want to appear in a running head or ina running foot.
3. Select the paragraph.
4. If you want to format the paragraph as a running head, press Ctrl+F2.

If you want to format the paragraph as a running foot, press Alt+F2.

Here are two general rules that will help you to successfully create a variety of running heads and feet:

- If you want to create running heads or feet that are more than one line long, press Shift+Enter at the ends of lines to enter a newline character and keep all the lines in the same paragraph.
- Put blank space (at least one space character) before a page, date, or time field. Otherwise, when you press F3, Word won't be able to identify the text as a field and you'll get an error message.

The following examples show some running heads or feet you might create. Don't type (page), (date), or (time)—these are fields entered according to the preceding instructions.

Type	To Create This When Printed
Feasibility Study (date) Page (page)	Feasibility Study 5/5/89 Page 45
Chapter 2 Scheduling 2 - (page)	Chapter 2 Scheduling 2 - 45
— (page) — Program Listing (date) (time)	— 45 — Program Listing 5/5/89 11:23 AM
((page))	(45)
Chapter 3: Planning for the Future — (page) —	Chapter 3: Planning for the Future — 45 —

Viewing Codes for Running Heads in the Style Bar

If you have the style bar displayed, you'll see codes identifying running heads and running feet next to the paragraphs you've entered. Figure 13-12 shows examples of these codes.

Here's what the codes mean:

Code	Meaning
tf	Running head on first page only ("t" for top, "f" for first).
to	Running head on odd pages only ("t" for top, "o" for odd).
te	Running head on even pages only ("t" for top, "e" for even).
t	Running head on both odd and even pages (t for top).
bf	Running foot on first page only ("b" for bottom, "f" for first).
bo	Running foot on odd pages only ("b" for bottom, "o" for odd).
be	Running foot on even pages only ("b" for bottom, "e" for even).
b	Running foot on both odd and even pages (b for bottom).

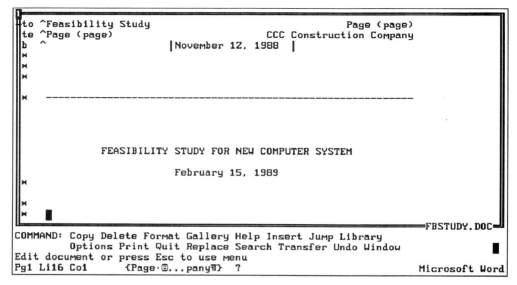

Figure 13-12.   **Codes identifying running heads and running feet in the style bar.**

To display the style bar:

1.   Choose the Options command.
2.   In the "show style bar" field choose Yes.
3.   Press Enter or click the command name.

Editing and Formatting Running Heads or Running Feet

All of Word's editing and formatting commands affect running heads just like they affect other text in a document. You just:

1.   Move the cursor into the running head or running foot paragraph you want to affect.
2.   Select text as necessary and choose the appropriate editing or formatting commands or key combinations.

You can add character formats such as italic, bold, underlining, different fonts or sizes. To apply a character format to the text in a field, you select the entire field and apply the format. You can also use paragraph formats, such as borders, indents, alignments, and tabs to format running heads or running feet—centered alignment is a popular option.

Word uses an automatic paragraph style, the Running head style, to format running heads and running feet. You can change this Running head style in NORMAL.STY if you want Word to use a different format automatically for all running heads and feet (see "Changing the Running Head Automatic Style" later in this chapter). Or you may want to develop several special styles to format different running heads or feet.

For more information about editing and formatting:

See	For Information About
Chapter 4	Editing
Chapter 7	Character formats
Chapter 8	Paragraph formats, including borders
Chapter 9	Setting Tabs
Chapter 11	Styles

Changing the Position of Running Heads or Running Feet

Word automatically positions running heads .5 inch from the top of the page, and running feet .5 inch from the bottom of the page, measuring from the edge of the page to the top of the first line of a running head or running foot. If you want to change this default position, use the following procedure:

1. Choose the Format Division Margins command.
2. To position running heads in the division, you type a new measurement in the "running head position from top" field. For example, to position the top of a running head one inch from the top edge of the page, you type *1* here. To position running feet in the division, you type a new measurement in the "from bottom" field. For example, to position the top of a running foot one and 1/2 inch from the bottom edge of the page, type *1.5* here.

Repeating Running Heads or Running Feet from Division to Division

If your document is separated into divisions and you want to repeat the same running head or running foot throughout your document, copy the

---

Example

Say you want to create a "mirrored" running head like the following:

| 10 | 5/5/89 | Progress Report | | Progress Report | 5/5/89 | 11 |

Here's what you'd do:

1. At the beginning of the document press Enter twice to insert two paragraph marks, then select the first paragraph mark. You're going to create the even-page running head first.
2. Choose the Format Running-head command, and choose Top in the "position" field, No in the "odd" field and "first page" fields, Yes in the "even" field, and Left-margin in the "alignment" field, then press Enter.
3. Type *page*, press F3, press Tab, type *date*, press F3, press Tab, then type *Progress Report*. You've created the even running head. Next, you'll create the running head for the odd pages.
4. Select the second paragraph mark (the second blank paragraph you created when you pressed Enter).
5. Choose the Format Running-head command, and choose Top in the "position" field, Yes in the "odd" field, No in the "even" field and "first page" fields, and Left-margin in the "alignment" field, then press Enter.
6. Type *Progress Report*, press Tab, type *date*, press F3, press Tab, then type *page* and press F3.
7. Select the first running-head paragraph, then use the Format Tab Set command to set tabs in appropriate spots to position the text between margins. For the best-looking results, set a centered tab to position the date and a right-aligned tab at the right margin to make the running-head text align with the right margin.
8. Select the second running-head paragraph, then use the Format Tab Set command to set tabs in appropriate spots to position the text between margins, and press Enter. For the best-looking results, set a centered tab to position the date (use the same position as you used for the even running head) and a right-aligned tab at the right margin to make the running-head text align with the right margin.

Now you've got your "mirrored" running heads. The date and page fields will be filled in when you print. To add running feet, you'd use a similar procedure, but choose Bottom in the "position" field of the Format Running-head command.

paragraphs that create the running heads or running feet and insert them at the beginning of each division, like this:

1. Select the running head paragraph(s) that you want to repeat.
2. Choose the Copy command and press Enter to copy the paragraph(s) to the scrap.
3. Move the cursor to the beginning of the next division.
4. Press Ins to insert the copied paragraph(s). Repeat steps 3 and 4 as necessary.

Changing the Running Head Automatic Style

Word automatically applies its Running head style to all running-head and running-foot paragraphs. You can format the paragraphs and apply new styles to make them look just the way you want, but if you find yourself always changing the format the same way, you might want to change the Running head automatic style in NORMAL.STY. That way, Word would automatically apply the format you want to all running-head paragraphs.

To change the automatic Running head style:

1. Choose the Gallery command to go to the Gallery.
2. Make sure NORMAL.STY is loaded (you should see the name NOR-MAL.STY in the lower right corner of the Gallery window). If necessary, use the Transfer Load command to load NORMAL.STY.
3. Choose the Insert command.
4. In the "usage" field, choose Paragraph.
5. In the "variant" field, press F1. You should see a list of all the paragraph styles in NORMAL.STY.
6. Select Running head.
7. Press Enter or click the command name to insert that style into the style sheet.
8. Choose Format commands from the Gallery menu to change the style the way you want.
9. Press Enter or click the command name to change the style.
10. Use the Transfer Save command from the Gallery menu to save the style sheet.

Example: Changing the Automatic Running Head Style

Say you'd like to change the Running head style to contain a centered tab that would center text in the middle of the running head, and a right-aligned tab that would align text with the right margin. For example, in the sample running head below the position of the date is controlled by a centered tab and the position of the page number is controlled by a right-aligned tab set at the right margin:

Chapter 2   5/5/89   Page 13

The following procedure assumes that you're using Word's default margin settings of 1.25 inches for the left and right margins, that you have no gutter margin, and that you're using inches as the unit of measurement. If you're not using these settings, you'll have to adjust the measurements used below to make sure they line up with the center of the page and the right margin.

To change the Running head automatic style to the format specified above:

1. With NORMAL.STY loaded in the Gallery window, choose the Insert command.
2. In the "usage" field choose Paragraph.
3. In the "variant" field press F1, then select Running head from the list and press Enter to insert the Running head style in the style sheet.
4. Choose the Format Tab Set command from the Gallery menu.
5. Type *4.25* in the "position" field, choose Centered in the "alignment" field, and press Enter, creating the centered tab in the middle of the running head.
6. Choose the Format Tab Set command again.
7. Type *7.25* in the "position" field, choose Right in the "alignment" field, and press Enter, creating the right-aligned tab at the right side of the running head.
8. Use the Transfer Save command from the Gallery menu to save the changes to NORMAL.STY.

Now, whenever you create a running head or running foot, Word will automatically apply this format. The first time you press the Tab key in a header or footer, it will take you to the centered tab character, which will center any text you type there. The second time you press the Tab key, it will take you to the right-aligned tab character, and align any text you type there with the right margin. So if you don't have three parts to a running head or running foot, just press a tab character to align the text the way you want. For example, if you wanted to add a footer containing only a centered document title, you could just press Tab, then type the document title at the centered tab. If you wanted only text aligned with the right margin, just press Tab twice, then type the text.

Removing Running Heads or Running Feet

To remove a running head or running foot from your document:

1. Select the entire paragraph that creates the running head or running foot.
2. Press the Del key.

ADDING FOOTNOTES

Word has four commands that affect footnotes:

Command	Description
Format Footnote command	Inserts a footnote reference mark at the cursor position, then jumps to the end of the document so you can type the footnote text.
Jump Footnote command	Moves the cursor to the next footnote reference mark, or if a reference mark or footnote text is selected, moves the cursor back and forth between the reference mark and the text.
Window Split Footnote command	Opens a window at the bottom of the screen to allow you to view or edit footnotes and see document text at the same time.

Format Division   Controls whether footnotes print at the bottoms
Layout command   of pages or print at the ends of divisions.

You'll learn more about these commands and their uses in the following sections.

Inserting Footnotes

There are two parts to a footnote: the footnote reference (that number or mark in text that tells you to look for a footnote), and the footnote text, as shown in Figure 13-13.

When you insert footnotes, you can have Word number your footnotes automatically, you can insert your own reference characters, or you can use a combination of both methods. If you let Word number your footnotes, Word will update the references when you add or delete a footnote. If you insert your own numbers or characters, you'll have to keep track of the order yourself. If you combine your own reference marks and automatically-numbered reference marks, Word counts your reference marks when numbering footnotes. For example, if you insert an automati-

Figure 13-13.   **The parts of a footnote.**

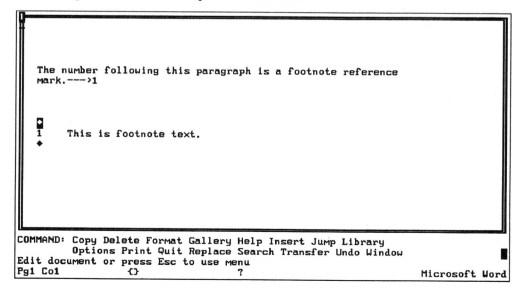

cally numbered reference, and insert an asterisk reference, then insert another automatically numbered reference, Word numbers the first reference as 1, counts the asterisk reference as 2, and numbers the third footnote reference as 3.

To insert a footnote:

1. Place the cursor where you want the footnote reference mark to appear.
2. Choose the Format Footnote command.
3. Do one of the following:
   - If you want Word to automatically number the footnote, press Enter or click the command name.
   - If you don't want Word to number your footnotes automatically, type the character you want to use instead in the "reference mark" field, then press Enter or click the command name. For example, if you want to mark your footnote with an asterisk, type * in the "reference mark" field.

   Word inserts the reference mark and moves the cursor to the end of the document where you can enter the footnote text.
4. Type the text for your footnote. The text can be as long as you want it to be.
5. To add more footnotes, move the cursor to the next place you want to add a footnote in your document, then repeat steps 2 through 4. Figure 13-14 illustrates adding footnotes to a document.

Moving Between Reference Marks and Footnote Text

The Jump Footnote command quickly moves the cursor to the next footnote reference mark, or back and forth between reference marks and their associated footnote text.

Here's how the command works:

To Jump to	Do This
The next reference mark	1. Move the cursor into the document text.
	2. Choose the Jump Footnote command.
The footnote text associated with a reference mark	1. Select the reference mark.
	2. Choose the Jump Footnote command.
The reference mark associated with footnote text	1. Move the cursor into the footnote text.
	2. Choose the Jump Footnote command.

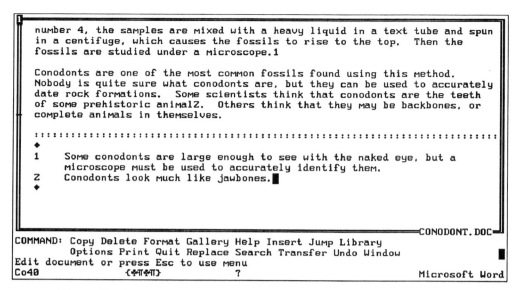

```
 number 4, the samples are mixed with a heavy liquid in a text tube and spun
 in a centifuge, which causes the fossils to rise to the top.  Then the
 fossils are studied under a microscope.1

 Conodonts are one of the most common fossils found using this method.
 Nobody is quite sure what conodonts are, but they can be used to accurately
 date rock formations.  Some scientists think that conodonts are the teeth
 of some prehistoric animalZ.  Others think that they may be backbones, or
 complete animals in themselves.

 :::::::::::::::::::::::::::::::::::::::::::::::::::::::::::::::::::::::::::
 ◆
 1    Some conodonts are large enough to see with the naked eye, but a
      microscope must be used to accurately identify them.
 Z    Conodonts look much like jawbones.█
 ◆
                                                           CONODONT.DOC
COMMAND: Copy Delete Format Gallery Help Insert Jump Library
         Options Print Quit Replace Search Transfer Undo Window        █
Edit document or press Esc to use menu
Co40            {✷T✷T}            ?              Microsoft Word
```

Figure 13-14.   **Adding footnotes to a document.**

Using a Footnote Window

If you'd like to see your document text at the same time you view your footnotes, you can use the Window Split Footnote command to open a window that displays footnotes at the bottom of the screen. Opening a footnote window is just like opening any other window on the Word screen; you can scroll in either window, use F1 or the mouse to move the cursor back and forth between windows, and change the size of the windows. Figure 13-15 shows a footnote window. You can open a footnote window with keys or with a mouse.

To open a footnote window using keys:

1. Choose the Window Split Footnote command.
2. In the "at line" field, type a line number at which you want to split the Word window, or press F1 to display a highlight in the selection bar, then use the Down or Up arrow keys to move the highlight to where you want to split the window.
3. Press Enter or click the command name. Word draws the footnote window at the bottom of the document window.

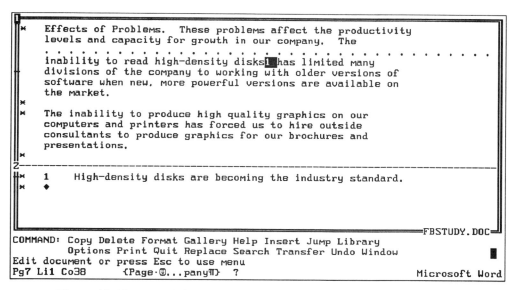

Figure 13-15.   **Using a footnote window allows you to view your text and your footnotes at the same time.**

To open a footnote window using the mouse:

1. Point to the right border of the document window where you want to split the window.
2. Hold down the Shift key and click either mouse button to open the footnote window.

Changing the Size of the Footnote Window

Like any other window, you can make a footnote window larger or smaller by moving the horizontal border, the vertical border, or both.

To change the size of the footnote window with the keys:

1. Choose the Window Move command.
2. In the "window #" field, type the number that appears in the upper left corner of the footnote window.
3. To move the horizontal border, type a number in the "to row" field, or press F1 to put a highlight in the window border, then use the direction keys to move the highlight to where you want the border to be. To move the vertical border, type a number in the "to column" field,

or press F1 to put a highlight in the window border, then use the direction keys to move the highlight to where you want the border to be.

4. Press Enter to redraw the window.

To change the size of the footnote window using the mouse:

1. Point to the lower right corner of the window.
2. Hold down either mouse button and drag the window to a new size. You'll see a dotted outline of the window move along with your mouse pointer to show you the changing dimensions of the window.
3. Release the mouse button to redraw the window.

For more information about working with multiple windows, see "Working with More Than One Window" in Chapter 4.

Closing the Footnote Window

When you close a footnote window, Word expands the document window to its previous size. You can use either the keyboard or the mouse to close the window.

To close a footnote window using keys:

1. Move the cursor to the footnote window.
2. Choose the Window Close command.
3. Press Enter or click the command name.

To close a footnote window using the mouse:

1. Point to the right border of the footnote window.
2. Click both mouse buttons simultaneously.

Editing Footnotes

You can edit and format the text of footnotes just as you would any other text in your document.

Editing Footnote Text
To edit the text of a footnote:

1. If you want to display a footnote window, choose the Window Split Footnote command as described in "Using a Footnote Window" earlier in this chapter.

2. Select the reference mark of the footnote whose text you want to edit.
3. Choose the Jump Footnote command to move the cursor to the footnote text.
4. Edit the text.

Editing the Footnote Reference Mark

You can change a footnote reference character. For example, you might want to change from an ampersand to an asterisk, or change from a character you've specified to an automatically numbered footnote.

To edit a footnote reference mark:

1. Select the reference mark in your document.
2. Choose the Format Footnote command.
3. If you want to specify a new character, type the new character in the "reference mark" field. If you want to change to an automatically numbered reference, delete any text in the field. (Word assumes you want a number when this field is blank.)
4. Press Enter or click the command name.

Restoring an Automatic Reference Number You Accidentally Deleted

If you accidentally delete an automatic footnote reference number when you're editing the footnote text, you can put the number back this way:

1. Move the cursor to where you want the number to appear.
2. Type *footnote*.
   "Footnote" is the name of an entry in Word's standard glossary. If you'd like to learn more about glossaries, see "Saving Text and Graphics for Later Use: Using Glossaries" in Chapter 4.
3. Press F3.
   Word converts the word "footnote" to the correct automatic number.

Formatting Footnotes

You can use Word's formatting commands to change the appearance of both the footnote text and of the footnote reference marks. For the reference marks, you can use the Format Character command or the shortcut keys, such as Alt+B for bold. For the footnote text, you can use both the Format Character and the Format Paragraph commands, any shortcut keys that format characters or paragraphs, as well as the Format Tab Set command to add tabs.

If you don't want to change individual reference marks or footnotes, you can change Word's automatic footnote styles. Word uses two automatic styles to format footnotes: the Footnote ref character style for reference marks, and the Footnote paragraph style for the footnote text. You can change these styles in the NORMAL.STY file to change the format Word automatically applies to footnotes. For example, you might want to change the Footnote ref style to make all footnote references into tiny superscripts. Or you might want to change the Footnote style to format all footnote text using a different font or indents. See "Changing Word's Automatic Styles" in Chapter 11 for more information.

Controlling Where the Footnote Text Prints

Although the text for footnotes is stored at the end of the document, it won't necessarily appear there when you print your document. By default, Word prints footnotes at the bottom of the pages on which their reference marks appear, as shown in Figure 13-13. If there's not enough room to print all the footnotes at the bottom of the page, Word prints the rest on the next page. If you don't like this arrangement, you can tell Word to print the footnotes at the end of each division, or, if your document is not divided into divisions, at the end of the document.

To control the position of footnote text in your document:

1. Choose the Format Division Layout command. The command's fields are shown in Figure 13-16.
2. In the "footnotes" field choose one of the following options:

Option	Positions Footnotes
Same-page	At the bottom of the page on which the footnote references appear.
End	At the end of the division containing the cursor. If you have not divided your document into divisions, Word prints the footnote text at the end of the document.

3. Press Enter or click the command name.

```
┌─────────────────────────────────────────────────────────────────────┐
│█                                                                      │
│ ⋅⋅⋅⋅⋅⋅⋅⋅⋅⋅⋅⋅⋅⋅⋅⋅⋅⋅⋅⋅⋅⋅⋅⋅⋅⋅REFERENCES⋅⋅⋅⋅⋅⋅⋅⋅⋅⋅⋅⋅⋅⋅⋅⋅⋅⋅⋅⋅⋅⋅⋅⋅⋅⋅⋅⋅│
│  "State-of-the-Art Computers," COMP-YOU-T Magazine, Vol. XX,          │
│  March 1989.                                                          │
│  ^Page (page)                         CCC Construction Company        │
│  ^Page (page)                         CCC Construction Company        │
│  "Best Computer Buys," PC Value Reports, Vol. 22, February            │
│  1989.                                                                │
│                                                                       │
│                               INDEX                                   │
│                                                                       │
│ ::::::::::::::::::::::::::::::::::::::::::::::::::::::::::::::::::::::::│
│  ◆                                                                    │
│  1     High-density disks are becoming the industry standard.         │
├───────────────────────────────────────────────────────────────────── │
│FORMAT DIVISION LAYOUT footnotes: ▓Same-page▓ End                      │
│        number of columns: 1          space between columns: 0.5"      │
│            division break:(Page)Continuous Column Even Odd         █   │
│Select option                                                          │
│Pg15 Li20 Col      {Page·⊕...pany¶}  ?              Microsoft Word     │
└───────────────────────────────────────────────────────────────────────┘
```

Figure 13-16.   **The Format Division Layout command controls the position of footnotes.**

Moving Footnotes

To move a footnote:

1. Select the footnote reference mark.
2. Press the Del key.
3. Move the cursor to the new position.
4. Press the Ins key.

Deleting Footnotes

To delete a footnote:

1. Select the footnote reference mark.
2. Press the Del key. Word automatically deletes the footnote text and renumbers footnotes as appropriate.

PERFECTING YOUR PAGES

This Chapter Contains the Following:

When you've finished editing and formatting your document, you'll want to see the finished pages before you print. Word has two commands that help you to see just what your printed document will look like:

Command	Description
Options command, "show layout" and "show line breaks" options	The "show layout" option displays a full-size view of multiple columns, with text and graphics paragraphs correctly positioned, and allows you to edit your text. It doesn't show finished graphics, running heads, page numbers, footnote text, or annotation text. The "show line breaks" option puts line breaks exactly where they will be when printed. It's useful when you're using a proportional font that doesn't match the spacing of the screen font.
Print preView command	Displays a miniature version of your pages with all elements (including page numbers, footnotes, running heads, and graphics) in place, but doesn't allow you to edit your text.

This chapter shows you how to use Word's show layout and print preview features to check and change page layout. Normally you'll want to make a few changes to perfect your pages after you check them; changing page breaks, line breaks, positioning objects, and so forth. In this chapter, you'll also learn how to control page breaks and line breaks, how to position graphics and text objects exactly where you want them, and how to use hyphenation to make line breaks more even.

USING SHOW LAYOUT VIEW

Word's show layout view helps you work with text in multiple columns and with paragraphs you've positioned using the Format pOsition command (covered later in this chapter). Unless you have multiple columns or positioned paragraphs in your document, you won't notice any difference between document view and show layout view.

You can edit text in show layout view just as you would in document view. However, because Word redraws the screen when you make changes in show layout view, this feature may slow down operations considerably. For this reason, you'll probably want to make most of your changes in document view, then switch to show layout view to see the effect.

Switching to and from Show Layout View

To switch to and from show layout:

- Press Alt+F4.
  or
- Choose the Options command, choose Yes or No in the "show layout" field, then press Enter.

Figure 14-1 shows a document that contains two columns and a positioned paragraph displayed in show layout view.

If you display the ruler in show layout view, the ruler begins at zero (0) for each paragraph containing the cursor. This lets you measure indents and set tabs more easily.

Figure 14-1. Show layout view helps you work with multiple columns and precisely positioned paragraphs.

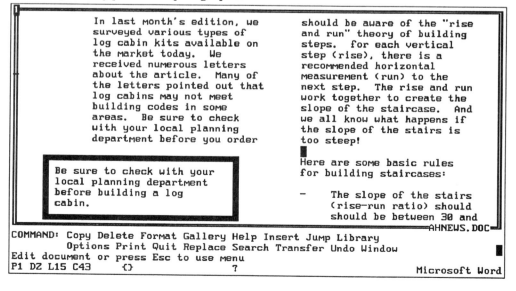

Moving the Cursor in Show Layout

You can use the normal commands to move the cursor around in show layout, and you can also use the following keys to jump from column to column:

To Jump to   **Press**
Next object or column   Ctrl+5 on numeric keypad+Right arrow key
Previous object or column   Ctrl+5 on numeric keypad+Left arrow key

USING PRINT PREVIEW

Most of the time you'll enter, edit, and format your text in document view—Word's default view, which you see when you first start Word. But you can't see some parts of a document in document view or in show layout view, like headers and footers, page numbers, footnotes, and graphics. To check all aspects of your document before you print, you can

Figure 14-2.   **Print preview shows entire pages.**

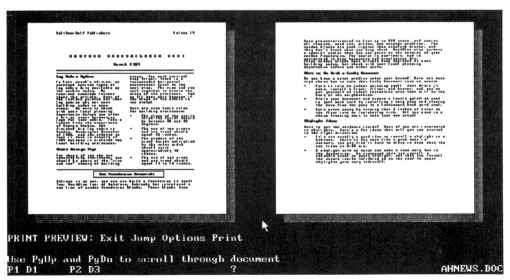

switch to print preview, the view that shows you a miniature version of your formatted pages, as in Figure 14–2.

In order to use print preview, you must have a video adapter with graphics capabilities installed in your computer. You can find a list of appropriate video adapters in the *Using Word* manual.

Print preview allows you to view your pages as they will be printed. You can see the placement and appearance of the following elements, as well as the normal character and paragraph formatting that see in document view:

- running heads and feet
- page numbers
- margins
- multiple columns
- footnotes
- line numbers
- side-by-side paragraphs
- graphics
- paragraphs positioned with the Format pOsition command
- proportionally spaced text

Options you choose with the Print Options command affect the display of pages in print preview. For example, if you've chosen Yes in the "draft" field of Print Options, Word displays only empty spaces at the positions of graphics. Otherwise, Word scales graphics to fit the size of their frames.

As the command's name implies, you use print preview to look at your documents before printing. You can't edit or format text in print preview. You've got to switch back to document view to make any changes to your document.

Switching to and from Print Preview

To switch to print preview from document view:

- Press Ctrl+F9.
  or
- Choose the Print preView command from the main menu (Esc, P, V).
  To switch back to document view from print preview:
- Press Ctrl+F9.
  or
- Choose the Exit command from the Print preView menu.

Viewing Pages in Print Preview

When you first switch to print preview, Word displays a two-page view (if you have at least two pages of text), starting with the page containing the cursor. The current page numbers are shown in the status line at the bottom of the screen. You can flip back and forth through all the pages in your document, and you can also jump to a specific place in your document.

Scrolling Through the Document

To display another page, you can use keys or use the mouse in the "invisible" scroll bar at the left side of the print preview window. You may see only a little dash—the elevator bar—in the scroll bar area of the window, but if you move your mouse pointer into the area, it will become a two-headed arrow. The position of the elevator bar lets you know the relative position of the displayed pages in the document. For example, if the elevator bar is in the middle of the scroll bar area, you're looking at pages in the middle of the document.

To Scroll	Do This
To the next page	Press PgDn or click the right mouse button on the scroll bar.
To the previous page	Press PgUp or click the left mouse button on the scroll bar.
To the end of the document	Press Ctrl+PgDn or drag the elevator bar to the bottom of the scroll bar.
To the beginning of the document	Press Ctrl+PgUp or drag the elevator bar to the top of the scroll bar.

Jumping to Specific Pages or Bookmarks

To display a particular page or jump to a bookmark:

1. Choose the Jump command from the Print preView menu.
2. In the "to" field, choose Page if you want to specify a page number, or choose bookmarK (press K) if you want to find the position of a bookmark you've entered.
3. Type the page number in the "number" field, or type the bookmark name in the "name" field. If you're typing page numbers and your document has multiple divisions, you need to type the division number after the page number. For example, you'd type *10D2* to see page 10 in the second division.

4. Press Enter or click the command name. Word displays the appropriate page. You can see the page number in the status line.

You can find out more about bookmarks in Chapter 17.

Displaying One or Two Pages in Print Preview

You can choose from three different displays in print preview:

Option	Displays
1-page	A single page, as in Figure 14–3.
2-page	Two pages.
Facing-pages	Two pages positioned as if in an open book, with the odd-numbered page on the right.

To switch displays:

1. Choose the Options command from the Print preView menu.
2. In the "display" field, choose a new option.
3. Press Enter or click the command name. Word redraws the screen.

Printing from Print Preview

Once you've made sure all your pages look OK, you're ready to print. You can use the Print command from print preview just like the Print command from Word's main menu.

To print from print preview:

1. Choose the Print command from the Print preView menu.
2. Choose subcommands and options as necessary, then press Enter or click the command name.

For more information about printing commands and options, see Chapter 15, "Printing."

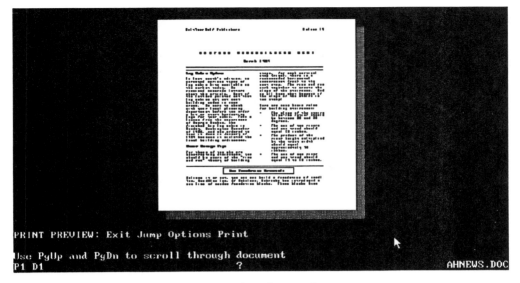

PRINT PREVIEW: Exit Jump Options Print

Use PgUp and PgDn to scroll through document
P1 D1   ?   AHNEWS.DOC

Figure 14-3.   **One-page display in print preview.**

POSITIONING OBJECTS ANYWHERE ON A PAGE

You can use the Format pOsition command to tell Word exactly where to position paragraphs on a page. As paragraphs can contain not only text, but graphics and tables, you can move almost anything anywhere on a page. Want that graphic placed 3 inches from the top of the page and 2 inches from the left margin? You can specify exactly those measurements. You provide both horizontal and vertical positions; tell Word to align paragraphs with columns, margins, or page edges; and specify paragraph widths. You can also move more than one paragraph as a unit. This feature allows you to extend paragraphs into margins, position paragraphs side-by-side, put a paragraph into the center of a page, and precisely control page layout. Figure 14-4 shows a page in print preview in which a graphic has been centered with the Format pOsition command.

When you use the Format pOsition command to position a paragraph, Word automatically adjusts any surrounding text to "flow" around the positioned paragraph.

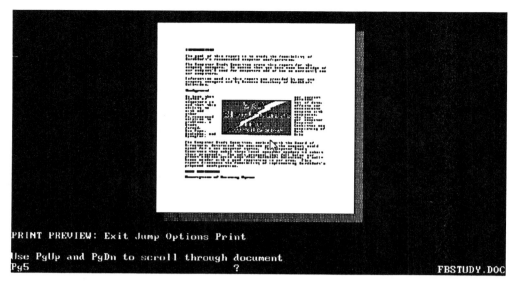

PRINT PREVIEW: Exit Jump Options Print

Use PgUp and PgDn to scroll through document
PgS   ?   FBSTUDY.DOC

Figure 14-4.   **The graphic on this page has been positioned with the Format p-Osition command.**

The Format pOsition command draws an invisible boundary or "frame" around a paragraph. Within this boundary, Word keeps any paragraph formats that affect the paragraph;ch consequently, a paragraph's line spacing, indents, and alignment move with the paragraph. Because these frames can make positioning paragraphs confusing, you may want to remove space-before and space-after formats, as well as indents, from paragraphs before positioning them with the Format pOsition command.

You can specify two types of position in the Format pOsition command fields.

• Specific position (exact measurements from the top and left margins or page edges).
• Relative position (left, right, center, inside, outside, top, and bottom positions, relative to margins or page edges).

You can also use a combination of the two. For example, you could specify a vertical position of 2 inches from the top margin and choose a centered horizontal position.

Typing Specific Measurements

When you want to be specific, you type measurements in the "horizontal frame position" and "vertical frame position" fields. You can specify inches, centimeters, points, or picas by using the abbreviations *in, cm, pt,* and *pi,* respectively. If you don't use one of these abbreviations, Word assumes the measurement is in inches, unless you've changed the default unit of measurement with the Options command. Type a measurement in the "horizontal frame position" field, then choose whether that measurement is relative to the left column margin (if you're working with multiple columns), the left document margin, or the left edge of the page. Next, type a measurement in the "vertical frame position" field, then choose whether that measurement is relative to the top margin or to the top edge of the page.

Choosing a Relative Position

When you want to choose a relative position, you'll do this:

1. In the "horizontal frame position" field, choose a left, right, or centered position. (If your document is formatted to have facing pages, you can also choose inside or outside positions.)
2. Choose whether the horizontal position is relative to the columns, the document margins, or the edges of the page.
3. In the "vertical frame position" field, choose a top, center, or bottom position.
4. Choose whether the vertical position is relative to the margins or page edges.

All measurements are between the relative page position and the closest edge of the paragraph boundary. For example, when you specify a position from the top of the page, you type a measurement that you want between the top of the page and the top edge of the paragraph boundary; when you specify a Bottom position relative to the Margin, that means you're asking Word to place the bottom edge of the paragraph even with the bottom margin of your document.

```
can now put a graphic or text paragraph anywhere you want on

a page.  With Word 5.0, you can now put a graphic or text

paragraph anywhere you want on a page.  With Word 5.0, you

can now put a graphic or text paragraph anywhere you want on

a page.  With Word 5.0, you can now put a graphic or text

paragraph anywhere you want on a page.

.G.C:\PBRUSH\ZAP.SCR;4";3.75";PCX
```

```
FORMAT POSITION
      horizontal frame position: Left        relative to: Column(Margins)Page
      vertical frame position: In line       relative to:(Margins)Page
      frame width: Single Column             distance from text: 0.167"
Enter measurement or press F1 to select from list
Pg1 Li27 Co1        {With·W...·page.} ?                      Microsoft Word
```

Figure 14-5. **The Format pOsition command fields.**

Basic Procedure

Because moving a paragraph with indents and spacing may be confusing, you might want to use the Format Paragraph command to remove any indents and spacing before or after a paragraph before using the Format pOsition command to position the paragraph.

To position a paragraph on a page:

1. Select the paragraph to position.
2. Choose the Format pOsition command from the main menu.
   Word displays the Format pOsition command fields as shown in Figure 14–5.
3. In the "horizontal frame position field" do one of the following:
   - If you want to use a specific position, type a measurement here. For example, if you want to position the left edge of the paragraph 1/2 inches from the left margin or the left edge of the page, type *.5 in.*
   - If you want to specify a relative position, press F1, then highlight an option in the list then press F1 to return to the command field. For example, if you want to align the right edge of the paragraph with the right margin or right edge of the page, choose Right.

- If you want to return the paragraph to its original horizontal position, press F1 and choose Left.

4. In the following "relative to" field, choose whether the horizontal position relates to the Column containing the paragraph, the Margins, or the Page edges. For example, to position a paragraph 1/2 inch from the left edge of the page, you'd type *.5 in* in the "horizontal frame position" field and choose Page here.

5. In the "vertical frame position field" do one of the following:
   - If you want to specify a vertical measurement from the top page edge or from the top margin, type a measurement here. For example, to position the top edge of the paragraph 2 inches down from the top margin or the top edge of the page, type *2 in* here.
   - If you want to specify a relative position, press F1, highlight a position option in the list then press F1 to return to the command field. For example, to align the bottom edge of the paragraph with the bottom margin or the bottom edge of the page, choose Bottom.
   - If you want to return the paragraph in its original vertical position, press F1 and choose In line.

6. In the following "relative to" field choose whether the vertical position relates to the Margins or the Page edges. For example, to position the top edge of the paragraph 2 inches from the top margin, type *2* in the "vertical frame position" field and choose Margins here.

7. If you want to change the width of a text paragraph, type a new measurement in the "frame width" field. This field has no effect on graphic paragraphs. For example, if you want to make a text paragraph 2 inches wide, type *2 in* here. If you want to return the paragraph to its original width, press F1 and choose Single Column from the list then press F1 to return to the command field.

8. In the "distance from text" field, type a measurement for the amount of white space you want between the paragraph's boundary and the surrounding text, or accept Word's default measurement of .167 inch.

9. Press Enter or click the command name.

In document view, you won't see the paragraph change position. You'll have to switch to show layout or to print preview to see the true position of the paragraph. No matter how the paragraph looks on the screen, it will print in the position you've assigned to it with the Format pOsition command.

Figures 14-6 and 14-7 show some examples of boxed paragraphs positioned with the Format pOsition command, along with the command field options that specified those positions.

If you don't want text to wrap around a "positioned" paragraph, press Enter before and after the paragraph to put blank paragraphs around it.

Returning a Paragraph to Its Original Position

To return a paragraph you've moved with the Format pOsition command to its original position, you can do one of the following procedures. This procedure changes only the position of the paragraph:

1. Select the paragraph.
2. Choose the Format pOsition command.
3. In the "horizontal frame position" field, press F1 highlight Left then press F1 again.
4. In the following "relative to" field, choose Margin.
5. In the "vertical frame position" field, choose In line.
6. Press Enter or click the command name.

The following procedure changes not only the position, but will also change other paragraph formats, such as indents and line spacing:

1. Select the paragraph.
2. Press Alt+P (or press Alt+XP if you have a style sheet attached to your document) to return all paragraph formats to the default style.

Using the Format pOsition Command to Simplify Page Layout

If you want to use the same position for paragraphs of text or graphics over and over again, you don't have to use the Format pOsition command to position each individual paragraph. If you want to save a position to use occasionally, you can save that position (and any other formats) as a style that you can apply to a selected paragraph with a few quick keystrokes. If you want to position the same object in the same place on every page of a division or of your entire document, you can make the positioned paragraph into a running head.

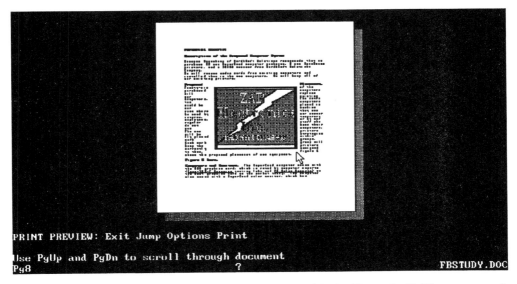

Figure 14-6.   **A boxed paragraph centered with the Format pOsition command.**

Figure 14-7.   **A sidebar paragraph positioned with the Format pOsition command.**

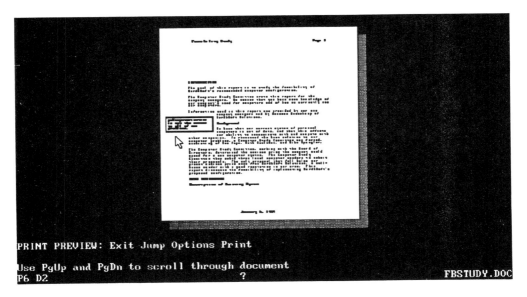

Saving a Paragraph Position as a Style

If you think you'll be a using specific position to format paragraphs over and over again, you can save time by using the Format pOsition command once, then saving that paragraph format as a style that you can apply to other paragraphs. You can also add any other sort of paragraph or character formatting you might want to save in the style.

Say, for example, that you want to create a style for an italic-text paragraph that's centered on the page, 3 inches wide, and surrounded with a double border. Just format a paragraph the way you want it using the Format Character, Format Paragraph, Format Border, and Format pOsition commands, then select the formatted paragraph and save it as a style with the Format Stylesheet Record command. You might name the style CP for "centered paragraph." Then you can easily apply the CP style to paragraphs in the future to make them look just the same. See Chapter 11 for more information about creating and applying styles.

Positioning a Paragraph in the Same Place Throughout Your Document

If you want to position the same paragraph in the same place throughout your document, you don't have to format every page separately. Just make the positioned paragraph a running head. Yes, that sounds strange, but you can can position a running head anywhere on a page, and you can specify whether running heads appear on every page of a division, every even page, or every odd page. Figure 14-8 shows how such a positioned paragraph might look on facing pages.

To position a paragraph in the same place throughout your document:

1. Move the paragraph to the beginning of the division (or the beginning of the document, if you don't have divisions). Running head paragraphs must be at the beginning of a division.
2. Select the paragraph.
3. Choose the Format Running-head command, choose the options you want, then press enter. It doesn't really matter if you choose the Top or Bottom position here, because you're going to use the Format pOsition command to set the position.
4. Use the Format pOsition command to set the position of the paragraph. If you want facing pages to "mirror" each other, as shown in the preceding figure, choose Inside or Outside in the "horizontal frame position" field.

You can have normal running heads and running feet as well as a paragraph positioned in this way. Just make sure to put the running head

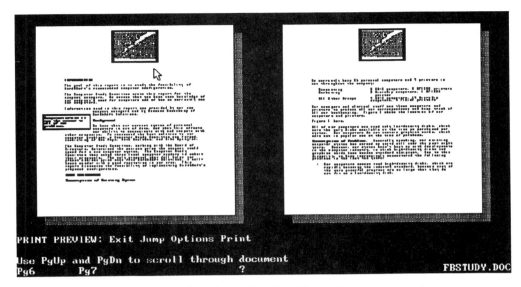

Figure 14-8.   A "positioned running-head" graphic appears on every page.

paragraphs one right after another at the beginning of a division or of a document. Take care that you don't specify positions that overlap. For more information about running heads and running feet, see "Adding Running Heads and Running Feet" in Chapter 13.

CONTROLLING WHEN WORD REPAGINATES

By default, Word calculates page breaks only when it needs to—when it needs to make a table of contents or an index, display pages in print preview, or print a document, for example. However, you can choose to repaginate whenever you want to see page breaks or count pages, and you can also choose to have Word repaginate automatically as you work.

Repaginating on Demand

To calculate pages on demand:

1.   Choose the Print Repaginate command.

Example: Positioning a Paragraph on Every Page

Say that you want a graphic to appear on each page, 2 inches down from the top page edge and 1 inch from the left page edge.

To position the graphic as described above:

1. Move the graphic paragraph to the beginning of the division (or the beginning of the document, if you don't have divisions). Running head paragraphs must be at the beginning of a division. Remember, you can't see a positioned paragraph in its true location in document view.
2. Select the paragraph.
3. Choose the Format Running-head command, choose the options you want, then press Enter. It doesn't really matter if you choose Top or Bottom position here, because you're going to use the Format pOsition command to set the position.
4. Choose the Format pOsition command and set the command fields as follows:

For the Command	Do This
"horizontal frame position"	Type *1*.
"relative to" field	Choose Page.
"vertical frame position"	Type *2*.
"relative to"	Choose Page.

5. Press Enter or click the command name.
6. If desired, press Ctrl+F9 or choose the Print preView command to see the page layout you've created. See "Using Print Preview" earlier in this chapter for instructions on using print preview.

---

2. In the "confirm page breaks" field, choose Yes if you want Word to pause and ask you if each page break is OK, or choose No if you want Word to break all pages automatically.
3. Press Enter or click the command name to start repagination.

Confirming Page Breaks

If you choose Yes in the "confirm page breaks" field of the Print Repaginate command, Word will pause each place a page break occurs and ask you to confirm the page break or to move it. If Word originally entered the page break, you'll see the message: *"Enter Y to confirm or use direction keys."*
To respond, do one of the following:

- To confirm the page break (represented by a dotted line), press Y.
- To move the page break up, press the Up arrow key until the cursor is in the line before which you want the page break to occur, then press Enter. (You can't move a page break down because Word can't make one page longer than the margin settings will allow.)

If you entered the page break by pressing Shift+Enter, you'll see the message: *"Enter Y to confirm or R to remove"*.
To respond, you'd do one of the following:

- To confirm the page break press Y.
- To remove the page break press R.
  Word will then calculate a new page break and ask you to confirm or move it.

Note: When you confirm page breaks, Word displays line breaks as they will be when printed, so don't be shocked if the screen suddenly looks a little different. If you've set the "show line breaks" field of the Options command to No, Word changes the display back to its previous state when you've finished repaginating.

Repaginating Automatically as You Work

You can choose to recalculate pages automatically as you work by specifying background repagination:

1. Choose the Options command.
2. In the "paginate" field, choose Auto.
3. Press Enter or click the command name.

Word adjusts page breaks whenever there's a pause between typing or choosing commands. This option can slow down Word somewhat, so if you find the program is too slow, choose the Options command again and choose Manual in the "paginate" field to turn off background repagination.

How Hidden Text Affects Pagination

If you are displaying text you've formatted as hidden at the time Word repaginates, Word counts the hidden text when calculating page length. If you don't plan to print hidden text, choose the Options command and choose No in the "show hidden text" field before choosing any command that causes Word to repaginate.

CONTROLLING PAGE BREAKS

You can control where Word inserts a page break by inserting your own page break, by choosing options that prevent page breaks within or between paragraphs, or by confirming each page break before it's entered.

Inserting a Page Break

To insert a page break:

1. Place the cursor where you want to insert a page break.
2. Press Ctrl+Shift+Enter.

Figure 14-9 shows how a page break you enter looks different from a page break entered by Word. The first dotted line, where the dots are widely spaced, is a page break calculated by Word. The second dotted line has been inserted with Ctrl + Shift + Enter.

Deleting a Page Break that You Inserted

You can't delete a page break calculated by Word, but you can delete one that you've inserted.
To delete a page break you inserted:

1. Select the page break marker.
2. Press the Del key.

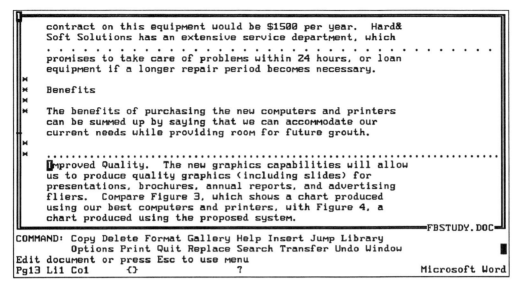

```
    contract on this equipment would be $1500 per year.  Hard&
    Soft Solutions has an extensive service department, which
    . . . . . . . . . . . . . . . . . . . . . . . . . . . . . . . . . .
    promises to take care of problems within 24 hours, or loan
    equipment if a longer repair period becomes necessary.
×
×   Benefits
×
×   The benefits of purchasing the new computers and printers
    can be summed up by saying that we can accommodate our
    current needs while providing room for future growth.
×
×   ..............................................................
    Improved Quality.  The new graphics capabilities will allow
    us to produce quality graphics (including slides) for
    presentations, brochures, annual reports, and advertising
    fliers.  Compare Figure 3, which shows a chart produced
    using our best computers and printers, with Figure 4, a
    chart produced using the proposed system.
                                                    ═FBSTUDY.DOC═
COMMAND: Copy Delete Format Gallery Help Insert Jump Library
         Options Print Quit Replace Search Transfer Undo Window     ■
Edit document or press Esc to use menu
Pg13 Li1 Col       {}              7                  Microsoft Word
```

Figure 14-9.   **Pressing Ctrl+Shift+Enter inserts a page break.**

Controlling Page Breaks Within and Between Paragraphs

Normally, you don't want Word to leave only one line of a paragraph on a page— the page will look odd. To prevent this, Word has in effect a "widow/orphan control" option ("widows" and "orphans" are typesetters' terms for lonely lines and words left by themselves on a page). However, there may be special occasions when you'll want to turn off this option to allow one line of a paragraph to print on a page.

Not only can you prevent Word from leaving one line of a paragraph on a page, you can also make sure that Word doesn't split a paragraph between pages at all, or that Word doesn't put page breaks between related paragraphs. You can also tell Word to put a page break before a specific paragraph to make sure it comes at the top of a page.

To control leaving one line of a paragraph on a page ("widows" or "orphans"):

1. Choose the Print Options command.
2. In the "widow/orphan control" field, choose No to allow one line of a paragraph to print on a page, or choose Yes (the default) to prevent leaving one line on a page.

To control page breaks anywhere within paragraphs or between related paragraphs:

1. Select the paragraphs in which you want to control page breaks.
2. Choose the Format Paragraph command.
3. Choose Yes in the appropriate command fields:

Command	Description
"page break before"	Puts a page break immediately before the paragraph.
"keep with next"	Prevents a page break between the paragraph and the following paragraph.
"keep together"	Keeps the entire paragraph together. If a page break would normally occur within the paragraph, Word puts the page break before theparagraph.

4. Press Enter or click the command name.

CONTROLLING LINE BREAKS BETWEEN WORDS

At times you may want to keep two or more words together on a line. You can always press Shift+Enter to insert a newline character to break a line, but if you later change margins or add or delete text, you may end up with a funny looking break. A better way to keep words together is to use a *nonbreaking space* to link the words.

To insert a nonbreaking space between words:

• Press Ctrl+spacebar.

You can control the display of space characters (and all other format characters) with the "show nonprinting symbols" field of the Options command. If this field is set to None or Partial, you'll see only blank spaces between words. If this field is set to All, you'll see a dot for regular spaces between words and a blank space for a nonbreaking space.

CHANGING MARGINS OR PAGE SIZE

Margins are the white space between your text and the edges of your page. By default, Word assumes you're using a 8-1/2 x 11 inch page and sets the following margins:

Top   1 inch
Bottom   1 inch
Right   1.25 inches
Left   1.25 inches
Gutter*   0 inch

    * A gutter margin is the space reserved for binding pages in a notebook or cover.

The amount of space available for text on a page is, of course, affected by the size of the page and the horizontal or vertical orientation of the paper. When you change margins, it affects every page in your document, even though you can only see one or two pages at a time. If you want only one page to have more white space around the text than other pages, you have to indent the paragraphs on that page (see "Indenting Paragraphs" in Chapter 8) or keep that page in a separate division (see Chapter 10 for more information about division formatting).

To change the margins or the page size in your document:

1. Choose the Format Division Margins command.
2. In the "top," "bottom," "right," and "left" fields, type new measurements. Word measures from the corresponding edge of the page, so if you type 2 in the "right" field, the right margin will be set 2 inches from the right edge of the page.
3. If you want to add a gutter margin, type a measurement in the "gutter" field.
4. If necessary, type new measurements in the "page length" and "width" fields.
5. If you'd like Word to use the margins and page size you just specified as the default layout for all documents, choose Yes in the "use as default" field.
6. Press Enter or click the command name.

The best way to see your margins is to switch to print preview (Ctrl+F9).

Creating Mirrored Margins on Facing Pages

If your right and left margins are different, or if you're using a gutter margin, and your document will be printed double-sided (on both the fronts and backs of pages), you'll want to format your pages so that the margins mirror each other. Formatting your pages as mirror images makes inside and outside margins mirror each other (especially important if you have a gutter margin).

Note that making margins mirror each other does not affect running heads. If you want running heads to mirror each other, you'll have to create separate running heads for odd and even pages. For more information, see Chapter 13. Look at Figures 14-10 and 14-11 to see the difference between regular pages and mirror-image pages.

To make margins mirror each other on facing pages:

1. Choose the Format Divisions Margins command.
2. In the "left" and "right" fields type the measurements for the margins on odd pages. The even pages will "mirror" these settings. For example, if you want the inside margins of facing pages to be 2 inches wide and the outside margins to be 1 inch, type *2* in the "left" field and type *1* in the "right" field.
3. If you want a gutter margin to reserve space for binding, type a measurement in the "gutter" field.
4. In the "mirror margins" fields choose Yes.
5. Press Enter or click the command name.

Note: Word always makes even-numbered pages left-hand pages, and odd-numbered right-hand pages, so page 1 of your document will have no facing page.

USING HYPHENATION TO IMPROVE THE APPEARANCE OF PAGES

If your paragraphs are left-aligned or right-aligned and you think one margin looks too "ragged," you can:

• justify all the paragraphs
• hyphenate words to help fill the lines

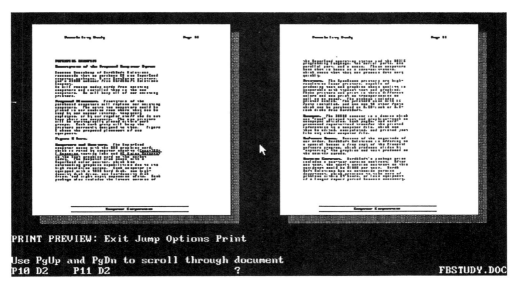

Figure 14-10.   **Regular pages with a gutter margin.**

Figure 14-11.   **Facing pages with a gutter margin.**

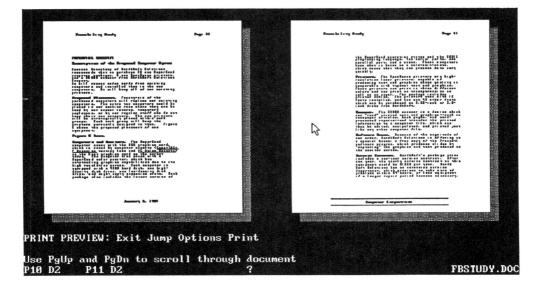

To justify paragraphs (make the left and right sides even), Word adds enough spaces between words to fill up the lines. This feature can put big gaps in your text and make your pages look as though they're filled with "holes." You can fill these "holes" by using a combination of justified paragraphs and hyphenated words.

You may also choose to keep left or right alignment, but use hyphenation to make the other margin less ragged. See how adding a couple of hyphens makes the right side of a paragraph more even in the example below:

It was a scorching, dismal, and stormy day, black as midnight even though it was only noon. Lightning crackled somewhere in the hazy distance, and the dusty, violently churning clouds on the horizon rose to unbelievable billowing heights.

It was a scorching, dismal, and stormy day, black as midnight even though it was only noon. Lightning crackled somewhere in the hazy distance, and the dusty, violently churning clouds on the horizon rose to unbelievable billowing heights.

For more information on aligning paragraphs, see "Aligning Paragraphs" in Chapter 8.

Using the Library Hyphenate Command

You can always press the hyphen key to add a hyphen to a word, but if you later add text or change margins or indents, the hyphen remains in the word even though the word may no longer be at the end of a line. A safer way to hyphenate is to let Word suggest where to put hyphens throughout your document, or just in selected text. Word inserts "optional hyphens" that are removed if the word is later relocated. This method also saves you the trouble of using a dictionary to determine where to break a word.

Word begins hyphenating at the cursor, so you may want to move the cursor to the beginning of your document before you choose the Library Hyphenate command. You can have Word hyphenate all the appropriate words in your document or selection automatically, or you can approve or reject each hyphenation Word proposes.

To have Word hyphenate all appropriate words:

1. To hyphenate only part of your document, select the text you want to hyphenate. If you don't select anything, Word hyphenates the entire document.
2. Choose the Library Hyphenate command.
   Word displays the command fields shown in Figure 14-12.
3. In the "confirm" field, choose Yes if you want to confirm each hyphenation Word suggests. Leave the field set to No if you want Word to automatically insert hyphens wherever it can.
4. Press Enter or click the command name to begin hyphenation.

Confirming Hyphenation

If you chose Yes in the "confirm" field of the Library Hyphenate command, Word will display each word for your approval before inserting a hyphen, as shown in Figure 14-13. You'll see this message in the com-

Figure 14-12.   **The Library Hyphenate command fields.**

```
      current needs while providing room for future growth.
 ×
 ×    Improved Quality.  The new graphics capabilities will allow
      us to produce quality graphics (including slides) for
      presentations, brochures, annual reports, and advertising
      fliers.  Compare Figure 3, which shows a chart produced
      using our best computers and printers, with Figure 4, a
      chart produced using the proposed system.
 ×
 ×    Figure 3 here.
 ×
 ×    Figure 4 here.
 ×
 ×    Increased Productivity.  The new computers are equipped with
      both high-density and low-density drives.  This will allow
      us to upgrade to new versions of our current software, which
      use the high-density drives, while maintaining the ability
      to use existing information stored on the low-density disks
      we use now.  The new high-density drives will also allow us
                                                    FBSTUDY.DOC
LIBRARY HYPHENATE confirm: Yes No          hyphenate caps: Yes(No)

Select option
Pg12 L110 Col      {}              ?              Microsoft Word
```

```
┌─────────────────────────────────────────────────────────────────────┐
│█══════════════════════════════════════════════════════════════════════
│    current needs while providing room for future growth.
│×
│×   Improved Quality.  The new graphics capabilities will allow
│    us to produce quality graphics (including slides) for
│    presentations, brochures, annual reports, and advertising
│    fliers.  Compare Figure 3, which shows a chart produced
│    using our best computers and printers, with Figure 4, a
│    chart produced using the proposed system.
│×
│×   Figure 3 here.
│×
│×   Figure 4 here.
│×
│×   Increased Productivity.  The new computers are equipped with
│    both high-density and low-density drives.  This will allow
│    us to upgrade to new versions of our current software, which
│    use the high-density drives, while maintaining the ability
│    to use existing information stored on the low-density disks
│    we use now.  The new high-density drives will also allow us
│                                                        ══FBSTUDY.DOC══
│LIBRARY HYPHENATE confirm:(Yes)No              hyphenate caps: Yes(No)
│
│Enter Y to insert hyphen, N to skip word, or use direction keys to reposition ▐
│Pg1Z Li1Z Co4      {}              ?                      Microsoft Word
└─────────────────────────────────────────────────────────────────────┘
```

Figure 14-13. **Confirming hyphenations before they're made.**

mand line: *"Enter Y to insert hyphen, N to skip, or use direction keys to reposition."*

Do one of the following:

- If you want to accept Word's placement of the hyphen, press Y.
- If you don't want to hyphenate the word, press N.
- If you want to hyphenate the word in a different place, press the Left arrow key to move the cursor to where you want the hyphen, then press Y. If you try to insert a hyphen that would extend a word beyond the margin.

Word won't insert a hyphen at all, but will just move the word down to the next line.

Stopping Automatic Hyphenation

If you've chosen the Library Hyphenate command but you want to stop the hyphenation process, you can do this:

1. Press Esc to stop hyphenation. Word displays a message asking you if you want to resume hyphenation.

2. Press Esc again to stop hyphenation without losing the hyphens already inserted.

Typing Optional Hyphens

If you don't want to use the Library Hyphenate command but you want to insert hyphens that will be removed if the word is not at the end of a line, you can insert optional hyphens to divide words at the ends of lines:
To insert an optional hyphen:

- Press Ctrl+ - (hyphen).

Using Nonbreaking Hyphens to Keep Words Together

If you don't care whether or not Word breaks up strings of words connected with hyphens, you can just insert normal hyphens wherever you want. If you have a string of words connected by hyphens that you don't want Word to break up—such as seventy-five, Stratford-upon-Avon, ill-fated—you can use a nonbreaking hyphen to keep the words together on a line.
To insert a nonbreaking hyphen:

- Press Ctrl+Shift+ - (hyphen).

Searching for Hyphens

If you've added hyphens and then you change the margins or delete or add text, you may need to go back and delete hyphens. You can search for all types of hyphens in Word. You may need to display all types of hyphens by first choosing the Options command and choosing Yes in the "show nonprinting symbols" field. Then choose the Search command (or the Replace command), and type the character you want to find in "for" field:

To Find	Type
Regular hyphen or nonbreaking hyphen	-
Optional hyphen	^-

CHAPTER

15

PRINTING

This Chapter Contains the Following:

.

When you're finished editing and formatting, you'll want to print your document. The instructions in this chapter show you how to use your printer effectively with Word, and how to check for problems when something goes wrong.

ABOUT .PRD FILES

What's a .PRD file? PRD is the extension Word uses for *printer driver files*. You must have the appropriate printer driver file installed for your computer before you can print from Word. You can use the Word SETUP program or the DOS COPY command to copy the .PRD file for your printer to your Word disk. If you're uncertain about which .PRD file is appropriate for your printer, or about the capabilities of your printer, see the *Printer Information for Microsoft Word* manual.

If you've used previous versions of Word, don't assume you can use your previous .PRD file with this new version of Word. This Word package contains the updated .PRD file you'll need to use new Word features such as print preview and importing graphics, so be sure to replace any old .PRD files with the most current ones.

CHECKING THE CAPABILITIES OF YOUR PRINTER

If you're not sure which characters your printer can produce, you can run Word's *character_test.mac* macro, which prints out all the characters your printer is capable of in a font you choose. The macro is stored in the MACRO.GLY file, which was shipped on the Utilities Disk 2.

To run the *character_test.mac* macro:

1. Choose the Transfer Glossary Load command.
2. In the "filename" field, type *macro* or press F1 to display the list of glossary files, then select the MACRO.GLY file.
3. Press Enter or click the command name to load the glossary file.
4. Choose the Insert command, then press F1 to see a list of glossary entries.
5. Highlight character_test.mac in the list.
6. Press Enter to start the macro. Follow the instructions that appear in the message line. The macro takes you to Print Options to check your

settings, then asks you to select one or more fonts. It will print its character set for each font.

PREPARING TO PRINT

Before you print, you may want to do the following:

- Use the Print Repaginate command to repaginate your document. Choose Yes in the "confirm page breaks" field if you want Word to pause and give you a chance to change the page breaks before they're entered.
- Choose the Options command and choose Yes in the "show line breaks" field so Word will break the lines in the document window just as they will be broken when printed.
- Check pages using print preview and (if appropriate) show layout view.
- Choose the Print Options command and check the options in the command fields to make sure they are what you want.

BASIC PRINTING

To print the active document:

- Choose the Print Printer command, or press Ctrl+F8.

Word displays a message telling you it's printing your document. Don't be alarmed if printing doesn't begin instantly. Word takes a few seconds to format pages and communicate with the printer, then your document should start to print. If it doesn't, read "What If It Doesn't Print?" later in this chapter for suggestions about how to find the problem.

After Word finishes printing, it displays a message telling you how many lines and words were printed.

PRINTING MORE THAN ONE COPY

To print more than one copy of your document:

1. Choose the Print Options command.
   Word displays the command fields shown in Figure 15-1.

2. Type the number of copies you want in the "copies" field.
3. Press Enter or click the command name.
4. Choose the Printer command to begin printing.

PRINTING TO A FILE

If you want to transfer a printed version of your document to another program or save a printed version on disk to take it somewhere to print on another printer, you can use the Print File command. If you want to create an ASCII version of a document, use the Transfer Save command as described in "Saving a Document in a Different File" in Chapter 3.

To print to a file:

1. Choose the Print File command.
2. In the "name" field, type a name for the file that will contain the printed version.
3. Press Enter or click the command name to print.

Figure 15-1. **Choosing print options.**

```
┌─┬────────────────────────────────────────────────────────────────────┐
│ │   of date, and that this affects our ability to communicate         │
│ │   with and compete with other companies.  To recommend the          │
│ │   best solution to our computer problems, a Computer Study           │
│ │   Committee was formed, consisting of Ren Pope, Ruth Hoolahan,       │
│ │   and Mike Spangler.                                                 │
│×│                                                                      │
│×│   The Computer Study Committee, working with the Board of            │
│ │   Directors, determined the maximum price the company could          │
│ │   spend for a new computer system.  The Computer Study               │
│ │   Committee then asked three local computer vendors to submit        │
│ │   their proposals.  The only proposal that fell below our            │
│ │   preset maximum price came from Hard&Soft Solutions, a well-        │
│ │   known vendor with a good reputation in our area.  This             │
│ │   report discusses the feasibility of implementing Hard&Soft's       │
└─┴────────────────────────────────────────────────────────────────────┘
PRINT OPTIONS printer: IBMGRAPH            setup: LPT1:
        model: IBM Graphics Printer        graphics resolution: 240 dpi
        copies: 1                          draft: Yes(No)
        hidden text: Yes(No)               summary sheet: Yes(No)
        range:(All)Selection Pages         page numbers:
        widow/orphan control:(Yes)No       queued: Yes(No)
        paper feed: Continuous             duplex: Yes(No)
Enter printer name or press F1 to select from list
Pg5 Li26 Col      {Comput...ems.¶}   ?                       Microsoft Word
```

CANCELING PRINTING

If you need to cancel printing at any time:

• Press Esc.

The printer may not stop immediately, because it continues to print whatever's in its memory until it receives the "Stop!" message from Word. If the paper is becoming jammed or another emergency situation has developed, turn off the printer.

CONTROLLING THE PAPER FEED TO THE PRINTER

You can use the Print Options command to tell the printer where to get paper, and whether or not to pause after every page.

1. Choose the Print Options command.
2. In the "paper feed" field type the option you want, or press F1 to display the list of options for your printer, then use the arrow keys to highlight the option you want. The list will include some of these options:

Option	Description
Manual	Printing stops at the end of every page, and Word displays a message asking you to press Y when you've inserted another piece of paper.
Continuous	Printing continues until the end of the document is reached.
Bin 1	The printer gets paper from bin 1.
Bin 2	The printer gets paper from bin 2.
Bin 3	The printer gets paper from bin 3.
Mixed	The printer gets paper from bin 1 for the first page, and gets paper from bin 2 for all following pages.
Envelope	The printer prints envelopes if it supports an envelope feeder.

3. Press Enter or click the command name.

CHANGING PRINTERS

The Word package comes with a great variety of printer driver (.PRD) files that you can use when you use different printers. Just copy the .PRD files you need to your Word directory. If you're unsure about which .PRD file a printer needs, check the *Printer Information for Microsoft Word* manual.

When you used Word's setup program, you told Word what kind of printer you're using. Word displays the command fields appropriate for that printer. If you have copied several .PRD files to your Word disk, you can use the Print Options command to switch to a different printer.

To switch to a different printer:

1. Choose the Print Options command. Word displays the command fields shown in Figure 15-1.
2. In the "printer" field, type a printer driver filename, or press F1 to display a list of the printer driver files installed on the disk, highlight the driver file you want to use, then press F1 again.
3. In the "model" field, type the model name of the printer, or press F1 to display a list of printer models, then use the arrow keys to highlight the appropriate model name, then press F1 again . (A .PRD file can support a variety of printer models.)
4. In the "setup" field, check the port setting to be sure that the printer you're choosing is connected to the port listed there. If necessary, press F1 and select a new port.
5. Press Enter or click the command name.

PRINTING PART OF YOUR DOCUMENT

You can use the Print Options command to tell Word to print a range of pages, or to print only the text you have selected at the time.

To print only part of your document:

1. If you want to print selected text only, select the part of your document you want to print.
2. Choose the Print Options command.
3. Choose options to tell Word what you want to print:

To Print	Do This
Selected text only	Choose Selection in the "range" field.
Certain pages	Choose Pages in the "range" field, then type the page numbers in the "page numbers" field. If you want to print a range of pages, type a hyphen between the page numbers, e.g., *5-9*. If you want to print nonsequential pages, put a comma between the page numbers, e.g., *3,7,10*. You can also combine nonsequential pages and ranges, e.g., *3,7,10-25*, and specify pages in divisions, e.g., *3-6D1, 15D2* (pages 3 through 6 in division 1, page 15 in division 2, respectively).

4. Press Enter or click the command name.
5. Choose the Printer command to print.

PRINTING ENVELOPES

If your printer is wide enough and if it supports a manual or envelope-feed mode, you can print on envelopes with Word. The method you use to print on envelopes depends on the type of printer you have. For some printers, you need to use a special landscape mode. Check the listing for your printer in the *Printer Information for Microsoft Word* manual to see what your printer supports.

To print on envelopes with a nonlaser printer:

1. Choose the Print Options command.
2. In the "paper feed" field select Manual if your printer doesn't have an evelope feeder, or select Envelope if your printer has an envelope feeder.
3. Press Enter or click the command name.
4. Use the Printer command from the Print menu to print on the envelope. Word also has a macro you can use to print on envelopes, *envelope.mac*. See Chapter 22 for more information about using Word's supplied macros.

To print on envelopes with a laser printer using a landscape PRD file:

1. Check Chapter 2 of *Printer Information for Microsoft Word* to find out the name of the landscape PRD file you need for your printer.

2. Use the COPY command to copy the PRD file to your Word disk.
3. Choose the Print Options command.
4. In the "printer" field, press F1 to see a list of PRD files. Use the arrow keys to highlight the landscape PRD file you need, then press F1 again.
5. In the "paper feed" field, select Manual if your printer doesn't have an evelope feeder, or select Envelope if your printer has an envelope feeder.
6. Press Enter or click the command name.
7. Use the Printer command from the Print menu to print on the envelope.

PRINTING GLOSSARIES, STYLE SHEETS, AND DOCUMENT SUMMARY SHEETS

You can use the Print command to print glossaries and style sheets attached to your document, and to print document summary sheets containing information about the file.

To print a glossary:

1. If necessary, use the Transfer Glossary Load command to load the glossary you want to print.
2. Choose the Print Glossary command.

See Chapter 4 for more information about working with glossaries.

To print a style sheet:

1. Choose the Gallery command. Word displays the style sheet attached to your document.
2. If necessary, use the Transfer Load command from the Gallery menu to load the style sheet you want to print.
3. Choose the Print command from the Gallery menu.

See Chapter 21 for more information about working with summary sheets.

To print a document summary sheet:

1. Choose the Print Options command.
2. In the "summary sheet" field, choose Yes.
3. Press Enter or click the command name.

4.   Choose the Printer command to begin printing.

See Chapter 11 for more information about working with style sheets.

SENDING KEYSTROKES DIRECTLY TO THE PRINTER

There may be times when you want to type something on the screen and have it go directly to the printer without any formatting.
To send keystrokes directly to the printer:

1.   Choose the Print Direct command.
2.   Type the text.
3.   Press Enter.
4.   When you're finished typing, press Esc.

Note: If you're sending keystrokes directly to a laser printer, use the form feed button to eject the page.

SPECIFYING RESOLUTION WHEN PRINTING GRAPHICS

If you're printing a document that includes graphics, you can set the graphics resolution, before printing, to specify how many dots per inch to use when printing graphics. The higher the resolution (dots per inch), the clearer the graphic. However, you must also keep in mind that higher resolutions require more memory in your printer.
To specify graphics resolution:

1.   Choose the Print Options command.
2.   In the "graphics resolution" field, type a number to specify the resolution, or press F1 to display the list of choices for your printer, then use the arrow keys to highlight the resolution you want then press F1 again.
3.   Press Enter or click the command name.
4.   Choose the Printer command to begin printing.

PRINTING ON BOTH SIDES OF PAGES

If your printer can print on both sides of a page, you can tell Word to print a double-sided version of your document.

To print on both sides of pages:

1. Choose the Print Options command.
2. In the "duplex" field, choose Yes.
3. Press Enter or click the command name.
4. Choose the Printer command to begin printing.

PRINTING WHILE YOU WORK

If you want to continue to work with Word while your document prints, you can use Word's queued printing feature. Queued printing does require a fair amount of disk space; because Word creates a temporary print file on your document disk, it may make Word run slower.

Note: If you're connected to a network, you're already using a different type of print queue. Don't use the following procedure.

To use queued printing:

1. Choose the Print Options command.
2. In the "queued" field, choose Yes.
3. Press Enter or click the command name. If there's not enough room on the document disk to create a temporary print file, Word displays a message saying the document disk is full. In that case, you'll have to use a different document disk, create some space, or not use queued printing.
4. Choose the Printer command to begin printing.

After you've chosen queued printing, you can use the Print Queue commands to control the printing:

Choose	To
Print Queue Pause	Stop printing temporarily (to add paper, or something like that).
Print Queue Continue	Continue printing after you've chosen Print Queue Pause.
Print Queue Restart	Start printing the current document in the queue at the beginning of the document (you might want to use this command if you've had a paper jam or other problem that has messed up some pages).
Print Queue Stop	Cancel printing.

PRINTING HIDDEN TEXT

If you have text that's formatted as hidden text in your document, you can tell Word to print that hidden text, whether or not it's visible on the screen.
    To print hidden text:

1.   Choose the Print Options command.
2.   In the "hidden text" field, choose Yes.
3.   Press Enter or click the command name.
4.   Choose the Printer command to begin printing.

PRINTING A DRAFT COPY

When you don't care about anything but for the words, you can print a draft copy of your document. Printing a draft copy is fast, because Word doesn't print graphics or do microspace justification and other time-consuming printing tasks. Word leaves an empty space where a graphic belongs.
    To print a draft copy:

1.   Choose the Print Options command.
2.   In the "draft" field, choose Yes.
3.   Press Enter or click the command name.
4.   Choose the Printer command to begin printing.

PRINTING SEVERAL FILES AT ONCE

You can use several techniques to print several files, one right after another. Here are the techniques from which you can choose and where to find more information about how to use them:

Technique	For More Information, See
Use the INCLUDE instruction to include one file in another	"Inserting Another Document" "Creating Form Letters and Address Labels: Print Merge" (You can use this technique even if you're not creating form letters.)

Use the *chainprint.mac* macro to print a list of files and number the pages sequentially	Chapter 22, "Using Macros."
Print all marked files from the document retrieval window	Chapter 21, "Using the Document Retrieval System."

WHAT IF IT DOESN'T PRINT?

If Word displays a message saying that your document is printing, but the printer is just sitting there silently, don't start cursing right away. It takes Word a few seconds to format pages and communicate with the printer—the length of time required depends on the length of your document and the speed of your computer. However, if you've waited a moment or two and it still isn't printing or Word has displayed an error message, go through the steps in the checklist below. This book can't foresee all the problems that could go wrong, but if you complete all the steps in the checklist in order, the odds are good that you'll find and fix your problem along the way.

1. Make sure the printer is plugged in and turned on.
2. Make sure the printer cable is securely plugged into the correct printer and computer ports.
3. Make sure the printer buttons are "on" if they should be.
4. Make sure there's paper positioned properly in the printer.
5. Make sure all pieces of the printer (covers, ribbon or cartridge, paper trays, etc.) are in place.
6. Choose the Print Options command and check the settings to make sure they're right.
7. Turn the printer off, wait a few seconds, then turn it back on and try again.
8. If you're using PostScript codes in your document, create another copy of the document, remove the PostScript codes, and try printing with the copy. An error in PostScript code can cause a document not to print.

   If you've gone through every step in this list and your document still doesn't print, call your printer manufacturer or call the customer support number at Microsoft.

PART V

Working With Complex Documents

Word has all the features you need to create books, long reports, and other complex documents. You can include calculations in your document and sort lists of information. You can use Word's outlining feature to set up the structure of your document, to view your document at different levels, and to easily rearrange or just to travel through your document. You can number paragraphs and lines for easy reference, and you can use bookmarks to name specific areas of text for later cross-referencing. You can link files or parts of files together to make printing and other tasks easier.

Word can also create indexes and tables of contents, collecting the page numbers along with the text you specify. And if you have a need to create form letters, Word allows you to do that easily as well.

Word's document retrieval system can help you manage your files. You can use it to search for files, to view information quickly about files, and to print a list of files. This part of the book shows you everything you need to know to handle complex documents.

CALCULATING AND SORTING

This Chapter Contains the Following:

When you want to do a calculation or sort a list, you don't need to switch to another program. Word can sum columns or rows, and perform simple addition, subtraction, multiplication, and division. Word can also sort an alphabetic or numeric list in ascending or descending order. This chapter shows you how to use these Word features.

PERFORMING CALCULATIONS

Although Word is not a spreadsheet program, you can use it to perform simple calculations. You can use this feature to check your arithmetic quickly, or to include calculations in your documents. For example, Word can solve mathematical expressions like these:

267+433+188.3	10555 - 290 * 3 / 15	99.45
		16.22
		(19.13)
		27.47

$19,300.55	13300021	$237.96+18%
*75%	-899	
	-206	

Order of Calculation

To add numbers, you don't have to type a plus sign (+) in front of the numbers: Word assumes you want to add the numbers unless you include another operator in front of a number or surround a number with parentheses to indicate subtraction (typing *(100)* is the same as typing *-100*). You can also use parentheses to change the order of calculations in a line, like this:

    3*2+5+4*3=45
    3*(2+5)+4*3=75

Word calculates numbers in order from right to left and from top to bottom, using floating-point arithmetic. If all the numbers to be calculated are whole numbers, Word displays the result with a maximum of two decimal places. If any of the numbers to be calculated contain decimal points, Word displays the result with the maximum number of decimal places used in the calculation, like this:

6/3.000=2.000
6/3.0=2.0

Word ignores most characters associated with numbers, such as $ and #. If you include a comma in a number in your calculation, Word includes a comma in the result.

Basic Procedure

When Word calculates an expression, it displays the result in the status area at the bottom of the screen. You can then paste this result into your document. However, if you include the result in your document, keep in mind that. Word cannot automatically update results; if you change a number in your expression, you'll have to recalculate, then paste in a new result.

Note: Word cannot perform calculations for which the result is greater than 14 digits. If you try to perform a calculation Word can't hold in memory, Word displays a message telling you that there is a "math overflow."

To perform a calculation:

1. Type the numbers you want to calculate. Use the following symbols to indicate the operation to perform:

Operation	Key
Addition	+ or no operator
Subtraction	- or parentheses around number
Multiplication	*
Division	/
Percentage	%

2. Select all the numbers to calculate.
3. Press F2. Word performs the calculation and places the result in the scrap. You can see the result in the scrap area at the bottom of the screen, as shown in Figure 16-1.
4. If you want to paste the result into your document, position the cursor, then press the Ins key to insert the result from the scrap.

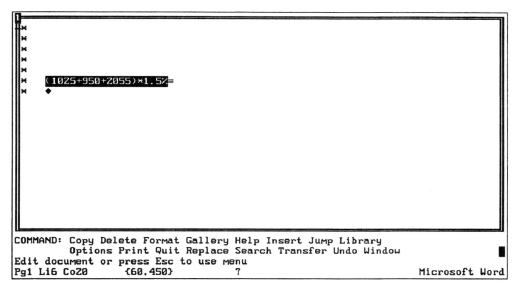

```
 (1025+950+2055)*1.5%=
 ◆
```

```
COMMAND: Copy Delete Format Gallery Help Insert Jump Library
         Options Print Quit Replace Search Transfer Undo Window  ■
Edit document or press Esc to use menu
Pg1 Li6 Co20      {60.450}           ?              Microsoft Word
```

Figure 16-1.   **Word performs calculations and stores the result in the scrap.**

SORTING IN ALPHABETIC OR NUMERIC ORDER

When you have a list of names or numbers, you don't have to arrange them yourself—use Word to sort the list. The only catch is that Word sorts only information arranged in a vertical pattern, such as a column of text or numbers. Word can't sort a horizontal row of information.

Sorting in Tables

In tables, you can choose to use any column as a sorting key and have Word rearrange all rows in the table based on the sorting-key column. For example, in the following table, you might choose to do an alphabetic sort based on the first column of names, or you might choose to do a numeric sort based on the second column of figures.

Garcia	$37, 300
Chung	$35, 500
MacAlester	$36, 125
Benson	$32, 900
Foster	$41, 200

Example: Perform a Quick In-line Calculation and Show Only the Results

---

Before calculation:
On orders of more than $1000.00, you'll receive a 5% discount (for example, if your order totals $3200.00, we'll subtract $<u>3200 * 5%</u>!).

After calculation:
On orders of more than $1000.00, you'll receive a 5% discount (for example, if your order totals $3200.00, we'll subtract $<u>160.00</u>!).

To calculate an in-line expression like the one underlined above:

1. Type the expression.
2. Select the numbers to calculate. In the example above, you'd select "3200*5%."
3. Press F2. Word displays the result in the scrap area at the bottom of the screen.
4. To replace the expression (which is still selected) with the result, press Shift+Ins.

If the columns in a table are not related to each other, you can also choose to have Word sort only the information in one column and not rearrange the information in other columns.

Note: If a column of numbers has an alphabetic column heading, such as "Sales Figures," "Part Numbers," "First Quarter '88," select only the numbers in the column (not the column heading), then do a numeric sort.

To sort in a table:

1. Press Ctrl+F6 to turn on column select mode, then use the arrow keys or the mouse to select the column you want to use as a sorting key.
2. Choose the Library Autosort command.
3. In the "by" field, choose Alphanumeric if you want to sort letters or combinations of letters and numbers (Word will put the letters first, then any numbers), or choose Numeric if you want to sort only numbers.

Example: Setting Up a Simple Spreadsheet

Stores	Quarter 1	Quarter 2
Dallas	122,513.50	135,223.15
Tulsa	144,599.22	140,288.33
Kansas City	98,930.93	98,500.62
	(result)	(result)

To set up a spreadsheet like this and have Word calculate the results:

1. Type the data, pressing the Tab key between columns, then set tabs to line up the columns. Be sure to leave space to paste in the results. See Chapter 9 for information about tabs and tables. To make sure decimal points line up when putting numbers of different lengths in columns, use decimal tabs.
2. Select the first column of numbers to calculate. If your data is in paragraphs with tabs, see "Selecting Text: Telling Word Where to Make Changes" in Chapter 4, for information about selecting rectangular portions of text.
3. Press F2. Word displays the result in the scrap area at the bottom of the screen.
4. To paste in the result, position the cursor then press the Ins key.
5. Repeat steps 2 through 4 to calculate and paste in the results of the next column.

Word can also calculate numbers in a row.

---

4. In the "case" field, choose Yes if you want to arrange uppercase letters in front of lowercase letters, or choose No if you want Word to treat uppercase and lowercase letters the same.
5. In the "sequence" field, choose Ascending if you want the results in order from A to Z or from 0 to 9, or choose Descending if you want the results to descend in order from Z to A or from 9 to 0.
6. In the "column only" field, choose Yes if you want to rearrange only the items in the selected column, leaving other columns in the table

alone, or choose No if you want the rest of the rows to move along with the items in the selected column.

7. Press Enter or click the command name.

Sorting Outside of Tables

Word can also sort paragraphs that are not in a table. For example, you might want to sort a long list of names with each name in a separate paragraph. When sorting ordinary paragraphs, Word sorts based on the first letter or number in each paragraph.

To sort paragraphs outside of a table:

1. Select the paragraphs to sort. If you don't select paragraphs, Word sorts the entire document.
2. Choose the Library Autosort command.
3. In the "by" field, choose Alphanumeric if you want to sort letters or combinations of letters and numbers (Word will put the letters first, then any numbers), or choose Numeric if you want to sort only numbers.
4. In the "case" field, choose Yes if you want to arrange capital letters in front of lowercase letters, or choose No if you want Word to treat capital and lowercase letters the same.
5. In the "sequence" field, choose Ascending if you want the results in order from A to Z or from 0 to 9, or choose Descending if you want the results to descend in order from Z to A or from 9 to 0.
6. Press Enter or click the command name.

Helpful Hint

To sort an alphabetic list in which there are articles (a, an, the) or titles (Dr., Mr., Ms., Mrs.) you don't want included in the alphabetized list, put the list in a table, and put the articles or titles in a separate column, as shown in Figure 16-2. Then you can select any column to sort, and the articles or titles won't mess up the alphabetic order.

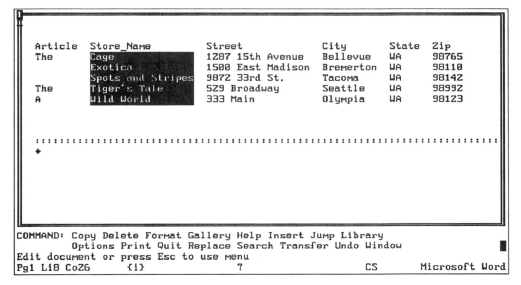

Figure 16-2.   **Putting articles and titles in a separate column in a table allows you to sort alphabetic items more easily.**

Reversing a Sort

If you accidentally select the wrong text when sorting, Word can really scramble your document. Don't tear your hair out if this happens to you. If you change your mind *immediately* after you sort (before doing anything else), you can reverse the action by choosing the Undo command. If you're working with a document that you've saved at least once and you've moved the cursor or made other changes after sorting, then discover that you don't like the result of the sort, you might consider quitting Word without saving the document—you'll lose all your changes since the last time you saved and be able to start over again with the previous version of the document.

For information about sorting records in a data document (used when creating form letters), see Chapter 20, "Creating Form Letters and Address Labels: Print Merge."

WORKING WITH LONG DOCUMENTS

This Chapter Contains the Following:

Using Outlines In Word
   Switching to and from Outline View
   Using the Two Outline Modes
   Creating an Outline
   Changing Heading Levels
     Demoting Headings
     Promoting Headings
   Entering Body Text
   Viewing Different Levels of Your Outline
     Displaying Only Specific Levels of Headings
     Collapsing All Subheadings and Body Text Beneath a Heading
     Expanding Subheadings and Body Text Below a Heading
     Displaying All Levels of Headings
   Rearranging a Document by Rearranging Its Outline
   Using Outline View to Navigate Through a Long Document
   Numbering Outline Headings
     Numbering Headings with the Traditional Numbering Format
     Numbering Headings with a Legal Numbering Format
     Updating Heading Numbers
     Removing Heading Numbers
   Printing an Outline

When you're creating a long document, from a Ph.D. dissertation to a research report for the office, you'll want to develop special techniques for keeping track of all the text. For example, you may want to use outlining to create and view the basic structure of your document. Outlining also lets you easily rearrange sections of your document, number paragraphs, change heading levels, and create a table of contents when you're all finished.

To keep track of exactly where you are in a long document, you can display line numbers on the screen and later include them in your printed document as well. When you need to refer to different sections within a document, you can use Word's new bookmark feature to name part of your text. Then you can use that bookmark name to jump to that section, to link that section with other documents, and to create cross-references that Word will automatically keep up to date.

The sections in this chapter will show you how to handle long documents effectively.

USING OUTLINES IN WORD

Most people have created outlines in high school or college as a means of developing a structure for a document. However, there's a big difference between creating an outline on paper and creating an outline with Word. In Word, an outline *is* the document, or to be more accurate, Word uses *outline view* as one way to view a document. A Word outline not only shows the structure and the order of topics in a document, but serves as a tool that allows you to move the cursor quickly, to display and print only certain levels of text, and to rearrange whole sections of a document quickly. You'll learn how to do all these tasks in the following sections.

Not all of Word's commands work in outline view, but one important command is available: the Undo command. So if something unexpected happens when you're working with an outline, just choose Undo to reverse your last action.

Switching to and from Outline View

To switch to and from outline view:

- Press Shift+F2. Word displays the outline view screen, as shown in Figure 17-1.

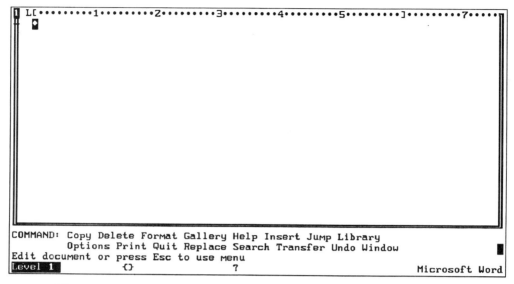

Figure 17-1.   **The outline view screen.**

Using the Two Outline Modes

Outline view has two modes you can use to do two kinds of tasks:

- Outline edit mode, in which you can type and edit the text of headings. In outline edit mode, Word displays the level of the selected heading in the status line.
- Outline organize mode, in which you can move headings to restructure your document. In outline organize mode, Word displays the word "ORGANIZE" in the status line.

To switch back and forth between these modes; Press Shift+F5. You'll learn how to use these modes in the following sections.

Creating an Outline

The easiest way to use Word's outlining function is to create an outline before you type the text for your document. When you create an outline in outline view, Word assigns automatic styles to your text. These styles are named Paragraph Heading level 1 through Paragraph Heading level 7. Each lower level is indented 1/4 inch from the previous level, as shown in Figure 17-2.

You can change the appearance of these Heading level styles by changing the styles in the NORMAL.STY style sheet, or by attaching the OUTLINE.STY style sheet to your document and changing the styles in OUTLINE.STY. For example, you might want to make level 1 heads all caps and bold, level 2 heads bold, and level 3 heads underlined. That way you can easily distinguish the levels of headings even when you switch back to document view. If you change the styles in the NORMAL.STY style sheet, the styles will automatically be applied to every outline you create. See Chapter 11 for more information about changing styles.

One advantage of using these Heading level styles is that Word can easily create a table of contents by collecting paragraphs with level styles. (For more information about styles and how to apply them or change them, see Chapter 11. For information about creating a table of contents, see Chapter 19.)

To create an outline:

1. Press Shift+F2 to switch to outline mode.
    Word displays the outline view screen.
2. Type the first outline heading paragraph, then press Enter.
    Word assigns the first heading the Level 1 style.
3. Type the rest of the outline heading paragraphs, assigning levels as follows before you press Enter. You can see the level of the selected paragraph in the status line at the bottom of the screen.
    *   To make a paragraph one level lower than the preceding paragraph, press Alt+0 (zero) after typing the text, then press Enter. (Use the zero key in the top row, not the one on the numeric keypad.)
    *   To make a paragraph one level higher than the preceding paragraph, press Alt+9 after typing the text, then press Enter. (Use the 9 key in the top row, not the one on the numeric keypad.)
    *   To make the paragraph the same level as the preceding paragraph, just type the text, then press Enter.

If you make a mistake, don't worry—you can always change the heading levels and rearrange an outline. You'll learn how to do that in the following sections.

```
┌─┌───────────────────────────────────────────────────────────────────┐─┐
│▌│L[•••••••••1•••••••••2•••••••••3•••••••••4•••••••••5•••••••••]•••••••••7••••┐│
│▌│  PART·I:··INTRODUCTION¶                                                │
│ │      What·You'll·Learn·From·this·Book¶                                │
│ │      What·We·Expect·You·to·Know¶                                      │
│ │      How·This·Book·is·Organized¶                                      │
│ │  PART·II:··ORGANIZING·YOUR·INFORMATION¶                               │
│ │      Hardware·and·Software·Requirements¶                              │
│ │          Description¶                                                 │
│ │          Form¶                                                        │
│ │      The·Audience¶                                                    │
│ │          Description¶                                                 │
│ │          Form¶                                                        │
│ │      The·Goals·of·the·Manual¶                                         │
│ │          Basic·Skills¶                                                │
│ │              Description¶                                             │
│ │              Form¶                                                    │
│ │          Advanced·Skills¶                                             │
│ │              Description¶                                             │
│ │              Form█                                                    │
│ │      ¶                                                                │
│ │                                                            ═BOOKZ.DOC═┘│
└─┴───────────────────────────────────────────────────────────────────────┘
COMMAND: Copy Delete Format Gallery Help Insert Jump Library
         Options Print Quit Replace Search Transfer Undo Window
Edit document or press Esc to use menu                                  █
▐Level 4▌           {Descri...Form¶}   ?                   Microsoft Word
```

Figure 17-2. **Creating an outline.**

Changing Heading Levels

A Word outline can include up to seven levels of headings, plus *body text*—the paragraphs, graphics, etc., that are not headings and that make up the majority of your document.

Demoting Headings

To demote a heading to the next lower level:

1. Select the heading.
2. Press Alt+0 (zero). Use the zero key in the top row, not the one on the numeric keypad.

Word indents the text and assigns it the Heading level style for the next lower level. You can make a heading only one level lower than the preceding heading.

To demote a heading to body text:

1. Select the heading.
2. Press Alt+P (or Alt+XP if you have a style sheet other than NOR-MAL.STY attached).

Word returns the paragraph to the default standard paragraph style.

Promoting Headings
To promote a heading to the next higher level:

1.   Select the heading.
2.   Press Alt+9. Use the 9 key in the top row, not the one on the numeric keypad.

Word shifts the text left and assigns it the Level style for the next higher level.

Entering Body Text

You can enter or edit the body of your document (all text except headings) in outline view, but you'll generally find it more convenient to switch back to document view to work on the main text of your document. You can switch back to outline view any time you want to see the structure of the document.
To enter body text:

1.   Press Shift+F2 to switch back to document view.
2.   Type the body text.

Viewing Different Levels of Your Outline

You can collapse or expand all or part of an outline to view different levels of text. Collapsing and expanding doesn't remove text from or add text to a document: it just displays or hides specific levels of text on the outline view screen. You can use keys or the mouse to expand or collapse headings.

Displaying Only Specific Levels of Headings

To display specific levels of your outline:

• Press Ctrl+plus (+) key on the numeric keypad, then type the number of the lowest heading level you want to display. To type the level number, use the number keys in the top row, not the keys on the numeric

```
 PART·I:··INTRODUCTION¶
        What·You'll·Learn·From·this·Book¶
        What·We·Expect·You·to·Know¶
        How·This·Book·is·Organized¶
 PART·II:·ORGANIZING·YOUR·INFORMATION¶
 +      Hardware·and·Software·Requirements¶
 +      The·Audience¶
 +      Features·Analysis¶
 +      The·Goals·of·the·Manual¶
 +      User·Interface¶
 PART·III:··PROJECT·MANAGEMENT¶
 +      Writing·Design·Specifications¶
 +      Tracking·Changes·to·the·Design·Specifications¶
 PART·IV:··TYPES·OF·USER·DOCUMENTATION¶
        Overview¶
 +      Tutorial¶
 +      Guide·to·Mastery¶
 +      Reference·Guide¶
 +      Quick·Reference·Materials▓
                                           ═BOOKZ.DOC═
 COMMAND: Copy Delete Format Gallery Help Insert Jump Library
          Options Print Quit Replace Search Transfer Undo Window
 Edit document or press Esc to use menu
 Level 2              {¶}              ?                Microsoft Word
```

Figure 17-3.   **You can expand and collapse an outline to show only the heading levels you want.**

keypad. Word hides all headings and text beneath that level. For example, press Ctrl+plus (+) on the numeric keypad, then press 3 (using the key in the top row) to see only levels 1 through 3.

Word displays plus signs (+) to the left of headings that have "collapsed" subheadings or text, as shown in Figure 17–3.

Collapsing All Subheadings and Body Text Beneath a Heading
To collapse all subheadings and text beneath a heading with keys:

1. Select the heading whose subheadings and body text you want to collapse.
2. Press the minus (-) key on the numeric keypad.

To collapse all subheadings and text beneath a heading with the mouse:

1. If necessary, press Shift+F5 to switch to outline organize mode. Word displays "ORGANIZE" in the status line.
2. Point to the heading whose subheadings and body text you want to collapse.

3.   Click both mouse buttons simultaneously.

Word displays plus signs (+) to the left of headings that have "collapsed" subheadings or text.

Expanding Subheadings and Body Text Below a Heading

To expand headings and text below a heading with keys:

1.   Select the heading whose subheadings and body text you want to expand.
2.   Do one of the following:
     • To expand the text to show the next lower level, press the plus (+) key on the numeric keypad.
     • To expand the text to show all levels of subheadings beneath the heading, press the asterisk (*) key on the numeric keypad.

To expand headings and text below a heading with the mouse:

1.   If necessary, press Shift+F5 to switch to outline organize mode. Word displays "ORGANIZE" in the status line.
2.   Point to the heading whose subheadings and body text you want to expand.
3.   Click the right mouse button to expand the text to the next level.

Displaying All Levels of Headings

To display all levels of your outline:

1.   Press Shift+F10 to select the entire document. Word switches to outline organize mode and displays "ORGANIZE" in the staus line
2.   Press the asterisk (*) key on the numeric keypad to display all subheadings.
3.   Press Shift+plus (+) key on the numeric keypad. Word displays all headings and text in the document.

Rearranging a Document by Changing Its Outline

You can change the order of headings in outline view and rearrange your document at the same time. When you move or copy a heading, Word relocates or copies that heading, all of its subordinate headings, and all of its associated text. (Remember, the outline is just another view of the document.)

To make rearranging easier and faster, you should switch to outline organize mode, which displays only headings, not the associated body text.
To move or copy headings and rearrange your document:

1. If you're using document view, press Shift+F2 to switch to outline view.
2. Press Shift+F5 to switch to outline organize mode. Word displays "ORGANIZE" in the status line.
3. Select the headings you want to move or copy:

To Select	Do This
Previous heading, no matter what level	Press the Left arrow key.
Next heading, no matter what level	Press the Right arrow key.
Another heading at the same level	Press the Up or Down arrow key.

   To select several headings press F6 to turn on extend mode, then use the keys listed above. Press F6 again when you're ready to turn off extend mode.
   You can also use a mouse, to select headings by clicking the left button on a heading to select one at a time, or holding down the left mouse button and dragging to select several headings at once.
4. If you want to move the selected headings, press the Del key to delete the selected headings to the scrap. If you want to copy the selected headings, choose the Copy command, then press Enter to put a copy in the scrap.
5. Move the cursor to the new location.
6. Press the Ins key to insert the headings from the scrap.

Using Outline View to Navigate Through a Long Document

You can use an outline to travel quickly through a long document:

1. If you're using document view, press Shift+F2 to switch to outline view.
2. Collapse the outline to its major headings by pressing Ctrl+ plus (+) key on the numeric keypad, then press 1 to display only first level

headings, or press 2 to display first and second level headings. (Use the keys in the top row to type the heading level number.)

3.   Select the heading where you want to move the cursor.

4.   Press Shift+F2 to switch back to document view.

Numbering Outline Headings

You can use the Library Number command to number headings in outline view. Word numbers all headings in an outline, whether or not they are displayed. By default, Word numbers outlines using the scheme described in the *Chicago Manual of Style* (University of Chicago Press), like this:

I.   First Level Heading
   A.   Second Level Heading
      1.   Third Level Heading
         a.   Fourth-Level Heading

If you don't want to use this outline scheme, you can choose to use a legal numbering format or set the numbering format for each different level.

Use the following procedures to number all headings originally, or to renumber headings when you've rearranged an outline.

Numbering Headings with the Traditional Numbering Format
To number outline headings using the default numbering format:

1.   If you're using document view, press Shift+F2 to switch to outline view.

2.   Choose the Library Number command. Figure 17-4 shows the command fields of the Library Number command.

3.   Press Enter or click the command name. Word displays numbers both in outline view (Figure 17–5)and in document view

Numbering Headings with a Legal Numbering Format
To number outline headings using a legal (see Figure 17–6) numbering format:

1.   If you're using document view, press Shift+F2 to switch to outline view.

2.   Before the first heading in the outline, type *1*. (one-period) followed by a space or a tab.

3.   Select the *1*. (Be sure to select the period.)

```
┌─────────────────────────────────────────────────────────────────────┐
│ L[••••••••1••••••••2••••••••3••••••••4••••••••5••••••••]••••••••7••••• │
│  PART·I:··INTRODUCTION¶                                               │
│       What·You'll·Learn·From·this·Book¶                              │
│       What·We·Expect·You·to·Know¶                                    │
│       How·This·Book·is·Organized¶                                    │
│  PART·II:·ORGANIZING·YOUR·INFORMATION¶                               │
│ +     Hardware·and·Software·Requirements¶                            │
│ +     The·Audience¶                                                  │
│ +     Features·Analysis¶                                             │
│ +     The·Goals·of·the·Manual¶                                       │
│ +     User·Interface¶                                                │
│  PART·IV:···TYPES·OF·USER·DOCUMENTATION¶                             │
│       Overview¶                                                      │
│ +     Tutorial¶                                                      │
│ +     Guide·to·Mastery¶                                              │
│ +     Reference·Guide¶                                               │
│ +     Quick·Reference·Materials¶                                     │
│ + PART·III:···PROJECT·MANAGEMENT¶                                    │
│   TERMS¶                                                             │
│   INDEX◆                                                             │
│                                                     BOOKZ.DOC        │
│LIBRARY NUMBER: Update Remove          restart sequence:(Yes)No       │
│                                                                      │
│Select option                                                     ▮   │
│Level 1            {PART·I...ment¶}   ?              Microsoft Word   │
└─────────────────────────────────────────────────────────────────────┘
```

Figure 17-4.   **The Library Number command fields.**

Figure 17-5.   **An outline with numbered headings.**

```
┌─────────────────────────────────────────────────────────────────────┐
│ L[••••••••1••••••••2••••••••3••••••••4••••••••5••••••••]••••••••7••••• │
│  I.·PART·I:··INTRODUCTION¶                                           │
│       A.·What·You'll·Learn·From·this·Book¶                          │
│       B.·What·We·Expect·You·to·Know¶                                │
│       C.·How·This·Book·is·Organized¶                                │
│  II.·PART·II:·ORGANIZING·YOUR·INFORMATION¶                          │
│ +     A.·Hardware·and·Software·Requirements¶                        │
│ +     B.·The·Audience¶                                              │
│ +     C.·Features·Analysis¶                                         │
│ +     D.·The·Goals·of·the·Manual¶                                   │
│ +     E.·User·Interface¶                                            │
│  III.·PART·IV:···TYPES·OF·USER·DOCUMENTATION¶                       │
│       A.·Overview¶                                                  │
│ +     B.·Tutorial¶                                                  │
│ +     C.·Guide·to·Mastery¶                                          │
│ +     D.·Reference·Guide¶                                           │
│ +     E.·Quick·Reference·Materials¶                                 │
│ + IV.·PART·III:···PROJECT·MANAGEMENT¶                               │
│   V.·TERMS¶                                                         │
│   INDEX◆                                                            │
│                                                     BOOKZ.DOC        │
│COMMAND: Copy Delete Format Gallery Help Insert Jump Library          │
│         Options Print Quit Replace Search Transfer Undo Window       │
│Edit document or press Esc to use menu                           ▮    │
│Level 1            {PART·I...ment¶}   ?              Microsoft Word   │
└─────────────────────────────────────────────────────────────────────┘
```

4. Choose the Library Number command.

5. Choose Update.

6. In the "restart sequence" field choose Yes.

7. Press Enter or click the command name

Updating Heading Numbers

To update heading numbers after you add or delete text from your outline:

1. Choose the Library Number command.

2. Press Enter or click the command name.

Removing Heading Numbers

To remove numbers from headings:

1. Select the first character in the outline if you want to remove numbers from the entire outline, or select a portion of the outline if you want to remove numbers from only part of the outline.

2. Choose the Library Number command.

Figure 17-6.   **An outline that uses the legal numbering format.**

```
│L[•••••••••1•••••••••2•••••••••3•••••••••4•••••••••5•••••••••]•••••••••7•••••│
│ ▌.·PART·I:··INTRODUCTION¶                                                    │
│      1.1.·What·You'll·Learn·From·this·Book¶                                  │
│      1.2.·What·We·Expect·You·to·Know¶                                        │
│      1.3.·How·This·Book·is·Organized¶                                        │
│ 2.·PART·II:·ORGANIZING·YOUR·INFORMATION¶                                     │
│      2.1.·Hardware·and·Software·Requirements¶                                │
│          2.1.1·Description¶                                                  │
│          2.1.2·Form¶                                                         │
│      2.2.·The·Audience¶                                                      │
│          2.2.1·Description¶                                                  │
│          2.2.2·Form¶                                                         │
│      2.3.·Features·Analysis¶                                                 │
│          2.3.1·Features·in·Common·with·Competitors¶                          │
│              2.3.1.1·Description¶                                            │
│              2.3.1.2·Form¶                                                   │
│          2.3.2·Features·Better·than·Competitors¶                            │
│              2.3.2.1·Description¶                                            │
│              2.3.2.2·Form¶                                                   │
│      2.4.·The·Goals·of·the·Manual¶                                           │
│                                                                ═BOOK2.DOC═   │
│COMMAND: Copy Delete Format Gallery Help Insert Jump Library                  │
│         Options Print Quit Replace Search Transfer Undo Window          ▐    │
│Edit document or press Esc to use menu                                        │
│Level 1            {¶}              ?                    Microsoft Word        │
```

3. Choose Remove.
4. Press Enter or click the command name.

Printing an Outline

Word prints only the headings that are in outline view, so make sure you can see everything you want to print is on the screen.
To print an outline:

1. Expand or collapse text as necessary to display the text you want to print.
2. Use the Print Printer command to print your outline.

Displaying Non-outline Text in Outline View

If you didn't use outline view to create an outline, you can still display your document in outline view, although this won't be of much use to you unless you have formatted your headings using Word's Level 1 through Level 7 styles, or unless you want to reformat your headings using these styles. Word uses the Level styles to keep track of the levels of text in an outline. If your text contains no Level styles, Word can't distinguish between the levels of text, so it simply displays "T" (for text) next to the paragraphs in outline view. Word displays all non-outline text as body text in outline view, as shown in Figure 17-7.

If you want to convert a document for use in outline view, you can assign key codes to Word's Level 1-Level 7 automatic styles, then apply them to your headings (see Chapter 11 for details), or use the procedure described previously in this chapter to assign heading levels and rearrange text in your document.

NUMBERING PARAGRAPHS

To have Word number the paragraphs in your document, you must use outline view and format your headings as levels 1, 2, 3, etc. This procedure is explained in "Numbering Outline Headings" earlier in this chapter. The only other way to add numbers is to type them yourself.

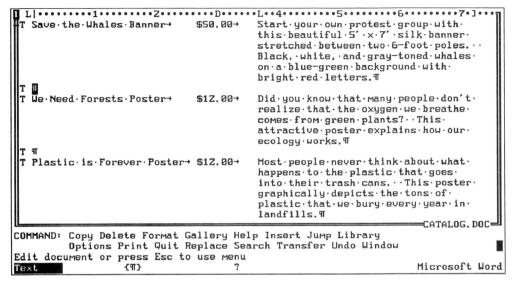

Figure 17-7. **Non-outline text in outline view.**

To type numbers yourself, use one of the following formats, followed
by a period, then a space or tab:

1., 2., 3., etc.
I., II., III., etc.
i., ii., iii., etc.
A., B., C., etc.
a., b., c., etc.

Updating Paragraph Numbers

Once you've added numbers, whether you did it with outline view or you
typed them yourself, you can make Word renumber the paragraphs, either
in outline view or in document view. This feature is handy if you've added
or deleted text since numbering. New text must include either a number
or letter followed by a period, then a space or tab at the beginning of the
paragraph (e.g. III. Training Your Porpoise); or must be formatted using
a Level heading from the OUTLINE.STY style sheet. Word renumbers
from the cursor position to the end of the document.

To update paragraph numbers:

1. Make sure all paragraphs you want to renumber are preceded by a
   number.

2. Select the first character of the portion you want to renumber.
3. Choose the Library Number command.
4. Press Enter or click the command name. Word renumbers any paragraphs that already have numbers.

Removing Numbers from Selected Paragraphs

Sometimes your document may include paragraphs that you don't want to number. You can use the following procedure to remove numbers from selected paragraphs. You'll get in trouble if you remove the number from the first paragraph, however, because Word uses the first number it encounters to determine how to number the rest of the document.

To remove numbers from selected paragraphs:

1. If you're in outline view, press Shift+F2 to switch to document view.
2. Select the paragraphs from which to remove numbers.
3. Choose the Library Number command.
4. Choose Remove.
5. Press Enter or click the command name.
6. To update the numbers so they'll be sequential, choose the Library Number command again, then press Enter.

NUMBERING LINES

You can add line numbers to your document when you need to count lines at a glance or to make text easier to refer to on a page. Line numbers are commonly used in legal documents and military specifications. You use the Options command to display line numbers in the status line in document view, and you use the Format Division line-Numbers command to print line numbers when you print your document.

Word runs more slowly when it has to calculate line numbers, so you may want to turn off line numbers when you don't need them.

Displaying Line Numbers in the Status Line

To display line numbers in the status line in document view:

1. If you don't have automatic pagination turned on, use the Print Repaginate command to repaginate your document.

2. Choose the Options command. The command fields are shown in Figure 17–8.
3. In the "line numbers" field, choose Yes.
4. In the "count blank space" field, choose Yes if you want Word to count blank lines; or choose No if you want Word to count only lines that contain text.
5. Press Enter or click the command name.

When line numbers are turned on, Word displays in the status line the number of the line containing the cursor, as well as the usual page number and column number.

Making Line Numbers on the Screen Match Printed Line Numbers

Because you use two different commands to display line numbers on the screen and to print line numbers, the screen display and the printed version may not be the same. To make the screen match the printout:

1. Choose the Options command.

Figure 17-8. **The Options command controls line numbering.**

```
┌── L[•••••••••1•••••••••2•••••••••3•••••••••4•••••••••5•••••••••]•••••••••7•••┐
│ ⊦   PART·I:··INTRODUCTION¶                                                  │
│ ⊦   What·You'll·Learn·From·this·Book¶                                       │
│ ⊦   What·We·Expect·You·to·Know¶                                             │
│ ⊦   How·This·Book·is·Organized¶                                             │
│ ⊦   PART·II:·ORGANIZING·YOUR·INFORMATION¶                                   │
│ ⊦   Hardware·and·Software·Requirements¶                                     │
├─────────────────────────────────────────────────────────────────────────────┤
│ WINDOW OPTIONS for window number: 1        show hidden text:(Yes)No          │
│            show ruler:(Yes)No      show non-printing symbols: None Partial(All)│
│            show layout: Yes(No)            show line breaks: Yes(No)          │
│            show outline: Yes(No)           show style bar:(Yes)No            │
│                                                                              │
│ GENERAL OPTIONS mute: Yes(No)              summary sheet:(Yes)No             │
│            measure:(In)Cm P10 P12 Pt       display mode: 1                ▮   │
│            paginate:(Auto)Manual           colors:                           │
│            autosave:                       autosave confirm: Yes(No)         │
│            show menu:(Yes)No               show borders:(Yes)No              │
│         date format:(MDY)DMY               decimal character:(.),            │
│         time format:(12)24                 default tab width: 0.5"           │
│         line numbers: Yes No               count blank space: Yes(No)        │
│         cursor speed: 3                    linedraw character: (|)           │
│         speller path: C:\WORD5\SPELL-AM.LEX                                  │
│ Select option                                                                │
│ Pg1 Li1 Co1          {}              ?                        Microsoft Word │
└───────────────────────────────────────────────────────────────────────────┘
```

2. In the "line numbers" field choose Yes.
3. In the "count blank space" field choose No.
4. In the "show line breaks" field choose Yes.
5. Press Enter or click the command name.

Printing Line Numbers

To print line numbers, you'll use the Format Division line-Numbers command. This command controls only the printing of line numbers. To display numbers on the screen, use the procedure described in "Adding Line Numbers and Column Numbers to the Screen" earlier in this chapter.

Word counts only lines containing text in the body of the document—running heads, running feet, and footnotes are not counted. By default, Word positions the line numbers .4 inch from the left margin, and begins the line numbers on each page with 1. However, you can change both of these settings, as described in the following procedure.

To print line numbers:

1. Choose the Format Division line-Numbers command (Esc, F, D, N).
2. Choose Yes.
3. If you want to change the position of the line numbers (to allow room for revision marks, for example), type a measurement less than the left margin. For example, if the left margin is set at 1.25 inches and you want line numbers positioned .75 inch before the left margin, type .5.
4. If you don't want line numbers to start at 1 on each page, choose one of the following options:

Option	Description
Division	Starts line numbers at 1 in each division and numbers lines continuously to the end of the division.
Continuous	Numbers lines continuously to the end of the document.

5. If you don't want Word to print a number next to every line of text, type the increment you want in the "increments" field. For example, if you want Word to number only every tenth line, type 10. Then Word prints numbers next to lines 10, 20, 30, etc.

```
 1    RISKS

 2

 3    The only risk we can foresee to purchasing the new computer

 4    system is the speed at which the computer industry changes.

 5    At this time, the proposed system would seem to fulfill our

 6    needs for many years to come.  However, no company can

 7    foresee new developments which would make a computer system

 8    outdated.

 9

10    COSTS

11

12    The cost of the new system is $72,950.00.  This includes all

13    installation costs, as well as a one-year service contract

14    with Hard&Soft Solutions company.  Our current insurance

15    coverage is adequate to protect our investment.

16

17    To buy new versions of our existing software programs and a

18    new page-layout program, we estimate a maximum of $2000.00.
```

Figure 17-9. **Line numbers in a printed document.**

6. Press Enter or click the command name to tell Word that you want to add line numbers when printing.

Note: If you want to print line numbers for some divisions of your document, but not for others, move the cursor into each division, then choose the Format Division line-Numbers command. Set the first command field to Yes in those divisions where you want line numbers, and set it to No in those divisions where you don't.

NUMBERING TABLES, FIGURES, AND OTHER SEQUENTIAL ITEMS

If you have a lot of tables, figures, charts, or illustrations in your document, you'll want to number them so you can refer to them in the text. For example, the figures in this book are numbered according to the chapter and the number of figures in that chapter, so we can say things like, "Figure 17-5 shows this. . ."

As you edit your text, add new figures or tables and maybe delete old ones, keeping the numbers sequential can become a real hassle. To make your life easier, you can make Word number figures, tables, and other sequential items by inserting a field that Word will update at printing time. You could even use this technique to number chapters or sections in a long document. Word fills in the fields with purely sequential numbers—1, 2, 3, and so forth.

To number tables, figures, or other sequential items:

1. Move the cursor to where you want to insert the sequential number. For example, you probably want to put a figure or table number in a caption above or below each figure or table.
2. Type any text you want to precede the sequential number, press the spacebar, then type an appropriate code name, followed by a colon, like these:

    table: *figure*:   *chart*:   *illustration*:   *section*:

Don't put any space between the code name and the colon (:). Here are some examples of series items you might create. For simplicity's sake, we've given all of these items the number 3.

Type This	To Print This
Table table:.	Table 3.
Figure 10-figure:.	Figure 10-3.
Chart chart:. Quarterly	Chart 3. Quarterly Sales Figures.
Sales Figures:.	
Section section:.	Section 3.

3. Press F3. Word encloses the code name in parentheses (for example, (table:) or (chart:) creating a field that the program will update with a sequential number when you print the document. Figure 17-10 shows examples of series codes for figures in Word.

Of course, if you want Word to sequentially number all the tables, figures, and so forth, you have to give the same categories of items all the same code name. You'll have to code all tables with the same code (table:, for example); all figures with the same code (figure:, for example); and so forth. It really doesn't matter what code you give the items (you could call them fred: or spike: if you wanted), as long as you give all the items in the same category the same code.

```
┌─────────────────────────────────────────────────────────────┐
│┌───────────────────────────────────────────────────────────┐│
││ Accounting        5 EZ-X computers, 2 MT1200 printers       ││
││ Marketing         3 MicroZip computers, 1 MT1200            ││
││                      printer                                ││
││ All Other Groups  4 EZ-X computers, 14 MicroZip             ││
││                      computers, 4 FluidT printers           ││
││                                                             ││
││ Our managers and clerical staff use these computers and     ││
││ printers to produce all our correspondence and keep track of││
││ all our bookkeeping.  The following figures show the        ││
││ location of our computers and printers, and the proposed    ││
││ location for new equipment.                                 ││
││                                                             ││
││ Figure (figure:).  Location of Existing Equipment.          ││
││ Figure (figure:).  Proposed Location of New Equipment.█     ││
││                                                             ││
││ All of our computers can read only low-density disks, which ││
││ were the only disks available at the time we purchased our  ││
││ system.  Our computers do not contain graphics cards, which ││
│└───────────────────────────────────────────FBSTUDY.DOC──────┘│
│COMMAND: Copy Delete Format Gallery Help Insert Jump Library   │
│         Options Print Quit Replace Search Transfer Undo Window│  █
│Edit document or press Esc to use menu                         │
│Pg7 Co55          {s}              ?            Microsoft Word │
└─────────────────────────────────────────────────────────────┘
```

Figure 17-10.   **Series codes for figures in a Word document.**

To make it easier to add exactly the same code to each item in a category (all tables, for example), you could make the code into a glossary entry, then insert it from the glossary wherever you want. See Chapter 4 for more information about using glossaries.

If you want to create cross-references to items that Word numbers in this way, you can add bookmark names to the items as well. The following section tells you how to use the bookmarks.

NAMING PARTS OF YOUR DOCUMENT: USING BOOKMARKS

When you need to keep track of sections or items of text within your document, you can use *bookmarks*. In Word, bookmarks are names that you attach to selected text. For example, you might want to name a section of a report "Quarterly_Sales," or a section of your great American novel "Torrid_Love_Scene." A bookmark can contain anything—a table of figures, a graphic and its caption, a paragraph, or several chapters of text.

Once you've created a bookmark (named a graphic or a piece of text), you can use that bookmark name to move the cursor quickly to that spot, to include that section of text in another document, or to set up a cross-reference that Word will automatically update. If you're accustomed to working with spreadsheets, you'll find that using bookmarks in Word is much like using named ranges in a spreadsheet program.

It's a good idea to wait until your text is nearly perfected to assign bookmarks to sections, because if you need to delete or expand text that you've named as a bookmark, you may have to go through the process all over again.

Creating a Bookmark

To create a bookmark:

1. Select all of the section of your document you want to name. Be sure to select the entire section, especially if you want to use bookmarks to insert the text into other documents.
2. Choose the Format bookmarK command (Esc, F, K).
3. Type a name for your bookmark. The name can be up to 31 characters long, and can contain letters, numbers, underscores (_), periods, and hyphens (although you cannot begin or end a bookmark name with an underscore, a period, or a hyphen). A bookmark name cannot contain a colon (:) or a space.
    Here are some examples of bookmark names: Introduction, Price-List, Meeting_Schedule, 1-8-89_Minutes. Each bookmark name must be unique within a document. If you've already created several bookmarks within the document, you can press F1 to see a list and make sure that you don't duplicate a name already assigned.
4. Press Enter or click the command name.

That's all there is to it! Don't expect to see any changes on the screen, however; bookmarks are invisible. Word uses the first and the last characters of the selected text to mark the beginning and end of the bookmark. If you later delete one of these characters, Word moves the beginning or end of the bookmark to the next letter within the bookmark.

You can assign more than one bookmark name to the same text, so you can have bookmarks within bookmarks within bookmarks, if you like.

Jumping to a Bookmark

One convenience associated with using bookmarks is that you can tell Word to jump to the section of text you've named.

To jump to a bookmark:

1. Choose the Jump bookmarK command (Esc, J, K).
2. Type the bookmark name or press F1 to display a list, then select a name.
3. Press Enter or click the command name. Word selects the section of text with that name.

Cross-Referencing a Bookmark

When you've created a bookmark in your document, you can insert a cross-reference to that bookmark in another part of your document. This feature creates a field that Word will update when you print the document. You can use bookmarks to create cross-references to paragraph numbers, footnotes, and figure and table captions, as well as to the pages that contain the bookmark text.

Cross-Referencing Pages

The most common use for cross-referencing bookmarks is when you want to refer to the pages on which the bookmark text is located. For example, if you've named a table of sales figures with the bookmark "Sales," you can create a cross-reference to that table that Word will update with the correct page number upon printing. If the table is split across several pages, Word will print a page range (such as 8-10).

To cross-reference the pages on which a bookmark is located:

1. Place the cursor where you want to insert the cross-reference.
2. Type any text you want to precede the page number, press the spacebar, then type

    Page:<bookmarkname>

where *<bookmarkname>* is the name you assigned to the text, then type any text you want to follow the reference. Be sure to include the colon (:), and don't leave any space between the colon and the bookmark name. Here are some examples that refer to a bookmark named Sales on page 11:

Type This	To Print This
See page page:Sales for more information.	See page 11 for more information.
(See also the table on page page:Sales.)	(See also the table on page 11.)
Page page:Sales contains the figures supporting this.	Page 11 contains the figures supporting this.
(See Table 1-3 on p. page: Sales.)	(See Table 1-3 on page 11.)

3. Press F3. Word encloses the page: code and the bookmark name in parentheses (for example (page:Sales)), creating a field that the program will update when you print the document.

Cross-Referencing a Paragraph Number
When you're using paragraph numbers in a document such as a military specification or a legal document, you'll want to refer to the number of the paragraph where the bookmark text begins. You must add paragraph numbers before using the following procedure.

To cross-reference the paragraph where the bookmark text begins:

1. Place the cursor where you want to insert the cross-reference.
2. Type any text you want to precede the paragraph number, press the spacebar, then type *para-num:<bookmarkname> where <bookmarkname>* is the name you assigned to the text, then type any text you want to follow the reference. Be sure to include the colon (:), and don't leave any space between the colon and the bookmark name. Here are some examples that refer to a bookmark named Background in paragraph 2.1 on page 10:

Type This	To Print This
See paragraph para-num: Background for more information.	See paragraph 2.1 for more information.
(See also the background information in paragraph para-num:Background.)	(See also the background information in paragraph 2.1.)
Paragraph para-num: Background contains the pertinent background information.	Paragraph 2.1 contains the pertinent background information.

(See paragraph para-num: (See paragraph 2.1 on page 10.)
Background on page page:
Background.)

3. Press F3. Word encloses the para-num: code and the bookmark name
    in parentheses (for example (para-num:Background)), creating a
    field that the program will update when you print the document.

Cross-Referencing Footnotes

If you're using footnotes, you can cross-reference the text of a particular
footnote to which you've attached a bookmark name. To attach the bookmark name to the footnote, you'd move to the end of the document, select
the footnote text after the reference mark or number, then apply a bookmark name, as described in "Creating a Bookmark" earlier in this chapter.

   To cross-reference the footnote containing the bookmark text :

1. Place the cursor where you want to insert the cross-reference.
2. Type any text you want to precede the footnote number, press the
    spacebar, then type *para-num:<bookmarkname> where <book-
    markname>* is the name you assigned to the text, then type any text
    you want to follow the reference. Be sure to include the colon (:), and
    don't leave any space between the colon and the bookmark name.
    Here are some examples that refer to a bookmark named Obelisk in
    footnote 16 on page 20:

Type This	To Print This
See footnote footnote:Obelisk for more information.	See footnote 16 for more information.
(See also the description in footnote footnote:Obelisk.)	(See also the description in footnote 16.)
Footnote footnote:Obelisk describes the origin of the word "obelisk."	Footnote 16 describes the origin of the word "obelisk."
(See footnote footnote:Obelisk on page page:Obelisk.)	(See footnote 16 on page 20.)

3. Press F3. Word encloses the footnote: code and the bookmark name
    in parentheses (for example, footnote:Obelisk, creating a field that
    the program will update when you print the document.

Cross-Referencing Table or Figure Captions

If you're using automatically numbered table or figure captions, you can cross-reference the caption of a particular table or figure to which you've attached a bookmark name. To attach the bookmark name to the table or figure, you select table or figure text immediately preceding the caption code ((table:) or (figure:)), then apply a bookmark name, as described in "Creating a Bookmark" earlier in this chapter.

To cross-reference the table or figure caption containing the bookmark text :

1. Place the cursor where you want to insert the cross-reference.
2. Type any text you want to precede the table or figure caption number, press the spacebar, then type the appropriate code: *table:<bookmarkname>* or *figure:<bookmarkname>* where *<bookmarkname>* is the name you assigned to the text, then type any text you want to follow the reference. Be sure to include the colon (:), and don't leave any space between the colon and the bookmark name. Here are some examples that refer to a bookmark named Inventory in Table 5 on page 22:

Type This	To Print This
See Table table:Inventory for more information.	See Table 5 for more information.
(See also the inventory ratios in Table table:Inventory.)	(See also the inventory ratios in Table 5.)
Table table:Inventory summarizes the current inventory ratios.	Table 5 summarizes the current inventory ratios.
(See Table table:Inventory on page page:Inventory.)	(See Table 5 on page 22.)

3. Press F3. Word encloses the table: or figure: code and the bookmark name in parentheses (for example (table:Inventory), creating a field that the program will update when you print the document.

Removing a Bookmark

This procedure removes the bookmark designation from text. The text itself remains intact.

To remove a bookmark:

1. Choose the Jump bookmarK command (Esc, J, K).

2. Type the name of the bookmark you want to remove, and press Enter. Word jumps to the bookmark text and selects it.
3. Choose the Format bookmarK command (Esc, F, K).
4. Leave the "name" field blank, and press Enter. Word displays the message *"Enter Y to confirm deletion of bookmark(s)."*
5. Type Y.

Using an Existing Bookmark Name for a Different Section of Text

If you've mistakenly named one section of your document as a bookmark, but you want to use that name for a different section:

1. Select the new text to which you want to assign the existing bookmark name.
2. Choose the Format bookmarK command (Esc, F, K).
3. Type the existing bookmark name or press F1 and select it from the list.
4. Press Enter or click the command name. Word displays a message asking you to *"Enter Y if you want to overwrite the bookmark."*
5. Press Y.

Using a Named Section from One Document in Another Document

You can use the Library Link Document command to import a section of text named as a bookmark from one document into another document. You can also create a link between the two documents to make Word update the information as it changes. For example, you might want to include a table of sales figures from SALES.DOC in an annual report named YEAR-END.DOC. For more information about linking documents together, see "Importing and Linking Information from Another Word File" in Chapter 18.

18

LINKING WITH SPREADSHEETS AND OTHER DOCUMENTS

This Chapter Contains the Following:

$\mathbf{W}$ant to put some spreadsheet information in your Word document? You can import any part of a spreadsheet from Microsoft Multiplan, Microsoft Excel, or Lotus 1-2-3. You can also link that spreadsheet information to its source file, and update the information in the Word document whenever it changes in the source file. You can use the same process to import text from one Word document to another, and to update that text whenever it changes in the other document.

IMPORTING INFORMATION FROM SPREADSHEETS

When you import information from a spreadsheet created with Multiplan, Microsoft Excel for Windows, or Lotus 1-2-3, you use Word's Library Link Spreadsheet command to tell Word which part of a spreadsheet you want to copy. To specify a block of cells, you can use either a name you've assigned with the spreadsheet program, or a range that you specify using the standard format of the spreadsheet program.

Word can import up to 32K of information at a time. If the spreadsheet you want is bigger than 32K, divide it up horizontally into pieces, then import the pieces and insert them one after another in the Word document. They'll look as though they're all in the same table. Figure 18-1 shows a Multiplan spreadsheet that's been imported into a Word document.

To import information from a spreadsheet:

1. Move the cursor to where you want to insert the information.
2. Choose the Library Link Spreadsheet command. The command fields are shown in Figure 18-2.
3. In the "filename" field, type the name of the spreadsheet file, including any drive name or pathname Word needs to find the file. You can also press F1 to see a list of files in the current directory, then highlight the filename, then press F1 again.
4. In the "area" field type the area name or the range of cells if you want to import part of a spreadsheet, or leave the field blank if you want to import the entire spreadsheet. You can press F1 to see a list of named areas in the spreadsheet, then highlight the name you want, then press F1 again. If you want to type a range of cells, use the standard format described in the spreadsheet documentation (like R5C5:R10C5 for Multiplan or Excel and B5..D10 for Lotus 1-2-3 or Excel).
5. Press Enter or click the command name to import the information.

```
┌─────────────────────────────────────────────────────────────────────────┐
│█ L[•••••••••1•••••••••2•••••••••3•••••••••4•••••••••5•••••••••]•••••••••7••••█
│  ¶
│  ¶
│  I think we're doing pretty well.  This little spreadsheet
│  should give you a rough idea of how things went in the first
│  quarter of this year.¶
│  ¶
│  .L.C:\MP\QTR1.,↓
│  Month      Income     Expenses  Net Income↓
│  ↓
│  January    $5000.00   $3200.00  $1800.00↓
│  February   $4000.00   $2900.00  $1900.00↓
│  March      $4675.00   $2950.95  $1724.05↓
│  .L.¶
│  ¶
│  And here's how we did in the second quarter:¶
│  ¶
│  █
│  ◆
│
├─────────────────────────────────────────────────────────────────────────
│COMMAND: Copy Delete Format Gallery Help Insert Jump Library
│         Options Print Quit Replace Search Transfer Undo Window       █
│Microsoft Word Version 5.0 release 17
│Pg1 Col          {}                   ?               Microsoft Word
└─────────────────────────────────────────────────────────────────────────┘
```

Figure 18-1.   **A Multiplan spreadsheet in a Word document.**

Word displays a message telling you that it's importing the information.

- If Word can't find the file, it will display a message saying that the
  file is not available. Check the filename and pathname you typed
  to make sure everything is correct.
- If Word can't find the area you specified, it will display a message
  saying that the area name is not valid. Check the information you
  typed in the "area" field to make sure that it's correct.
- If Word finds a protected section in the specified area, it will display a message asking you to type a password before it imports the
  data

When Word imports the spreadsheet information, it creates a table, inserting tab characters between each column and a newline character at the
end of each row. This method makes the imported information a separate
paragraph. You may need to adjust the tab settings in the spreadsheet
paragraph.

Word puts special codes, formatted as hidden text, at the beginning and
end of the spreadsheet information. The beginning code is *.L. pathname,
area <newline character(↓)>*, and the ending code is *.L. <paragraph*

```
L[·········1·········2·········3·········4·········5·········]·········7·····

   I think we're doing pretty well.  This little spreadsheet
   should give you a rough idea of how things went in the first
   quarter of this year.

   .L.C:\MP\QTR1..
   Month      Income     Expenses  Net Income

   January    $5000.00   $3200.00  $1800.00
   February   $4800.00   $2900.00  $1900.00
   March      $4675.00   $2950.95  $1724.05
   .L.

   And here's how we did in the second quarter:

   ■
   ◆


LIBRARY LINK SPREADSHEET filename: ■              area:

Enter filename or press F1 to select from list                     ■
Pg1 Col            {}               ?              Microsoft Word
```

Figure 18-2.   **The Library Link Spreadsheet command fields.**

mark(¶)>. Word uses these codes to locate the spreadsheet source file, so don't change or delete these codes if you want to update the spreadsheet information. Before moving the spreadsheet paragraph, be sure to choose the Options command and choose Yes in the "show hidden text" field so that you can see these codes. Before printing, be sure to reverse this process and choose No in the "show hidden text" field of the Options command so that the codes won't print.

Word gets its currency symbols from the operating system, so you may need to adjust the dollar signs ($) or other symbols after importing information.

Formatting and Moving Spreadsheet Information

When you import spreadsheet information, it loses any character or paragraph formatting it had in the spreadsheet file. You can use the commands on Word's Format menu to add bold, italic, indents, borders, and so on, to the imported information. You can also edit the information if you don't want to update it later. (Updating overwrites any changes you've made.)

If you move or copy the imported information, be sure to select the hidden codes at the beginning and end of the paragraph and move them along with the paragraph. These codes tell Word where to find the source file so that it can update the information.

Updating Spreadsheet Information

When you update information you've copied from a spreadsheet, Word overwrites the imported area between the .L. codes, but keeps the paragraph mark at the end. Thus, the paragraph formatting is retained, but you'll lose any character formatting you've applied since importing the information into Word, unless that formatting is part of a style.

To update spreadsheet information in your document:

1. Press Shift+F10 to select the entire document, or select the area (including the beginning and ending .L. codes) that you want to update.
2. Choose the Library Link Spreadsheet command.
3. Press Enter or click the command name. If necessary, Word scrolls to the first imported area and displays any hidden codes. Word displays a message asking you if you want to update or skip the area.
4. Press Y to update the information, or press N if you want to skip the area.

Word scrolls to the next imported area (if any) and asks you if you want to update it. If Word can't find the .L. codes, it displays a message saying that it cannot find any links.

IMPORTING AND LINKING TEXT FROM ANOTHER WORD FILE

You can use the Copy and Insert commands to copy information between Word files, as described in Chapter 4; and the INCLUDE instruction to insert one file into another at printing time, as described in Chapter 20. You should use the following procedure only if you want to *link* information in one document to another. For example, if you want to include a list of products and prices in a brochure you're creating, you could copy that list from a main product file, and link the two Word files so that when the prices change in the main product file you can easily update them in the brochure file.

You can import part of another Word file by assigning a bookmark name to the area you want to import (bookmarks are described in detail in "Naming Parts of Your Document: Using Bookmarks" in Chapter 17). You can also import an entire Word file into another.

To import and link part of the text in another Word file:

1. Load the document that contains the text you want to copy.
2. Select the text you want.
3. Choose the Format bookmarK command.
4. In the "name" field, type a name for the marked text. For example, you could name a price list *PRICE*. See "Creating a Bookmark" in Chapter 17 for rules about naming bookmarks.
5. Press Enter or click the command name.
6. Load the document into which you want to insert the copy.
7. Choose the Library Link Document command. The command fields are shown in Figure 18-3.
8. In the "filename" field, type the name of the document in which you've marked text to be copied. Include any drive name and path-

Figure 18-3.   **The Library Link Document command fields.**

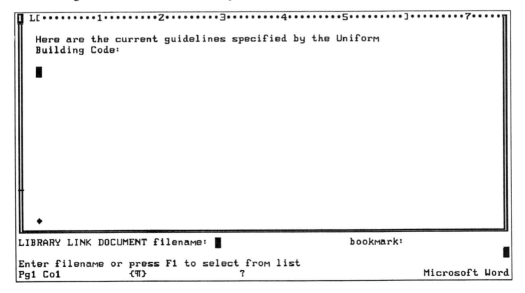

name Word will need to find the other file. You can also press F1 and select from a list of documents, then type F1 again to return to the command field.

9. In the "bookmark" field type the bookmark name you assigned to the text in the other file. You can also press F1 and select from a list of bookmarks, then press F1 again.

10. Press Enter or click the command name to import the text.

To import and link all the text in another Word file:

1. Load the document into which you want to insert the text.
2. Choose the Library Link Document command.
3. In the "filename" field, type the name of the document whose text you want to copy. Include any drive name and pathname Word will need to find the file. You can also press F1 select from a list of documents, then press F1 again to return to the command field.
4. Press Enter or click the command name to import the text.

When you use the Library Link Document command to import text from another document, Word puts codes, formatted as hidden text, at the beginning and ends of the imported text. The code *.D.pathname;bookmark name* appears at the beginning of the text, and *.D.* at the end, as shown in Figure 18-4. Don't change or delete these codes. Word uses them to find the other file when you want to update the text. Before moving the imported text, be sure to choose the Options command and choose Yes in the "show hidden text" field so that you can see and select these codes. Before printing, be sure to choose No in the "hidden text" field of the Print Options command so that the codes won't print.

Formatting and Moving Imported Text

You can use all of Word's commands to format the imported text, just as if it were any other type of text. However, keep in mind that when you update the text, Word will overwrite any formats you've applied, unless they're paragraph formats or styles attached to the last imported paragraph.

If you move or copy the imported text, be sure to select the hidden codes at the beginning and end of the paragraph and move them along with the paragraph. These codes tell Word where to find the source file so that it can update the information.

```
█ L[••••••••••1••••••••••2••••••••••3••••••••••4••••••••••5••••••••••]••••••••••7•••••█
  Here·are·the·current·guidelines·the·company·uses·to·prevent·
  the·concrete·buckling·problem:¶
  ¶
  ¶
  .D.STANDARD.DOC,slab↓
        1.→  Build·a·raised·base·of·gravel·6·to·8·inches·above·
        the·normal·drainage·plane.¶
  ¶
  2.→  Position·a·vapor·barrier·3·to·4·inches·beneath·the·
        concrete·slab,·in·the·middle·of·the·raised·base.¶
  ¶
  3.→  Pour·a·reinforced·concrete·slab·6·to·8·inches·thick·on·
        the·raised·base.¶
  ¶
  4.··Do·not·pour·walls·so·that·they·rest·on·the·concrete·
        slab.¶
  ↓
  .D.¶
  █                                                    ═MEMO5-25.DOC═╝
COMMAND: Copy Delete Format Gallery Help Insert Jump Library
         Options Print Quit Replace Search Transfer Undo Window    █
Edit document or press Esc to use menu
Pg1 Co1            {}               ?              Microsoft Word
```

Figure 18-4.   **A Word document containing text imported from another Word file.**

Updating Imported Text

When Word updates imported text, it overwrites the text, but keeps the paragraph mark after the ending .D. code. Thus, you'll lose any formatting you've applied, except that styles or paragraph formatting you've applied to the last paragraph.

To upgrade imported text:

1.   Press Shift+F10 to select the entire document, or select the area (including the beginning and ending .D. codes) that you want to update.
2.   Choose the Library Link Document command.
3.   Press Enter or click the command name. If necessary, Word scrolls to the first imported area and displays any hidden codes. Word displays a message asking you if you want to update or skip the area.
4.   Press Y to update the information, or press N if you want to skip the area.

Word scrolls to the next imported area (if any) and asks you if you want to update it. If you haven't selected any .D. codes, Word will display a message saying that it cannot find any links.

CREATING TABLES OF CONTENTS AND INDEXES

This Chapter Contains the Following:

Two final steps in finishing a long document are creating a table of contents for the front of the document, and creating an index for the back. This chapter shows you how.

CREATING A TABLE OF CONTENTS

When you're finished writing and formatting a long document, you'll want to add a table of contents so readers can see the structure of your document at a glance and know where to find the various sections they're looking for.

If you used Word's outlining feature to create an outline for your document, or you formatted your headings using Word's Heading level 1 through level 7 paragraph styles, you can create a table of contents from your document's outline—that's by far the easiest way. (For more information about outlining, see Chapter 17.) For instructions, see "Compiling a Table of Contents" later in this chapter.

If your document doesn't have an outline as described above, you'll follow these two basic steps to create a table of contents with Word:

1. Insert table-of-contents entries throughout your document.
2. Compile the table-of-contents entries to create a table of contents (as shown in Figure 19–1).

You'll learn how to do these tasks in this section.

Inserting Table-of-Contents Entries

If you don't have your headings formatted with outline level styles, you can create a table of contents by designating existing text on a page as a table-of-contents entry. You designate a table-of-contents entry by inserting beginning and ending table-of-contents codes, which are formatted as hidden text. These codes won't appear in your document when printed.

Word has two ways to insert table-of-contents codes: by typing them yourself, or by using the *toc_entry.mac* macro.

Inserting Table-of-Contents Codes with a Macro
You can use Word's *toc_entry.mac* macro to automate the process of coding table-of-contents entries.

371

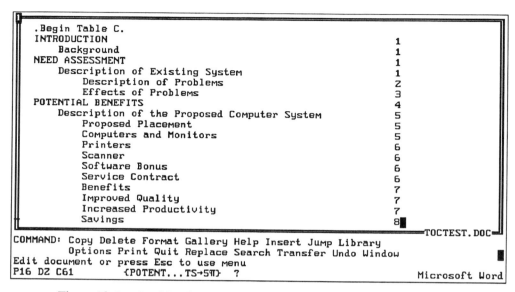

Figure 19-1.   **A table of contents created by Word.**

1. Use the Transfer Glossary load command to load the MACRO.GLY file, which contains the macro.

2. Select the text you want to appear as an entry in the table of contents. Don't worry if the text isn't exactly what you want—you can always edit it later.

3. Press Ctrl+TE to run the *toc_entry.mac* macro, which adds the hidden table-of-contents codes at the beginning and end of the selected text.

4. Repeat steps 2 and 3 to format all of the table-of-contents entries.

After you've inserted the first table-of-contents codes with the macro, you could use the repeat key, F4, instead of pressing Ctrl+TE to insert index codes around selected text.

Typing Table-of-Contents Codes

To designate existing text as a table-of-contents entry, as shown in Figure 19–2:

1. Choose the Options command.

2. In the "show hidden text" field, select Yes so you can see the table-of-contents codes as you insert them, then press Enter.

3. Select the first character of the text you want to appear in the table of contents.

4. Press Alt+E to turn on hidden text format. (If you have a style sheet other than NORMAL.STY attached, press Alt+XE.)

5. Type the beginning table-of-contents code, .c. (period-c-period), in front of the text.

6. If the table-of-contents text does not end in a paragraph mark (i.e., if it's not a complete paragraph in itself), move the cursor to the end of the text, press Alt+E (or Alt+XE), then type the ending table-of-contents code, a semicolon (;), to mark the end of the entry. This code is also formatted as hidden text, and won't appear in the printed document.

7. Repeat steps 3 through 6 for each table-of-contents entry. When you're through designating table-of-contents entries, press Alt+spacebar to turn off hidden text format.

Speed Tip: You can speed up this process by typing the .c. and semicolon codes once, then making each into a glossary entry assigned to a key. Then you can insert the glossary entries whenever and wherever you like, and do other editing tasks in between insertions without having to turn off and

Figure 19-2.   **Designating a table-of-contents entry.**

```
  their proposals.  The only proposal that fell below our
  preset maximum price came from Hard&Soft Solutions, a well-
  known vendor with a good reputation in our area.  This
  report discusses the feasibility of implementing Hard&Soft's
  proposed configuration.

  .c.NEED ASSESSMENT:

  .c.:Description of Existing System;█

  We currently have 26 personal computers and 7 printers in
  use throughout the company:

      Accounting          5 EZ-X computers, 2 MT1200 printers
      Marketing           3 MicroZip computers, 1 MT1200
                              printer
      All Other Groups    4 EZ-X computers, 14 MicroZip
                              computers, 4 FluidT printers
                                                      ══════FBSTUDY.DOC═══
  COMMAND: Copy Delete Format Gallery Help Insert Jump Library
          Options Print Quit Replace Search Transfer Undo Window      █
  Edit document or press Esc to use menu
  P7 D1 L9 C36       {;}                  ?              Microsoft Word
```

374 Working With Complex Documents

turn on the hidden text format. See Chapter 4 for more information about working with glossaries.

Specifying Different Levels

If the selected text should be a subentry in a table of contents, type one colon (:) for each level after the second period of the beginning table-of-contents code (.c.). For example, the entries

   .c.Lion Taming
   .c:.Capturing a Lion
   .c::.Using Tranquilizer Darts

would create first-, second-, and third-level entries in a table of contents like this:

   Lion Taming 15
      Capturing a Lion 18
         Using Tranquilizer Darts 18

Word assumes that each table-of-contents entry is a first-level entry unless you specify the levels with colons.

Compiling a Table of Contents

When you've finished your document and completed the outline or inserted table-of-contents entries throughout your document, you're ready to create the table of contents.

If you include page numbers in your table of contents, Word begins by repaginating your document. Hidden text displayed in your document will mess up the pagination, so use the Options command to make the hidden text invisible before you compile a table of contents.

After repaginating the document, Word collects the outline headings or table-of-contents entries, and places the table of contents in a new division at the end of your document. You can move, edit, and format a table of contents just like any text in a Word document.

To compile a table of contents:

1. If you're compiling a table of contents from an outline, display only those levels of headings you want to appear in the table of contents.

For example, if you want only first and second level headings in the table of contents, display only first and second level headings in the outline.

2. If necessary, choose the Options command and choose No in the "show hidden text" field to ensure that pagination will be correct.

3. Choose the Library Table command. Word displays the command fields shown in Figure 19-3.

4. If you're compiling the table of contents from outline levels, choose Outline in the "from" field. If you're compiling the table of contents from entries you inserted, choose Codes in the "from" field.

5. If you don't want to include page numbers in your table of contents, choose No in the "page numbers" field.

6. Press Enter or click the command name to start compiling the table of contents.Word repaginates the document before collecting the table-of-contents entries, so don't be surprised if this process takes a few minutes for a long document. When the process is complete, Word adds the table of contents to the end of the document.

Word adds the hidden text ".Begin Table C." as the first line of the table of contents and ".End Table C." as the last line. Leave these codes alone—

Figure 19-3. **The Library Table command fields.**

```
their proposals.  The only proposal that fell below our
preset maximum price came from Hard&Soft Solutions, a well-
known vendor with a good reputation in our area.  This
report discusses the feasibility of implementing Hard&Soft's
proposed configuration.

.c.NEED ASSESSMENT;

.c.:Description of Existing System;█

We currently have 26 personal computers and 7 printers in
use throughout the company:

    Accounting           5 EZ-X computers, 2 MT1200 printers
    Marketing            3 MicroZip computers, 1 MT1200
                         printer
    All Other Groups     4 EZ-X computers, 14 MicroZip
                         computers, 4 FluidT printers
```

```
LIBRARY TABLE from: Outline Codes           index code: C
        page numbers:(Yes)No                entry/page number separated by: ^t
        indent each level: 0.4"             use style sheet: Yes(No)          █
Select option
P7 D1 L9 C36        {;}              ?                       Microsoft Word
```

Word uses them to identify the table of contents. An existing table of contents is not automatically updated when you add or change material, so if you make changes to your document after compiling a table of contents, you'll have to update the table of contents to be sure it's accurate.

Formatting a Table of Contents Before Creating It

You can always change the appearance of a table of contents after it's created, just like any other Word text. But there are several things you can do to determine the look of the table of contents before it's created. These include:

- changing the leader character (the characters that fill in the space between the headings and their page numbers)
- changing the indents for subheadings
- using a style sheet to format the headings

Changing Leader Characters or Indents

By default, Word uses a right-aligned tab set at 6 inches to position the page number in a table of contents, and indents each subheading .4 inch from the previous heading level.

If you want to change the tab position or add leader characters before the tab, see "Formatting an Existing Table of Contents" later in this chapter. If you want to use spaces or something else instead of the tab character, use the procedure below.

To change leader characters or indents in a table of contents before it's created:

1. Choose the Library Table command.
2. In the "entry/page number separated by" field, type the leader character exactly as you want it. In other words, if you want the page number to appear three spaces after the heading, press the spacebar three times; if you want the page number to appear after five periods, type five periods.
3. In the "indent each level" field, type a new measurement.
4. Fill out other fields as necessary, then press Enter to create the table of contents.

Using a Style Sheet to Format a Table of Contents

If you've changed the automatic paragraph styles named Table level 1 through Table level 4 in NORMAL.STY or any other style sheet, you can use that style sheet to format your table of contents before it's created. Be sure to attach the style sheet to your document before creating a table of contents. Chapter 11 describes how to work with Word's automatic styles, how to attach style sheets, and how to create your own style sheets.

To use a style sheet to format a table of contents:

1.   If necessary, use the Format Stylesheet Attach command to attach the style sheet you want to use.
2.   Choose the Library Table command.
3.   In the "use style sheet" field, choose Yes.
4.   Fill out other fields as necessary, then press Enter to create the table of contents.

Formatting an Existing Table of Contents

You can use all of Word's formatting commands to change the appearance of an existing table of contents. Don't waste time formatting until you're sure you have the final table of contents, because each time a table of contents is updated, Word discards any formatting you've added. Here are two common tasks you might want to do:

• Change the position of the page numbers or change the leader characters that separate page numbers from the headings
• Change the margins to make lines wrap

Changing the Position of Page Numbers or the Leader Characters
The position of page numbers and the leader characters in a table of contents is determined by a tab setting at 6 inches.

To change the position of the page numbers of the leader characters:

1.   Select the entire table of contents.
2.   Press Alt+F1 to choose the Format Tab Set command and put a highlight in the ruler.
3.   Use the Down arrow key to highlight the tab at 6 inches.
4.   Use Ctrl+Right arrow key or Ctrl+Left arrow key to move the highlight to where you want page numbers to appear, then press F1.
5.   If you want to change the alignment at the tab, choose a new option in the "alignment" field.

6. If you want to change the leader characters that fill in the tab space, choose a new option in the "leader character" field.

7. Press Enter or click the command name to change the table of contents.

Changing the Margins

You can change the left and right margin of a table of contents to make the lines wrap or to make a table of contents narrower. Because a table of contents is in a separate division, its margins can be different from the rest of the document.

To change the margins in a table of contents:

1. Move the cursor into the table of contents.
2. Choose the Format Division Margins command.
3. Type new measurements in the "left" and "right" fields.
4. Press Enter or click the command name.

Creating One Table of Contents from Several Files

If you have inserted table-of-contents entries into a long document that you've kept in several files, you can merge those files together, then use Word to create a table of contents for the entire document. Keep in mind that the longer the file, the more memory Word needs for this process. Before creating the table of contents, Word will repaginate the entire document, so be sure to add any extra pages—such as chapter openings—that will be in the finished document before you create the table of contents.

1. Use the Transfer Load command to load the first file.
2. Press Ctrl+PgDn to move the cursor to the end of the file, then use the Transfer Merge command to append the second file to the first.
3. Repeat step 2 until all the files have been merged to create one huge file.
4. Use the process described in "Compiling a Table of Contents" earlier in this chapter to create the table of contents.

If your computer doesn't have enough memory to complete this operation, you can still create a complete table of contents. Just create a table of contents for the first file, note the ending page number, set the starting page number for the next file, then create a table of contents for it, and repeat this process until you have correctly paginated all the files and created a table of contents for each. Then move the table of contents from the end of each file into a new file, creating a complete, sequential table of contents.

Creating Tables of Figures and Other Tables

You can use the procedures described in "Typing Table-of-Contents Codes" and in "Compiling a Table of Contents" earlier in this chapter to create a table of figures or another table for of a document. The only difference is that you'll use another character instead of a "c" to code the entries. For example, you might use a ".f." code to designate figure captions for collection into a table of figures, or a ".t." code to designate table titles for a table of tables, like this:

.f.Figure 2-3. Carburetor assembly.
.t.Table 4.1. Average Rainfall In Major U.S. Cities.

You can use any letter other than i, l, d, or g—Word reserves these letters for other purposes.

To create a table of figures or another table:

1. Insert codes around all entries to be collected.
2. Choose the Library Table command.
3. In the "index code" field type the letter you chose to use as a code. For example, if you coded your entries with ".f.," type *f*.
4. Fill out the other fields as necessary, then press Enter or click the command name to begin compiling a table.

Updating a Table of Contents

Word doesn't automatically update a table of contents when you change the document. When all changes have been made, you need to compile the table of contents again to make sure it's current.

To update a table of contents:

1. If you're compiling a table of contents from an outline, display only those levels of headings you want to appear in the table of contents. For example, if you want only first-and-second level headings in the

table of contents, display only first-and-second level headings in the outline.

2. If necessary, choose the Options command and choose No in the "show hidden text" field, to ensure that pagination will be correct.

3. Choose the Library Table command.

4. If you're compiling the table of contents from outline levels, choose Outline in the "from" field. If you're compiling the table of contents from entries you inserted, choose Codes in the "from" field.

5. If you don't want to include page numbers in your table of contents, choose No in the "page numbers" field.

6. Press Enter or click the command name to start compiling the table of contents.

   Word repaginates the document before collecting the table-of-contents entries, so don't be surprised if this process takes a few minutes for a long document. When the process is complete, Word displays a message asking if you want to replace the existing table-of-contents. If you press N for No, Word appends the new table of contents to the existing table of contents at the end of your document. If you press Y for Yes, Word replaces the existing table of contents with the new one.

CREATING AN INDEX

When you're finished writing and formatting a long document such as your master's thesis or a voluminous report for the office, you may want to add an index to make it easier for readers to look up important information.

To create an index with Word, as shown in Figure 19–4, you follow two basic steps:

1. Insert index entries throughout your document.
2. Compile the index entries to create and insert an index.

You'll learn how to do these tasks in the rest of this chapter.

Inserting Index Entries

You'll put index entries on each page whose number you want to appear in the index. You can designate existing text on a page as an index entry, or you can type new text for an index entry. Either way, you mark the

```
::::::::::::::::::::::::::::::::::::::::::::::::::::::::::::::::::::::::::::::::
.Begin Index.
Background  6
BAZIK programming language  10
BIOS  4
Computer breakdowns  9
Computer Study Committee  5, 6
Developments in the computer industry  7
Disks
     double-density disks  4
     high-density disk  4
Existing System  7
EZ-X computers  7
FluidT printers  7
Graphics cards  8
Hard&Soft Solutions  5
High-density disks  4
Low-density disks  4
Machine room  10█
                                                         ═FBSTUDY.DOC═
COMMAND: Copy Delete Format Gallery Help Insert Jump Library
        Options Print Quit Replace Search Transfer Undo Window     ▐
Edit document or press Esc to use menu
P2Z D3 L18 C17    {→}                  ?                 Microsoft Word
```

Figure 19-4. **An index created by Word.**

entry by inserting index codes that are formatted as hidden text, which won't appear in your document when printed.

Word has three ways to insert index codes: by typing them yourself, by using the *index_entry.mac* macro, or by typing a list that Word can use in conjunction with the *index.mac* macro to designate index entries.

Inserting Index Codes with a Macro

You can use Word's *index_entry.mac* macro to automate the process of coding index entries.

1. Use the Transfer Glossary Load command to load the MACRO.GLY file, which contains the macro.
2. Select the text you want to appear as an entry in the index.
3. Press Ctrl+IE to run the *index_entry.mac* macro, which adds the hidden index codes at the beginning and end of the selected text.
4. Repeat steps 2 and 3 to format all of the index entries.

After you've inserted the first index codes, you can press the repeat key, F4, instead of pressing Ctrl+IE to insert more index codes around selected text.

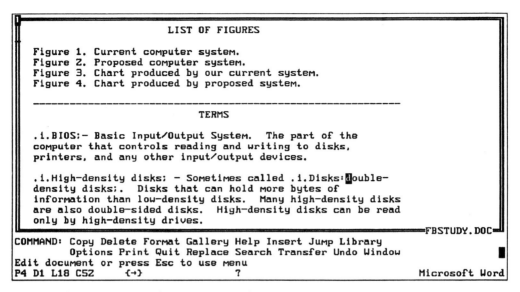

Figure 19-5. **Designating text as index entries.**

Typing Index Codes

To insert an index entry by designating existing text on a page:

1. Choose the Options command, choose Yes in the "show hidden text" field, and press Enter. This step will allow you to see the index codes as you type them.
2. Select the first character of the text you want to appear in the index.
3. Press Alt+E to turn on hidden text format. (Press Alt+XE if you have a style sheet other than NORMAL.STY attached.)
4. Type the beginning index code, *.i.* (period-i-period), in front of the text.
5. If the text does not end with a paragraph mark (i.e., is not a paragraph in itself), move the cursor to the end of the text, press Alt+E (or Alt+XE), then type the ending index code, a semicolon (;).
6. Repeat steps 3 through 5 for each entry you want to appear in the index.
7. When you're finished coding index entries, press Alt+Spacebar to turn off the hidden character format.

Speed Tip: You can speed up this process by typing the .i. and semicolon codes once, then making each into a glossary entry assigned to a key. Then you can insert the glossary entries whenever and wherever you like, and do other editing in between insertions without having to turn off and turn on the hidden text format.

Formatting Index Entries that Contain Colons, Semicolons, or Quotation Marks

If an index entry contains colons (:) or semicolons (;), enclose the entire entry in quotation marks fomatted as hidden text, like this:

.i."Africa: The Hungry Continent";

If an index entry contains quotation marks (""), enclose the entry in quotation marks formatted as hidden text, and type two quotation marks for each one that you want to appear in the index, like this:

.i."Africa: ""The Hungry Continent""";

Typing Your Own Index Entries

Sometimes the text in a document isn't worded exactly as you'd like it to appear in an index. In that case, you'll want to type new text for the index entry, and format the entire entry as hidden so it won't appear in the printed document.

To insert an index entry and type new text for the entry:

1. Position the cursor where you want to insert the index entry. It's important to put each entry as close as possible to the text it references, so that the text and the index entry won't be separated by a page break.
2. Press Alt+E to turn on hidden text format. (Press Alt+XE if you have a style sheet attached.)
3. Type the beginning index code, *.i.* (period-i-period), then the text you want to appear in the index, then the ending index code, the semicolon (;), like this:

A tamandua is a type of anteater. .i.Anteaters, types of;

Word assumes that each index entry is a first-level index entry unless you separate the index levels with a colon. You can have up to seven levels of index entries in a Word index. The following table shows how to type index entries to get different levels in the index.

Type	To Get This Result
.i.Indians;	Indians 7
.i.Indians:Navajos;	Indians
	Navajos.......7
i.Indian:Navajos:	Indians
weaving;	Navajos
	weaving.......7
i.Indians:navajos:	Indians
weaving:blanket designs;	Navajos
	weaving
	blanket designs.......7

4. Repeat steps 1 through 3 to add each entry you want to appear in the index.
5. When you're finished coding index entries, press Alt+Spacebar to turn off the hidden character format.

Using a List to Specify Index Entries

If you already know a lot of the items you want to include as entries in your index, you can create a list of these items, then use the *index.mac* macro to make Word go through your file and create an index entry for each occurrence of the list items. This process could save you a lot of time.

For example, if you're writing a report about plant growth, you might create a list something like this:

photosynthesis
chorophyll
growth rate
seed
fruit
flower
water absorption
soil nutrient

Then you could use this list in conjunction with the *index.mac* macro to make Word add index codes to every occurrence of these items in your document.

To use a list of terms and the *index.mac* macro to designate index entries:

1. Create the list in a separate document, typing one term per line and pressing Enter at the end of each line, then save the list document. Because Word will match the items you type with words in your document, be sure to use the exact terminology Word will find in the document. You can always edit the index later to give it exactly the wording you want. For example, if a term is normally used in the singular form in the document, don't make it plural in the list, and don't type "rainfall" if you want Word to find every occurrence of "rain." Just remember, the list and the terminology in your document must match for this technique to be effective.
2. If necessary, load the main document for which you're creating the index and move the cursor to the beginning of the document.
3. Use the Transfer Glossary Load command to load the MACRO.GLY file, which contains the macro.
4. Press Ctrl+IW to run the *index.mac* macro. Word will ask you for the name of the file containing the list of items.
5. Type the name of the list file you just created.
6. Press Enter. Word will go through the document and mark each occurrence of a list item as an index entry.

Compiling Index Entries

When you've inserted index entries throughout your document, you're ready to create the final index.

Because Word repaginates the document before collecting the index entries, you need to make hidden text invisible first so Word won't count it when calculating pages.

To create the index:

1. Choose the Options command, choose No in the "show hidden text" field, then press Enter. This step makes hidden text invisible so pagination will be accurate.
2. Choose the Library Index command. The command fields are shown in Figure 19-6.
3. Press Enter or click the command name to compile the index.

Word adds the hidden text ".Begin Index." as the first line of the index and ".End Index." as the last line. Leave these codes alone—Word uses

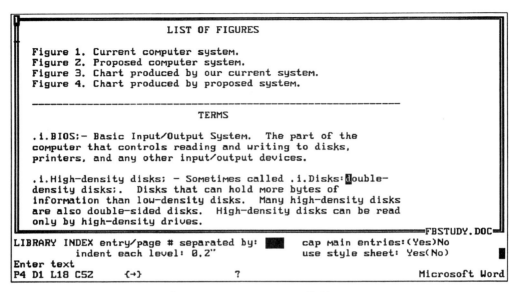

Figure 19-6.   **The Library Index command fields.**

them to identify the index. An existing index is not automatically updated when you add or change material, so if you make changes to your document after compiling an index, you'll have to update the index to be sure it's accurate.

Creating One Index from Several Files

If you have inserted index entries into a long document that you've kept in several files, you can merge those files together, then use Word to create an index for the entire document. Keep in mind that the longer the file, the more memory Word needs for this process. Before creating the index, Word will repaginate the entire document, so be sure to add any extra pages—such as chapter openings—that will be in the finished document before you create the index.

1.   Use the Transfer Load command to load the first file.
2.   Press Ctrl+PgDn to move the cursor to the end of the file, then use the Transfer Merge command to append the second file to the first.
3.   Repeat step 2 until all the files have been merged to create one huge file.

4. Use the process described in "Compiling Index Entries" earlier in this chapter to create the index.

Formatting an Index

Just like any other text, you can use all of Word's commands to edit and format an index after you create it. You can use the Format Character command to add bold or italic, for example, or use the Format Division Layout command to change the layout from two columns (the default) to three columns.

You can also choose options in the Library Index command fields to control these aspects of the appearance of the final index:

* Capitalization of first-level entries. By default, Word capitalizes the first letter of main entries and leaves the rest as typed.
* The characters that separate each entry from the following page number. By default, Word uses two spaces to separate entries and page numbers.
* Indents for subentries. By default, Word indents each subentry .2 inch.

You can also use a style sheet to format index entries.

Formatting an Index with the Library Index Command
To format an index before you create it:

1. Choose the Library Index command.
2. In the "entry/page # separated by" field, type the characters you want to separate the page numbers from the entries. If you want to change to use three spaces, for example, type three spaces.
3. In the "cap main entries" field, choose No if you want all entries to appear just as typed in the document.
4. In the "indent each level" field, type a new measurement to indent each level.
5. Press Enter or click the command name.

Using a Style Sheet to Format an Index
If you've defined the automatic paragraph styles named Index level 1 through Index level 4 in NORMAL.STY or in another style sheet, you can use that style sheet to format your table of contents. See Chapter 11 for

detailed information about changing Word's automatic styles and about using styles in general.

To use a style sheet to format an index:

1. If necessary, use the Format Stylesheet Attach command to attach the style sheet to the document.
2. Choose the Library Table command.
3. In the "use style sheet" field choose Yes.
4. Fill out other fields as necessary, then press Enter to create the table of contents.

Updating an Index

Word doesn't automatically update an index when you make changes in your document, so when you're all through, you may need to update the index.

To update an index, you just compile the index again:

1. Choose the Options command, choose No in the "show hidden text" field, then press Enter. This step makes hidden text invisible so pagination will be accurate.
2. Choose the Library Index command.
3. Press Enter or click the command name to compile the index.

After repaginating and collecting the entries, Word asks if you want to replace the index. If you press Y for Yes, Word replaces the existing index with the new index. If you press N for No, Word appends the new index to the end of the existing index.

CREATING FORM LETTERS AND ADDRESS LABELS: PRINT MERGE

This Chapter Contains the Following:

You can use Word to create form letters, invoices, and other merged documents using a list of names, addresses, and other information you supply, as shown in Figure 20–1.

To create form letters and other form documents, you follow three basic steps:

1. Create a *data document* containing the names, addresses, and other variable information to insert into the main document.
2. Create a *main document* containing the text that will remain the same and fields that will contain the names, addresses, and other variable information.
3. Use the Print Merge command to print the individual form letters.

You'll learn how to create these two documents and how to merge them together in the rest of this chapter.

Figure 20-1. **To create form letters, you create a data document and a main document and merge them together.**

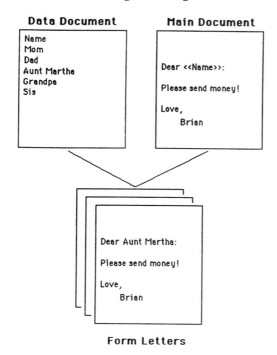

```
┌─────────────────────────────────────────────────────────────┐
│╷x   First_name,Last_name,Title,Address,City,State,Zip         │
│ x   Bo,O'Shea,Dr. ,123 Main Street,Sealth,WA,98126            │
│ x   Sally,Ramirez,Ms. ,456 Elm Avenue,Nouveau,WA,98134        │
│ x   M.L.,Wu,,9321 2nd Avenue SW,Reddick,WA,98132              │
│ x   Jesus,Rosario,Mr. ,7523 Roseview drive,Yakeema,WA,98149   │
│ x   Robert,Beason,Dr. ,932 43rd Street,Tulip,WA,98112         │
│ x   Joel,Geffs,Mr. ,4952 Redbud Avenue,Soome,WA,98134         │
│ x   J.D.,Collins,,1200 West Wayside Street,Nouveau,WA,98134   │
│ x   ◘                                                         │
│                                                               │
│                                                               │
│                                                               │
│                                                               │
│                                                               │
│                                                     ═ADDRESS.DOC═│
│COMMAND: Copy Delete Format Gallery Help Insert Jump Library    │
│         Options Print Quit Replace Search Transfer Undo Window │
│Edit document or press Esc to use menu                          │
│Pg1 Li9 Col      {¶}              ?            Microsoft Word   │
└─────────────────────────────────────────────────────────────┘
```

Figure 20-2.   **A sample data document.**

CREATING A DATA DOCUMENT

It really doesn't matter which document you create first for a form letter, but it's easier to understand how the two documents are related if you create the data document first. Figure 20–2 shows a data document.

A *data document* contains two elements:

- A paragraph of field names, called a *header record*.
- Data record paragraphs containing field entries in the same order as the header record.

If you know that you'll want to sort your information according to one of the entries in the records—zip codes or last names, for example—put that entry first in each data record paragraph. To enable sorting on a variety of fields when your records are not longer than one line, you may want to put your data document into a table.

Field names in the main document and in the header record must conform to these rules:

- A field name cannot contain spaces, mathematical symbols (+ - * / or %), or any of the following characters: & # ^ $ @ !

- A field name must begin with a letter, and can contain letters, numbers, or underscore characters.
- A field name can be up to 64 characters long.

To create a data document:

1. Type the header record paragraph, separating the field names with commas or tabs. The header record must be the first paragraph in the data document.
   Note: If you've set the "decimal character" field of the Options command to a comma, use a semicolon or a tab to separate the field entries of the records.

Helpful Hint

If you want to create a mailing list that you can easily sort, put your list into a table. (See Chapter 9 for information about creating tables.) Enter the header record as the first row in the table and make each record a separate row, like this:

Name	Address	City	State	Zip
Sam Chu	123 Elm Ln	Cedar	OH	94201
Jo Black	345 Oak Dr	Elma	WA	79213
Lila Obi	1982—14th	Tilsit	OR	68913

This format allows you to sort any column of the table, making it easy to add new records and create subsets of the mailing list. For example, if you wanted to mail form letters to customers in Cleveland, you could sort by City, then copy the Cleveland section to create a new data document to use during the print merge process. You could also sort by Zip, then divide the list into different data documents by zip code zones to make mass mailings easier.

If you have information in your list that you don't want to sort, such as titles (Ms., Mr., etc.) or articles that begin company names (The, A, An) be sure to put that information in a separate column so it won't be included when sorting.

Each record in a table must fit on one line. If your records are long, put the table in a separate division, then set the "width" field of the Format Division Margins command to the length you need for the longest record.

2. Type the data record paragraphs, separating the items with commas or tabs just like the header record, and putting the field entries in the same order as their field names in the header record.

If a field entry in a data record contains commas, tab marks, or quotation marks, enclose that entry in quotation marks. For example, if the customer name was "IQue, Inc.," enclose the customer name in quotation marks. Each record must be a separate paragraph, with no blank lines between records. If the field entries are so long that the lines in a record wrap, that's OK. Word assumes it's all the same record until it reaches the paragraph mark.

CREATING A MAIN DOCUMENT

Put the main document on the same disk and in the same directory as the data document.

A main document contains two elements:

1. The standard text, which remains the same in each letter.
2. Fields that tell Word where to find the variable information to insert into the main document from the data document.

You can enter and format the standard text of a main document just like any other Word document. Figure 20–3 shows a main document.

All fields in the main document must be enclosed in special bracket characters, <<>>. You can't use the angle-bracket keys on the keyboard

---

Helpful Hint

Use the key combinations listed above to type one pair of special bracket characters for fields (<<>>), then copy them and put them in a glossary, or use the Delete and Insert commands to insert them into your document wherever you need them.

See Chapter 4 for more information about working with glossaries and using the Delete and Insert commands.

```
█ L[•••••••••1•••••••••2•••••••••3•••••••••4•••••••••5•••••••••]•••••••••7•••••
   «DATA·ADDRESS.DOC»¶
   ¶
   ¶
   November·10,·1988¶
   ¶
   «First_name»·«Last_name»¶
   «Address»¶
   «City»,·«State»,·«Zip»¶
   ¶
   ¶
   Dear·«Title»«First_name»·«Last_name»:·¶
   ¶
   We'd·like·to·thank·you·for·your·generous·support·in·the·
   recent·election.··As·you·know,·the·cost·of·mounting·a·
   campaign·is·tremendous,··and·win·or·lose,·the·bills·have·got·
   to·be·paid.··If·you·could·contribute·a·few·dollars·to·help·
   us·defray·expenses,·we'd·be·mighty·grateful.··To·express·our·
   appreciation,·we've·enclosed·a·free·1989·calendar.¶
   ¶
                                                            MAIN.DOC
COMMAND: Copy Delete Format Gallery Help Insert Jump Library
         Options Print Quit Replace Search Transfer Undo Window
Edit document or press Esc to use menu
Pg1 Li19 Col       {}                      ?                Microsoft Word
```

Figure 20-3.   **A sample main document.**

to insert these. Instead, use these key combinations to create the special bracket characters:

To Create	Type
<<	Ctrl+[
>>	Ctrl+]

To create a main document:

1. Begin the letter with a field containing a DATA instruction and the name of your data document file. For example, if the data document was named ORDERS.DOC, the DATA instruction field would be:

    <<DATA ORDERS.DOC>>

    The field containing the DATA instruction must be the first paragraph in your document—it tells Word where to find information to insert into the fields.

2. Type and format the standard text.

3. Insert a field wherever you want Word to insert information from your data document. For example, insert the field <<last_name>> where you want the name in the data document's <<last_name>>field to be

---

Helpful Hint

To make sure that the field names you've used in your data document match the field names in your main document, use the Transfer Window Split command to create two windows, then load both documents so you can more easily compare them.

Figure 20-4 shows how this process would work. See Chapter 4 if you need more information about working with windows and multiple documents.

---

inserted. If you want the information to be inserted into the field to be formatted a certain way, format the text of the field. For example, if you want the customer's last name to be italic, make the words "last_name" in the <<last_name>> field italic: <<*last_name*>>.

Figure 20-4. **Using two windows makes it easier to compare field names in data and main documents.**

```
1 L[•••••••••1•••••••••2•••••••••3•••••••••4•••••••••5•••••••••]•••••••••7•••••
  «DATA·ADDRESS.DOC»¶
  ¶
  ¶
  November·10,·1988¶
  ¶
  «First_name»·«Last_name»¶
  «Address»¶
  «City»,·«State»,·«Zip»¶
  ¶
  ¶
  Dear·«Title»«First_name»·«Last_name»:¶
  ¶
                                                              MAIN.DOC
2 L[•••••••••1•••••••••2•••••••••3•••••••••4•••••••••5•••••••••]•••••••••7•••••
  First_name,Last_name,Title,Address,City,State,Zip¶
  Fred,Jones,Dr.,123·Main·Street,Sealth,WA,98126¶
  Sally,Ramirez,Ms.,456·Elm·Avenue,Nouveau,WA,98134¶
  M.L.,Wu,,9321·2nd·Avenue·SW,Reddick,WA,98132¶
  Jesus,Rosario,Mr.,7523·Roseview·drive,Yakeema,WA,98149¶
                                                              ADDRESS.DOC
COMMAND: Copy Delete Format Gallery Help Insert Jump Library
         Options Print Quit Replace Search Transfer Undo Window
407 characters
Pg1 Li1 Co1        {}                  ?                Microsoft Word
```

PRINTING FORM LETTERS

When you have created both the main document and the data document, you're ready to print your form letters. Word prints form letters in the same order as the records in your data document. If you want to print in a certain order, you can sort your records. For example, you might want to sort according to zip code to make it easier to mail the letters. For more information about sorting, see Chapter 16.

Printing Form Letters for All Records in a Data Document

To print form letters for all records in a data document:

1. Open the main document. Make sure the data document is on the same disk as the main document, and in the same directory.
2. Choose the Print Merge Printer command.
3. Press Enter or click the command name to start merging and printing. During this process, Word alternately displays two messages: "Merging. . ." and "Formatting page. . . ." Each form letter will be printed as soon as Word completes merging the information.

Here are two problems that can crop up when merging:

1. If Word can't find the data document, it displays a message saying the document is not a valid file. Make sure the DATA instruction at the top of the main document is exactly the same as the filename of the data document.
2. If Word can't match a field name in the main document with a field name in the data document, it prints "unknown field name" instead of the record entry in the form letter. Make sure the field name as typed in the main document is exactly the same as the field name in the header record of the data document.

Printing Only Certain Records from a Data Document

If you don't want to print form letters for all the records contained in a data document, you can use the Print Merge Options command to specify which ones to print.

```
1 L[••••••••1•••••••••2•••••••••3••••••••••4•••••••••5•••••••••]••••••••7••••┐
  First_name,Last_name,Title,Address,City,State,Zip¶
  Fred,Jones,Dr.,123·Main·Street,Sealth,WA,98126¶
  Sally,Ramirez,Ms.,456·Elm·Avenue,Nouveau,WA,98134¶
  M.L.,Wu,,9321·2nd·Avenue·SW,Reddick,WA,98132¶
  Jesus,Rosario,Mr.,7523·Roseview·drive,Yakeema,WA,98149¶
  Robert,Beason,Dr.,932·43rd·Street,Tulip,WA,98112¶
  Joel,Geffs,Mr.,4952·Redbud·Avenue,Soome,WA,98134¶
  J.D.,Collins,,1200·West·Wayside·Street,Nouveau,WA,98134¶
                                                         ══════════ADDRESS.DOC═
2 L[••••••••1•••••••••2•••••••••3••••••••••4•••••••••5•••••••••]••••••••7••••┐
  «DATA·ADDRESS.DOC»¶
  ¶
  ¶
  November·10,·1988¶
  ¶
  «First_name»·«Last_name»¶
  «Address»¶
  «City»,·«State»,·«Zip»¶
  ¶
                                                         ══════════MAIN.DOC═
PRINT MERGE OPTIONS range: All(Records)          record numbers: 3
Enter record numbers separated by commas; use colon for range
Pg1 Li1 Co1        {·}                ?                       Microsoft Word
```

Figure 20-5.   **The Print Merge Options command fields.**

To print only certain records from a data document:

1. Choose the Print Merge Options command. The command fields are shown in Figure 20-5.
2. In the "range" field, select Records.
3. In the "record numbers" field, type the numbers of the records for which you want to print form letters. To specify nonsequential records, you'd put a comma between the numbers, like this: 3,5,8. To specify a range of records, you'd put a colon between the first and last number, like this: 5:18. You can also combine nonsequential and range numbers, like this: 3,5,8,10:12.
4. Press Enter or click the command name.
5. Choose the Printer command to begin printing.

Pausing or Canceling Printing

To pause or cancel printing:

1. Press Esc to interrupt the merge process. Word displays a message asking you if you want to continue or cancel.

2. Press Y to continue the merge process, or press Esc to cancel the merge process.

SAVING FORM LETTERS IN A FILE

If you don't want to print your form letters directly from your data document, you can save all the letters in file. This feature allows you to edit, format, and print the completed form letters whenever you want.

To save form letters in a file:

1. Open the main document. Make sure the data document is on the same disk and in the same directory as the main document.
2. Choose the Print Merge command.
3. If you don't want to create form letters for all the records in the data document, choose the Options command, then select Records in the "range" field, then type the numbers of the records you want in the "record numbers" field.
4. Choose the Document command from the Print Merge menu.
5. In the "filename" field, type a name for the file that will contain the form letters.
6. Press Enter or click the command name to begin the merge process.

CREATING A DOCUMENT THAT ASKS YOU FOR INFORMATION

You can use the ASK instruction to create a main document that asks you for the information to put into fields immediately before printing a form letter. The basic form of the ASK instruction is <<ASK *field_name=?text* where *field_name* is the name of the field to fill with the information you type, and *text* is whatever information you want Word to print as a prompt. Figure 20-6 shows a main document that uses an ASK instruction to fill in its *first_prize* field.

You can also use multiple ASK instructions to fill in all fields, eliminating the need for a data document. Figure 20-7 shows a main document that uses only ASK instructions to fill in its fields.

```
L[••••••••1••••••••2••••••••3••••••••4••••••••5•••••••]••••••••7•••••
«DATA·LIST.DOC¶
«ASK·first_prize=?What's·the·first·prize·today?¶
¶
November·10,·1988¶
¶
«First_name»·«Last_name»¶
«Address»¶
«City»,·«State»,·«Zip»¶
¶
¶
Dear·«Title»·«First_name»·«Last_name»:¶
¶
Congratulations!··You·have·won·a·«first_prize»·in·our·
contest!¶
¶
Please·call·(202)938-7752·so·that·we·can·verify·your·address·
and·send·your·prize·to·you.¶
¶
▓
                                                      ═MAIN2.DOC═
RESPONSE:  trip to Tahiti█

What's the first prize today?
Pg1 Li19 Co1      {·}              ?              Microsoft Word
```

Figure 20-6.   **If you use the ASK instruction, Word prompts you for information to fill into the fields.**

Figure 20-7.   **A document that uses ASK to fill in all fields.**

```
L[••••••••1••••••••2••••••••3••••••••4••••••••5•••••••]••••••••7•••••
«ASK·First_name=?Type·customer's·first·name·or·initials¶
«ASK·Last_name=?Type·customer's·last·name¶
«ASK·Address=?Type·the·street·address¶
«ASK·City=?Type·the·city¶
«ASK·State=?Type·the·two-letter·state·code¶
«ASK·Zip=?Type·the·zip·code¶
«ASK·Amount=?Type·the·amount·donated▓¶
¶
November·10,·1988¶
¶
«First_name»·«Last_name»¶
«Address»¶
«City»,·«State»,·«Zip»¶
¶
Dear·«First_name»·«Last_name»:¶
¶
Thank·you·for·your·generous·donation·of·$«Amount».¶
¶
¶
                                                      ═MAIN3.DOC═
RESPONSE:  █

Type customer's first name or initials
Pg1 Li7 Co37      {»}              ?              Microsoft Word
```

To create a main document that asks you for information:

1. Type fields containing ASK instructions at the beginning of the document. Put the ASK instructions after the DATA instruction, if you're using a data document.
2. Type the text that will remain constant in each letter, and insert fields that will contain the variable information.
3. Choose the Print Merge command .
4. Choose the Printer command to print the form letters, or choose the Document command to save the form letters in a file.
5. When Word displays the text in each ASK instruction, type the information requested and press Enter. When Word has filled in all of the fields with the ASK instructions, it will create the first form letter, then it will display the ASK instructions for the second form letter.

INCLUDING INSTRUCTIONS FOR VARIABLE CONDITIONS: IF AND ELSE

If you want to print a clause in a form letter only when certain conditions are met, you can use IF and ELSE instructions.

You can use several variations of IF instructions when you use Word to check the contents of a field in your data document before inserting text in a form letter. Figure 20-8 shows a sample document that uses all types of IF instructions. These instructions are explained in greater detail in the following sections.

You can use an IF clause in three different ways:

1. To test if a field exists in the data document.
2. To test if text in a field matches text you specify in the IF clause.
3. To test if numbers in a field match numbers you specify in the IF clause.

Here's one element that all IF clauses have in common: Every IF clause must end with an ENDIF instruction.

Testing for Empty Fields

When you want to see if a field is empty or contains text in a data document record, you'll use a form of the IF clause that looks like the following:

<<IF field_name>>text to print<<ENDIF>>

```
L[••••••••1•••••••••2•••••••••3•••••••••4•••••••••5•••••••••]•••••••••7••••
 «DATA·garblist.doc¶
 ¶
 ¶
 November·10,·1988¶
 ¶
 «First_name»·«Last_name»¶
 «Address»¶
 «City»,·«State»,··«Zip»¶
 ¶
 Dear·«First_name»·«Last_name»:·¶
 ¶
 As·of·December·1,·1988,··your·garbage·pickup·rate·will·be·
 increased·from·$«rate»·to·«IF·rate=20»$22.00«ENDIF»«IF·
 rate=27»$29.70«ENDIF».¶
 ¶
 Sincerely,¶
 ¶
 GARBAGE·TO·GO,··INC.¶
 ▓
                                                       ═MAIN4.DOC═
COMMAND: Copy Delete Format Gallery Help Insert Jump Library
         Options Print Quit Replace Search Transfer Undo Window      ▓
Edit document or press Esc to use menu
Pg1 Li19 Co1      {Y}                  ?              Microsoft Word
```

Figure 20-8.   **IF instructions in a main document.**

For example, if you're using print merge to mail confirmation of orders and you don't know if one or two items have been ordered, you might want to tell Word something like "if there's text in the "item2" field, print that text here." You'd do this with an IF clause in your main document that might look something like this (the IF clause is in bold to make it stand out):

Thank you for your order for <<item1>><<**IF item2>> and <<item2>><<ENDIF>>.**

Here's how Word would deal with this clause. When Word checks a record, if the "item1" field contains "hula skirts" and there's nothing in the "item2" field, Word would print:

Thank you for your order for hula skirts.

If the "item1" field contains "tambourines" and the "item2" field contains "gypsy earrings," Word would print:

Thank you for your order for tambourines and gypsy earrings.

Using IF to Test the Text in a Field

When you want to see if a field contains specific text in a data document record, you'll use a form of the IF clause that looks like the following:

<<IF field_name="text to match">>text to print<<ENDIF>>

Be sure to put the "text to match" in double quotation marks. For example, if you're using print merge to mail confirmation of orders and want to include a sentence only if the customer has ordered a certain item, you might want to tell Word something like "if the "item1" field contains "Egyptian scarabs," print "We're sorry to inform you that we cannot ship Egyptian scarabs until August 1st." You'd do this with an IF clause in your main document that might look something like this (the IF clause is in bold to make it stand out):

Thank you for your order for <<item1>><<**IF item1="Egyptian scarabs">> We're sorry to inform you that we cannot ship Egyptian scarabs until August 1st.<<ENDIF>>**.

Here's how Word would deal with this clause. When Word checks a record, if the "item1" field contains "camel saddles," Word would print:

Thank you for your order for camel saddles.

If the "item1" field contains "Egyptian scarabs", Word would print this sentence like:

Thank you for your order for Egyptian scarabs. We're sorry to inform you that we cannot ship Egyptian scarabs until August 1st.

Using IF to Test Numbers in a Field

When you want to see if a field contains a specific number in a data document record, you'll use a form of the IF clause that looks like the following:

<<IF field_name=number>>text to print<<ENDIF>>

You can type a number to be matched exactly, or you can include the following symbols:

Comparison	Symbol to Type
Greater than	>
Less than	<
Equal to	=
Not equal to	<>
Greater than or equal to	>=
Less than or equal to	<=

For example, if you're using print merge to mail confirmation of orders and want to include a sentence only if the customer has ordered a certain item, you might want to tell Word something like "if the <<number1>> field contains a number greater than or equal to10, print "You qualify for our "10-Plus bonus—with each order of 10 or more, we give you an extra one free!." You'd do this task with an IF clause in your main document that might look something like this (the IF clause is in bold to make it stand out):

Thank you for your order for <<number1>> <<item1>>.**<<IF number1>=10>> You qualify for our 10-Plus bonus—with each order of 10 or more, we give you an extra one free!<<ENDIF>>**.

Here's how Word would deal with this clause. When Word checks a record, if the "number1" field contains 4 and the "item1" field contains "ant farms," Word would print:

Thank you for your order for 4 ant farms.

If the "number1" field contains 12, and the "item1" field contains "ant farms," Word would print:

Thank you for your order for 12 ant farms. You qualify for our 10-Plus bonus—with each order of 10 or more, we give you an extra one free!

Adding an ELSE Clause

The IF clauses described in the preceding sections instruct Word to print something only if a field matches certain conditions. There may be occasions when you want Word to print one phrase if one condition is met, or print another phrase if it's not met. In that case, you'd use an ELSE clause in the following general form:

<<IF field="text" or number>>text to print<<ELSE>>alternative text to print<<ENDIF>>

For example, you might want to tell Word "if the "state" field in the data document is equal to WA, print "The shipping fee is $4.50."; otherwise, print "The shipping fee is $5.00." To achieve this form, you'd write an IF statement like:

<<IF state="WA">>The shipping fee is $4.50.<<ELSE>>The shipping fee is $5.00.<<ENDIF>>

Here's how Word would deal with this clause. When Word checks a record, if the "state" field contains any text but WA, Word would print this:

The shipping fee is $5.00.

If the "state" field contains WA, Word would print this:

The shipping fee is $4.50.

Nesting IF Instructions

When you want to test a field to see if it meets several conditions, you can nest IF instructions:

<<IF field_name=first "text" or number>><<IF field_name=second "text" or number>><<ENDIF>><<ENDIF>>

Each IF clause must end with an ENDIF instruction. For example, you might want to tell Word something like "if the "number1" field is less than 10 and if the "item1" field contains "hula hoops," print "You must order a minimum of 10 hula hoops."'" You'd write an IF statement like this:

<<IF number1=10>><<IF item1="hula hoops">>You must order a minimum of 10 hula hoops.<<ENDIF>><<ENDIF>>

Here's how Word would deal with this clause. When Word checks a record, if the "number1" field contains 10 or any number greater than 10, Word simply skips the rest of the IF clause and adds nothing to the form letter.

If the "number1" field contains a number less than 10, Word checks the "item1" field. If "item1" does not contain "hula hoops," Word adds nothing to the form letter.

If the "number1" field contains a number less than 10 and "item1" contains "hula hoops," Word prints the following phrase in the form letter:

You must order a minimum of 10 hula hoops.

Using AND, OR, and NOT Operators in IF

As well as using the ELSE instruction and nesting IF instructions, you can use the following operators to refine IF expressions:

Operator	General Expression	Example
AND	<<IF field_name="text" or number AND field_name ="text"or number>>text to print <<ENDIF>>	<<IF city="Seattle" AND state ="WA">>Seattle, The Emerald City<<ENDIF>>
OR	<<IF field_name="text" or number OR field_name ="text" or number>>text to print<<ENDIF>>	<<IF zip=98126 OR city= "Seaside">> Seaside is facing a challenge!<<ENDIF>>
NOT	<<IF field_name NOT "text" or number>> text to print<<ENDIF>>	<<IF city NOT "Seaside">> This offer is only good in Seaside.<<ENDIF>>

Using IF to Print Only Certain Records in a Data Document

If you want to print form letters only if records in your data document meet certain conditions, you can use an IF instruction with a SKIP instruction, like:

<<IF field_name="text" or number>><<SKIP>><<ENDIF>>

This type of IF clause should be the second paragraph in your main document, right below the the DATA instruction paragraph. This clause tells Word to go on to the next record if the specified field does not meet the condition.

For example, you might want to print letters for those records that contain only a certain zip code. To do this task, you'd write an IF clause similar to this:

<<IF zip=98126>><<SKIP>><<ENDIF>>

This clause tells Word to check the "zip" field. If it contains "98126," Word prints a form letter. If the "zip" field contains anything else, Word goes on to the next record in the data document.

USING THE SET INSTRUCTION TO SUPPLY INFORMATION FOR A FIELD

If you want to supply information for a field in your main document instead of in the data document, you use a SET instruction. You might want to keep only a mailing list in the data document, and put the other variable information in your main document. For example, you were using print merge to produce notices for prize winners in a drawing. You could put the information to fill into the field in the body of the letter at the top of the main document, as shown in Figure 20-9.

Figure 20-10 shows a variation of the SET instruction in which Word prompts you for information before printing the form letters. If this isn't enough to prompt your memory, you can also type a message preceded by a question mark to cause Word to display the message, as shown in Figure 20-11.

```
L[••••••••1•••••••••2•••••••••3•••••••••4•••••••••5•••••••••]•••••••••7••••
«DATA·LIST1.DOC¶
«SET·first_prize=pony¶
¶
November·10,·1988¶
¶
«First_name»·«Last_name»¶
«Address»¶
«City»,·«State»,·«Zip»¶
¶
¶
Dear·«First_name»·«Last_name»:¶
¶
Congratulations!··You·have·won·a·«first_prize»·in·our·
contest!¶
¶
Please·call·(202)938-7752·so·that·we·can·verify·your·address·
and·send·your·prize·to·you.¶
¶
▯
                                                       MAINS.DOC
COMMAND: Copy Delete Format Gallery Help Insert Jump Library
         Options Print Quit Replace Search Transfer Undo Window
Edit document or press Esc to use menu
Pg1 Li19 Co1       {·}              ?                Microsoft Word
```

Figure 20-9.   **This type of SET instruction supplies information for a field in the main document.**

Figure 20-10.   **This type of SET instruction displays a default Word message to allow you to supply information for a field in the main document.**

```
L[••••••••1•••••••••2•••••••••3•••••••••4•••••••••5•••••••••]•••••••••7••••
«DATA·LIST1.DOC¶
«SET·first_prize=?▯
¶
November·10,·1988¶
¶
«First_name»·«Last_name»¶
«Address»¶
«City»,·«State»,·«Zip»¶
¶
¶
Dear·«First_name»·«Last_name»:¶
¶
Congratulations!··You·have·won·a·«first_prize»·in·our·
contest!¶
¶
Please·call·(202)938-7752·so·that·we·can·verify·your·address·
and·send·your·prize·to·you.¶
¶
¶
                                                       MAINS.DOC
RESPONSE: ▮

Enter text. Press Enter when done
Pg1 Li2 Co19       {y}              ?                Microsoft Word
```

```
█ L[••••••••••1•••••••••Z•••••••••3•••••••••4•••••••••5•••••••••]•••••••••7•••••█
 █ «DATA·LIST1.DOC¶
   «SET·first_prize=?Type·the·first·prize█
   ¶
   November·10,·1988¶
   ¶
   «First_name»·«Last_name»¶
   «Address»¶
   «City»,·«State»,·«Zip»¶
   ¶
   ¶
   Dear·«First_name»·«Last_name»:¶
   ¶
   Congratulations!··You·have·won·a·«first_prize»·in·our·
   contest!¶
   ¶
   Please·call·(Z0Z)938-775Z·so·that·we·can·verify·your·address·
   and·send·your·prize·to·you.¶
   ¶
   ¶
                                                    ═══════════MAINS.DOC═
RESPONSE:  █
                                                                         █
Type the first prize
Pg1 Li2 Co39      {y}                    ?                   Microsoft Word
```

Figure 20-11.   **A SET instruction that displays a message.**

You can use combinations of SET and ASK instructions in a main document to create form letters without using a data document.

INSERTING ANOTHER DOCUMENT

When you want to insert another document into a form letter (or into any other document) when it's printed, you can use the INCLUDE instruction. The basic form of the INCLUDE instruction is:

<<INCLUDE filename>>

You can use the INCLUDE instruction anywhere in your main document that you want to include another document. For example, if you were soliciting magazine subscriptions, you could keep your subscription form in a separate file, and type the following instruction where you want to insert the form:

<<INCLUDE SUBSCRPT.FRM>>

In form letters, you might want to combine the INCLUDE statement with an IF clause to test the value of a field before inserting a document, like this:

<<IF donation>1000>><<INCLUDE GOLDCLUB.DOC>>
<<ENDIF>>

MERGING MULTIPLE RECORDS INTO ONE DOCUMENT

Normally, Word prints one form for each record in a data file. However, there may be times when you want Word to print the information from all records on one copy of the form document. When you want to do this merge, you use a NEXT instruction.

The most common use of the NEXT instruction is to create a sheet of address labels. This NEXT instruction is shown in Figure 20-12.

Figure 20-12. **Using a NEXT instruction to merge multiple records into one document.**

```
L[••••••••1•••••••••2•••••••••3•••••••••4•••••••••5•••••••••]•••••••••7••••
«DATA·LABEL.DOC»¶
¶
«First_name»·«Last_name»¶
«Address»¶
«City»,·«State»,·«Zip»«NEXT»¶
¶
¶
«First_name»·«Last_name»¶
«Address»¶
«City»,·«State»,·«Zip»«NEXT»¶
¶
¶
«First_name»·«Last_name»¶
«Address»¶
«City»,·«State»,·«Zip»«NEXT»¶
¶
¶
«First_name»·«Last_name»¶
«Address»▊
                                                         ═NEXT.DOC═
COMMAND: Copy Delete Format Gallery Help Insert Jump Library
         Options Print Quit Replace Search Transfer Undo Window     ▊
Edit document or press Esc to use menu
Pg1 Li19 Co10     {}                  ?              Microsoft Word
```

CONTROLLING BLANK LINES IN FORM LETTERS

When IF and other instructions are included in separate paragraphs in form letters, more blank lines may appear than you may want in your form letters. To prevent the printing of blank lines between paragraphs, you replace the closing angle brackets (>>) at the end of the instruction paragraphs with paragraph marks, like:

<<IF state=WA>>"Keep Washington Green"<<ENDIF

This causes Word to read the next instruction as if it were on the same line.

CREATING ADDRESS LABELS

You can use the processes described in the previous section, "Merging Multiple Records into One Document" to create address labels by setting up a main document as an address label document. The tricky aspect of creating an address label document is to space the addresses appropriately so that they will print correctly on a sheet of stick-on labels. The basic idea is to create rows and columns of addresses that match the positions of the labels on the sheet. You can set tabs to create a table of addresses, like this:

Name1	Name2	Name3
Address1	Address2	Address3
Name4	Name5	Name6
Address4	Address5	Address6
Name7	Name8	Name9
Address7	Address8	Address9

The *Using Word* manual includes instructions for printing labels on various sizes of label sheets. However, as the sheets of labels and the labels themselves sometimes vary in size, you'll need to experiment a little to create perfect labels. To avoid wasting expensive sheets of labels, you should mark the outlines of the labels on a sheet of paper that's the same size as the label sheet, make several copies, then use these copies for experiments.

Using a Macro to Create Labels

Word comes with a macro named *mailing_label.mac* in the MACRO.GLY file. You can run the *mailing_label.mac* macro to merge the records in your data document into a "label" template (another glossary entry in MACRO.GLY), then save the mailing labels in a file so you can make any changes necessary before you print.

To run the *mailing-label. mac* macro:

1. If necessary, use the Transfer Glossary Load command or Transfer Glossary Merge command to load the MACRO.GLY file.
2. Choose the Insert command and press F1 to display the list of glossary entries.
3. Select *mailing-label.mac* from the list.
4. Press Enter to run the macro. Word asks you how many labels you want across the width of the page (1, 2, or 3 columns), then asks for the name of your data document and for the name of file where it will store the mailing labels, then creates the document containing the mailing labels. You can edit this document if you like, then use the Print Printer command to print the labels.

CHAPTER

21

USING THE DOCUMENT RETRIEVAL SYSTEM

This Chapter Contains the Following:

Using Summary Sheets
   Filling Out Summary Sheets
   Updating Summary Sheets
Controlling the Display of Documents
Marking Documents In the List
Searching For Documents
Loading a Document From the List
Moving Or Copying Documents
Printing Documents
Deleting Documents

When you first save a document, you see a summary sheet (shown in Figure 21-1), which asks you for more information about the document. You may ask yourself, "What's this for?" Well, when you save a document, Word automatically saves information such as the time and date of creation and revisions and, by displaying the summary sheet, Word allows you to enter information that will help identify the file. You can use this information later to search for certain types of documents. For example, you might want to see a list of all the files created by a certain person on a certain date, or a list of all files containing a key word such as a customer name.

When you want to use Word's document retrieval system, you choose the Library Document-retrieval command. This command replaces the Word screen with the screen shown in Figure 21-2. You can use commands on the Document-retrieval menu to search for documents, to load or print them, copy them to another location, or delete them. The rest of this chapter shows you how to do these tasks.

Figure 21-1. **The summary sheet Word displays the first time you save a document.**

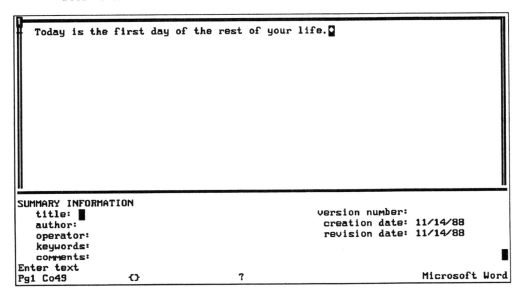

```
Path: C:\WORDS
C:\WORDS\AHNEWS.DOC                    C:\WORDS\OUTTEST.DOC
C:\WORDS\BORDERS.DOC                   C:\WORDS\PRICELST.DOC
C:\WORDS\CATALOG.DOC                   C:\WORDS\REPORT.DOC
C:\WORDS\CHARTEST.DOC                  C:\WORDS\SALES1.DOC
C:\WORDS\COLUMNS.DOC                   C:\WORDS\SALES2.DOC
C:\WORDS\CONODONT.DOC                  C:\WORDS\SBSPARAS.DOC
C:\WORDS\EXP-FORM.DOC                  C:\WORDS\STANDARD.DOC
C:\WORDS\FIG12-1.DOC                   C:\WORDS\STUFF.DOC
C:\WORDS\FIG9-5.DOC                    C:\WORDS\TAB&LNS.DOC
C:\WORDS\FRED.DOC                      C:\WORDS\TABLES.DOC
C:\WORDS\FREPORT.DOC                   C:\WORDS\TABS.DOC
C:\WORDS\GRTEST.DOC                    C:\WORDS\TEST.DOC




UPDATE SUMMARY filename: C:\WORDS\AHNEWS.DOC
    title: ah newsletter                   version number: 1█
    author: beason                         creation date: 10/31/88
    operator: beason                       revision date: 11/05/88
    keywords: log cabin, basement leaks, stair tips
    comments: January 1989 issue                                    █
Enter document version number
                                    ?                    Microsoft Word
```

Figure 21-2.   **The Document-retrieval screen.**

USING SUMMARY SHEETS

Because much of the information you use to search for documents comes
from the summary sheets, you'll need a good understanding of what types
of information you can enter and how you can use that information later.
Figure 21-3 shows a summary sheet that has been completely filled out.

Filling Out Summary Sheets

Unless you've set the "summary sheet" field of the Options command to
No, Word displays a summary sheet the first time you save a document.
In the summary sheet fields, you can type information that will help you
identify the file later.

Field Name	Type This
Title	A descriptive title for the document (up to 40 characters). The title does not need to be the same as the filename.

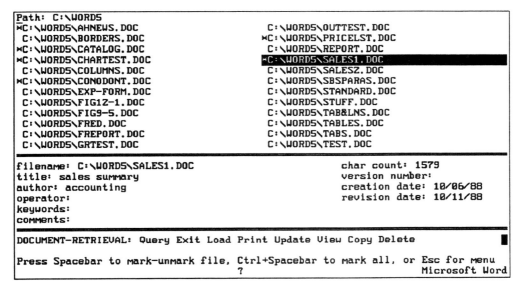

```
Path: C:\WORD5
*C:\WORD5\AHNEWS.DOC              C:\WORD5\OUTTEST.DOC
 C:\WORD5\BORDERS.DOC           *C:\WORD5\PRICELST.DOC
*C:\WORD5\CATALOG.DOC            C:\WORD5\REPORT.DOC
*C:\WORD5\CHARTEST.DOC          *C:\WORD5\SALES1.DOC
 C:\WORD5\COLUMNS.DOC            C:\WORD5\SALES2.DOC
*C:\WORD5\CONODONT.DOC           C:\WORD5\SBSPARAS.DOC
 C:\WORD5\EXP-FORM.DOC           C:\WORD5\STANDARD.DOC
 C:\WORD5\FIG12-1.DOC            C:\WORD5\STUFF.DOC
 C:\WORD5\FIG9-5.DOC             C:\WORD5\TAB&LNS.DOC
 C:\WORD5\FRED.DOC               C:\WORD5\TABLES.DOC
 C:\WORD5\FREPORT.DOC            C:\WORD5\TABS.DOC
 C:\WORD5\GRTEST.DOC             C:\WORD5\TEST.DOC

filename: C:\WORD5\SALES1.DOC              char count: 1579
title: sales summary                       version number:
author: accounting                         creation date: 10/06/88
operator:                                  revision date: 10/11/88
keywords:
comments:

DOCUMENT-RETRIEVAL: Query Exit Load Print Update View Copy Delete        ▌

Press Spacebar to mark-unmark file, Ctrl+Spacebar to mark all, or Esc for menu
                              7                         Microsoft Word
```

Figure 21-3.   **Updating a summary sheet in the document retrieval window.**

Author	The name of the person who created the document (up to 40 characters).
Operator	The name of the person typing the document or making revisions, if different from the author (up to 40 characters).
Keywords	Words or phrases that will help in identifying this document. If you wanted to keep track of all documents that involved a certain customer, product, legal case, or other topic, you could type the customer name, product name, legal case name, or words to identify a certain topic (up to 80 characters).
Comments	Any further information you want to add to clarify the document. For example, you might type something like "This letter responds to a query from the IRS about our fiscal year." You can type up to 220 characters.

When you revise a file, Word doesn't display the summary sheet, but the program automatically updates the "revision date" and "char(acter) count" fields. If you want to edit any of the other fields or add new information, use the following procedure.

Updating Summary Sheets

You may want to go back and update a summary sheet with new key words or other information that didn't occur to you at the time you saved the document.

To update a summary sheet:

1. Choose the Library Document-retrieval Query command.
2. Highlight the name of the document whose summary sheet you want to update.
3. Choose the Update command.
4. Edit or add new information to the summary sheet.
5. Press Enter or click the command name.

CONTROLLING THE DISPLAY OF DOCUMENTS

You can control which documents are displayed in the window with the Library Document-retrieval Query command; and you can control how they are displayed with the Library Document-retrieval View command. Word initally lists directories and files in alphabetic order, but you can sort the list any way you want.

To control which documents are displayed:

1. Choose the Library Document-retrieval Query command.
2. In the "path" field, type the directories, separated by commas, containing the files you want to see. (Example: \INVOICES,\NEWS, b:\DOCS\LETTERS); or press F1 to display a list of drives and directories, then highlight a drive name or directory name and press the comma (,) key to add the name to the list.
3. Press Enter or click the command name to display those files. If the list is long, you may need to scroll to find the files you want.

To control how the documents are displayed:

1. Choose the Library Document-retrieval View command.

2. Choose one of the following options to control how the window looks:

Option	Description
Short	Displays the list of documents.
Long	Displays the list of documents with additional author and title information.
Full	Displays the list of documents and a window containing the title summary sheet for the highlighted file—the default option.

3. In the "sort by" field, choose an option for how you want the names listed. For example, if you want to see a list of documents grouped according to their revision dates, choose Revision-date here.
4. Press Enter or click the command name.

MARKING DOCUMENTS IN THE LIST

When you choose the Library Document-retrieval command, you see a screen full of documents. Before you can load, print, or delete documents, you have to mark them on the screen to tell Word which ones you want. You can also mark documents when you want to search only those documents for specific information.

To mark a document:

1. Use the arrow keys to highlight the document name.Scroll up and down through the list, as necessary, to find the document name you want to mark.
2. Press the spacebar or press Enter. Word puts an asterisk (*) beside the document name.

You can mark as many documents as you like.
To mark all displayed documents at once:

• Press Ctrl+Spacebar.

Figure 21-4 shows marked documents on the screen. If you mark a document by mistake, you'll want to unmark that document before choosing a command.

To unmark a document:

1. Highlight the document name.
2. Press the spacebar or press Enter. Word erases the asterisk (*).

```
┌──────────────────────────────────────────────────────────────────────┐
│Path: C:\WORD5                                                          │
│×C:\WORD5\ADDRESS.DOC             C:\WORD5\MAIN5.DOC                     │
│ C:\WORD5\AHNEWS.DOC              C:\WORD5\MEMO.DOC                      │
│ C:\WORD5\AHOUT.DOC               C:\WORD5\MEMO5-25.DOC                  │
│×C:\WORD5\BORDERS.DOC             C:\WORD5\MEMOHIDD.DOC                  │
│ C:\WORD5\CATALOG.DOC            ×C:\WORD5\MERG.DOC                      │
│ C:\WORD5\CHARTEST.DOC           ×C:\WORD5\NEWMERG.DOC                   │
│×C:\WORD5\COLTEST.DOC            ×C:\WORD5\NEXT.DOC                      │
│ C:\WORD5\COLUMNS.DOC             C:\WORD5\NOTE.DOC                      │
│ C:\WORD5\CONODONT.DOC            C:\WORD5\NWMERG.DOC                    │
│ C:\WORD5\EXP-FORM.DOC           ×C:\WORD5\ORGCHART.DOC                  │
│ C:\WORD5\FBSTUDY.DOC             C:\WORD5\OUTTEST.DOC                   │
│ C:\WORD5\FIG12-1.DOC            ▐C:\WORD5\POSITION.DOC▌                 │
│ C:\WORD5\FIG9-5.DOC              C:\WORD5\PRICELST.DOC                  │
│ C:\WORD5\FRED.DOC                C:\WORD5\REPORT.DOC                    │
│ C:\WORD5\FREPORT.DOC             C:\WORD5\SALES1.DOC                    │
│ C:\WORD5\GARBLIST.DOC            C:\WORD5\SALES2.DOC                    │
│ C:\WORD5\GRTEST.DOC              C:\WORD5\SBSPARAS.DOC                  │
│ C:\WORD5\GTEST.DOC               C:\WORD5\SORT.DOC                      │
│ C:\WORD5\INVOICE.DOC             C:\WORD5\SSHEET.DOC                    │
│                                                                        │
│DOCUMENT-RETRIEVAL: Query Exit Load Print Update View Copy Delete       │
│                                                                        │
│Press Spacebar to mark-unmark file, Ctrl+Spacebar to mark all, or Esc for menu │
│                              ?                                         │
│                                               Microsoft Word           │
└──────────────────────────────────────────────────────────────────────┘
```

Figure 21-4.   **Marking documents on the screen.**

To unmark all marked documents:

• Press Shift+Ctrl+Spacebar.

SEARCHING FOR DOCUMENTS

To search for a single document or a list of documents, you use the Library Document-retrieval Query command to specify what you're looking for: a certain author, revision date, key words or phrases, and so forth.

If you want to search only specific documents, use the procedure described in the previous section, "Marking Documents in the List," to mark the documents you want to search. If you want to seach through all the documents in the system, you don't need to mark any documents before choosing the Document-retrieval Query command.

To tell Word what to look for, you fill in the fields of the Document retrieval-Query command. The command's fields are shown in Figure 21-5.

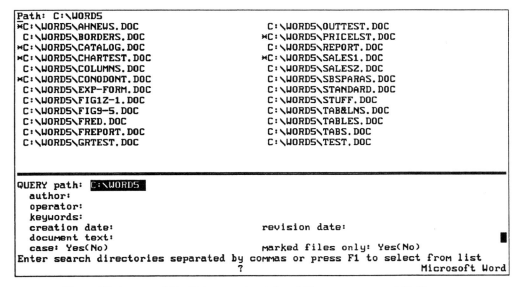

```
Path: C:\WORD5
×C:\WORD5\AHNEWS.DOC                      C:\WORD5\OUTTEST.DOC
 C:\WORD5\BORDERS.DOC                    ×C:\WORD5\PRICELST.DOC
×C:\WORD5\CATALOG.DOC                     C:\WORD5\REPORT.DOC
×C:\WORD5\CHARTEST.DOC                   ×C:\WORD5\SALES1.DOC
 C:\WORD5\COLUMNS.DOC                     C:\WORD5\SALES2.DOC
×C:\WORD5\CONODONT.DOC                    C:\WORD5\SBSPARAS.DOC
 C:\WORD5\EXP-FORM.DOC                    C:\WORD5\STANDARD.DOC
 C:\WORD5\FIG12-1.DOC                     C:\WORD5\STUFF.DOC
 C:\WORD5\FIG9-5.DOC                      C:\WORD5\TAB&LNS.DOC
 C:\WORD5\FRED.DOC                        C:\WORD5\TABLES.DOC
 C:\WORD5\FREPORT.DOC                     C:\WORD5\TABS.DOC
 C:\WORD5\GRTEST.DOC                      C:\WORD5\TEST.DOC



QUERY path: C:\WORD5
  author:
  operator:
  keywords:
  creation date:                   revision date:
  document text:                                                          ■
  case: Yes(No)                        marked files only: Yes(No)
Enter search directories separated by commas or press F1 to select from list
                              ?                                 Microsoft Word
```

Figure 21-5.   **The Document-retrieval Query command fields.**

To search for documents:

1. Choose the Library Document-retrieval Query command.
2. Fill in the fields with information you want to use as the search criteria. You can fill in as many fields as you like:

Field	What to do
"path"	Type one or more directories to search, separated by commas, like this: \Word\Legal, b:\Word\Invoices. or Press F1 to select from a list of drives and directories, then highlight the name and press the comma (,) key to add it to the search path. You can include up to 128 characters.

You can also type information that instructs Word to look for specific documents. For example, you could type *.INV to search for all documents with the .INV extension, or type CHAPTER* to search for

	all documents that begin with CHAPTER.
"author"	Type the first or last name(s)of theauthor(s),
"operator"	the first or last name(s) of the operator(s),
"keywords"	or the keywords you want to search for. Word will find all documents that contain these characters in their summary sheets. To specify more than one name or keyword, see "Searching for More than One Author, Operator, or Keyword" later in this chapter.
"creation date" "revision date"	Type the creation date or revision dateyou want to search for. The dates you type must match the format specified in the "date format" field of the Options command. To specify more than one date, see "Searching for More than One Date" later in this chapter.
"document text"	Type any text you want Word to search for in the files. For example, if you want to search for the phrase "erase the tapes," you'd type: erase the tapes. To specify more than one word or phrase, see "Searching for More than One Word or Phrase" later in this chapter.
"case"	Choose Yes if you want Word to search for the exact combination of upper and lowercase letters you type in the "document text" field. Choose No if you want Word to match letters only, and not pay attention to whether they're upper- case or lowercase.
"marked files only"	Choose Yes if you want Word to search only those files you've marked in the list. Choose No if you want Word to search all files in the list.

You can also use the ? and * wildcard characters in the "author," "operator," "keywords," and "document text" fields. Use ? to search for any single character in the question mark's position: For example, type Chapter? to find Chapter1, Chapter2, Chapters, etc. Use * to search for one or more characters in the asterisk's position: For example, type Jon* to find Jonathan, Jones, Jonson, etc.

To search for a question mark or an asterisk, precede it with a caret symbol (^? or ^*).

3. Press Enter or click the command name.

Word looks for documents matching the criteria you specified in the command fields, then displays a list of documents that match that criteria.

You can select documents from the list and load them to work on them, view them quickly to see what's in them, print them, or delete them. See the appropriate section later in this chapter for instructions on how to do these tasks.

Searching for More than One Author, Operator, or Keyword

To search for more than one author, operator, or keyword, use the following operators to tell Word exactly what you want:

Operator	Example
& or space to mean AND	Maria Jones or Maria&Jones means search for documents that contain both Maria and Jones in the field
, (comma) tomean OR	Smith, Chu means search for documents that contain either Smith or Chu in the field
~ (tilde) to mean NOT	Art~Article means search for Art, not for Article in the field

If the text you want to search for contains one of these operators (Jones & Co., for example), enclose the entire piece of text in quotation marks ("Jones & Co.").

Searching for More than One Date

To search for more than one date, use the following operators to tell Word exactly what you want:

Operator	Example
, (comma) to mean OR	1/05/88,1/06/88 means search for 1/05/88 or 1/06/88
~ (tilde) to mean NOT 1 1/05/88~	1/05/88~11/05/88 means search for 1/05/88, not for 11/05/88
>to mean LATER THAN	>1/05/88 means search for dates later than

	1/05/88
<to mean EARLIER THAN	<1/05/88 means search for dates earlier than 1/05/88

Searching for More than One Word or Phrase

If you want to search for more than one Word or phrase, use the following operators:

Operator	Example
& to mean AND	erase the tapes&hide the evidence means search for a document that contains both erase the tapes and hide the evidence
, (comma) to mean OR	vacation,holiday means search for a document that containsvacation or holiday
~ (tilde) to mean NOT	money~money-making means search for a document that containsmoney, not for money-making

If the text you want to search for contains one of these operators (Adventure, Inc., for example), enclose the entire piece of text in quotation marks ("Adventure, Inc.").

LOADING A DOCUMENT FROM THE LIST

You can load any document from the document retrieval list. You can highlight the document in the window, then load it, or you can type the name of the document, including pathnames and drive names, in the command field.

To load a document by highlighting it in the list:

1. Choose the Library Document-retrieval command.
2. Use the arrow keys or the mouse to highlight the filename you want.
3. Choose the Load command.
4. Press Enter or click the command name.

To load a document by typing its name in the command field:

1. Choose the Library Document-retrieval Load command.
2. Type the name of the file you want, including any drive names and pathnames Word needs to find the file.
3. Press Enter or click the command name.

Word returns to document view before loading the document. If the Word window contains a document that you've changed but haven't saved, Word asks you if you want to save that document before loading the new document.

For Network Users: When you try to load a document, you may see a message telling you that the file is in use. This message means that another user is using the file. Because only one person can change a file, network users must load files with the "read-only" field of the Transfer Load command set to Yes. Therefore, only the first person to load it can change the file, but others on the network may view the file at the same time.

MOVING OR COPYING DOCUMENTS

If you want to move or copy several files from one directory or disk to another directory or disk, you can use the document retrieval system to mark several files and move or copy them with one command.
   To move or copy documents:

1. Use the Library Document-retrieval Query command to list files you may want to move or copy.
2. Mark the documents you want to move or copy.
3. Choose the Copy command. The command fields are shown in Figure 21-6.
4. In the "marked files to drive/directory" field, type the path to the drive and/or directory to which you want to copy or move the files.
5. If you want to delete the documents after they've been copied (moving them), choose Yes in the "delete files after copy" field.
6. If you want to copy the style sheets attached to the marked documents, choose Yes in the "copy style sheets" field.
7. Press Enter or click the command name.

When Word has copied all of the files, it removes the asterisks from the screen and—if you deleted the documents—erases the names from the list.

If Word can't copy all the documents, it leaves the uncopied documents marked on the screen. This notation may happen if the destination disk is full, or if one of the documents is locked during network use.

PRINTING DOCUMENTS

You can print several documents, several summary sheets, or both summary sheets and documents at once using the document-retrieval system.

To print documents using the document retrieval system:

1. Choose the Library Document-retrieval command.
2. Mark the documents you want to print.
3. Choose the Print command.

Figure 21-6.   **The Library Document-retrieval Copy command fields.**

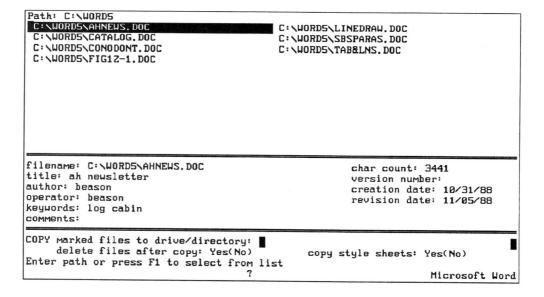

```
Path: C:\WORD5
C:\WORD5\AHNEWS.DOC                    C:\WORD5\LINEDRAW.DOC
C:\WORD5\CATALOG.DOC                   C:\WORD5\SBSPARAS.DOC
C:\WORD5\CONODONT.DOC                  C:\WORD5\TAB&LNS.DOC
C:\WORD5\FIG12-1.DOC




filename: C:\WORD5\AHNEWS.DOC              char count: 3441
title: ah newsletter                      version number:
author: beason                            creation date: 10/31/88
operator: beason                          revision date: 11/05/88
keywords: log cabin
comments:
COPY marked files to drive/directory: █
     delete files after copy: Yes(No)     copy style sheets: Yes(No)
Enter path or press F1 to select from list
                                ?                      Microsoft Word
```

4. In the "marked files" field, choose Summary to print only the summary sheets; choose Document to print only the documents; or choose Both to print both the documents and the summary sheets.
5. Press Enter or click the command name to begin printing.

DELETING DOCUMENTS

If you have a lot of old files that you want to remove from your system, you can use the document retrieval system to mark several files and delete them with one command.

To delete documents:

1. Use the Library Document-retrieval Query command to list files you may want to delete.
2. Mark the documents you want to delete.
3. Choose the Delete command.
4. Press Enter or click the command name. Just to be sure that you mean it, Word displays a message asking you if you want to delete the files.
5. Press Y for Yes. Word erases the files and removes the document names from the list.

PART VI

Customizing Word

If you find yourself using the same series of Word commands over and over again to perform common word-processing tasks, you can automate the process by recording a macro—a short program that can perform a series of Word instructions. It's as easy as making a tape recording. You can then play the macro with a quick key combination, and watch as the macro performs all your instructions in record time. You can also use the macros provided with Word to speed up various tasks.

If Word's default settings don't meet your needs, you can change them. If you want to work in centimeters rather than in inches, Word allows you to do that. If you want to change the way Word displays documents on the monitor screen, you can do that, too.

This part of the book shows you how to use Word's supplied macros, and how to customize Word to your satisfaction.

USING MACROS

This Chapter Contains the Following:

A *macro* is a set of instructions that automate Word tasks for you. You can use Word's supplied macros to do a variety of preset tasks, and you can also write your own macros to do exactly what you want. This chapter shows you how.

USING WORD'S SUPPLIED MACROS

Word comes with a long list of macros that you can use. These supplied macros are stored as glossary entries in the MACRO.GLY file. The following are descriptions of some of the macros that are included. There may be others. To see a description of them, you'd insert the glossary entry 1-README-FIRST from MACRO.GLY into a blank document.

Annotations Macros

Macro Name	Description
annot_collect.mac	Creates a separate list of annotations included in a document.
annot_merge.mac	Merges annotations from several copies of a document into one document.
annot_remove.mac	Removes all annotations from a document.

Printing Macros

Macro Name	Description
chainprint.mac	Prints several documents in succession and numbers the pages consecutively throughout the documents.
character_test.mac	Prints all of the characters your printer can produce in a font you select.
mailing_label.mac	Sets up a template to print mailing labels using addresses from a data document. See Chapter 20 for more information about using data documents and print merge.

Macros for Indexes and Tables of Contents

Macro Name	Description
authority_entry.mac	Marks a citation for inclusion in a table-of-authorities index. Asks you to select a citation and then select its scope from a list: previous case, constituition, statute, or other. Also prompts you to store the citation as a glossary entry so you can use it later.
authority_table.mac	Generates a table of authorities from entries coded with the *authority_entry.mac* macro described above, then replaces any existing index with the Table of Authorities.
index.mac	Adds index codes to a document using a list of terms you provide. See Chapter 19 for more information.
index_entry.mac	Adds index codes before and after selected text. See Chapter 19 for more information.
toc_entry.mac	Adds table-of-contents codes before and after selected text. See Chapter 19 for more information.

Macros that Move the Cursor

Macro Name	Description
next_page.mac	Moves the cursor to the beginning of the next page.
prev_page.mac	Moves the cursor to the beginning of the previous page.

Editing Macros

Macro Name	Description
copy_text.mac	Copies text you select to a destination you indicate.
move_text.mac	Moves text you select to a destination you indicate.
memo_header.mac	Inserts a header with "From," "To," and "Subject" fields, and asks you to fill in the fields.

repl_w_gloss.mac	Replaces text you specify with the contents of a glossary entry.
repl_w_scrap.mac	Replaces text you specify with the contents of the scrap.
3_delete.mac	Deletes text and saves it as a temporary glossary entry. You can recover up to three deletions that you've made this macro by using the *3_undelete.mac* macro.
3_undelete.mac	Lets you recover the three most recent deletions that you've made with the *3_delete.mac* macro.

Formatting Macros

Macro Name	Description
bulleted_list.mac	Formats a paragraph to create a bulleted list item preceded by a hyphen.
sidebyside.mac	Formats paragraphs as side-by-side paragraphs, asking you for the number of paragraphs, the space between paragraphs, and the alignment for each paragraph.
stop_last_footer.mac	Prevents the running foot on the last page of a document from being printed.
table.mac	Sets tabs for a table by asking you for the first table position and the distance between the following tabs.
tabs.mac	Sets tabs using positions and alignments you specify.
tabs2.mac	Sets tabs for a table by asking you for the number of columns in a table, the position of the first column, and the alignment of columns.

Macros that Convert or Save Text

Macro Name	Description
dca_load.mac	Converts a DCA-RFT document with the WORD_DCA.EXE program and loads the converted document into Word, giving it a .MSW extension.
dca_save.mac	Creates a copy of the current Word document

	and converts the copy to the DCA-RFT format, giving the converted file the .RFT extension.
freeze_style.mac	Converts all formatting applied with Word styles to direct formatting.
save_selection.mac	Save selected text to a file you name.

Loading the Supplied Macros

The first step in running one of Word's supplied macros is to load the file that contains them. Figure 22–1 shows the macro in the MACRO.GLY file.

To load the MACRO.GLY file:

1. Find the MACRO.GLY file. If you're using a hard disk system or a network, the file is probably on the hard disk or on the server. If you're using a floppy disk system, get the file from the Word Utilities Disk 2.
2. Start Word.
3. If you want to replace the current glossary with the MACRO.GLY file, choose the Transfer Glossary Load command. If you want to merge the entries in the MACRO.GLY file with the entries in the current file, choose the Transfer Glossary Merge command.
4. In the "filename" field, type *macro*, preceded by any necessary drive names or pathnames to tell Word where to find the file (examples: *b:macro, a:\word\util\macro*).
5. Press Enter or click the command name to load the file. If you chose the Transfer Glossary Load command and you've made any unsaved changes to the glossary you were using, Word asks you if you want to save the current glossary before loading the MACRO.GLY file. If you used the Transfer Glossary Merge command to merge glossary entries, you might want to use the Transfer Glossary Save command to save the combined entries so they'll be available for use whenever you load your document.

Running a Macro

Once you've loaded the glossary file that contains the macro, you can run a macro any time you want.

It's always a good idea to save your document before running a macro. Then, if the macro doesn't do what you want, you can just quit Word

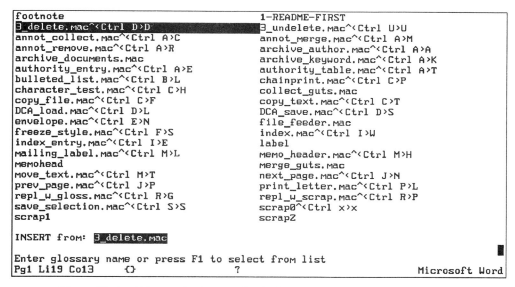

Figure 22-1. Macros in the MACRO.GLY file.

without saving the changes made by the macro. To run one of the supplied macros, you can use three different procedures, depending on whether you know a macro's name or its control code.

Running a Macro by Choosing It from a List

1. Move the cursor to where you want the macro to start running and select text if necessary.
2. Choose the Insert command.
3. Press F1 to display a list of the glossary entries.
4. Highlight the name of the macro you want to run. You may need to use the PageDown key to scroll to see all macros in the list.
5. Press Enter to run the macro.

Running a Macro by Typing Its Name

If you know the macro's name, you can run the macro without choosing a command first.

1. Move the cursor to where you want the macro to start running and select text if necessary.
2. Type the macro name.
3. Press F3. Word erases the macro name and runs the macro.

Running a Macro by Typing Its Control Code

If the macro you want to run has an assigned control code, you can run the macro without choosing a command first. Macro control codes are displayed along with the macro names when you press F1 to see a list of glossary entries. Here are two examples of control codes:

Code	Meaning
<Alt F2>	Hold down the Alt key while pressing F2, then release both keys.
<Ctrl p>x	Hold down the Ctrl key while pressing P, then release both keys and press X.

To type a control code, hold down the first key listed in the brackets while pressing the second key, then release both keys and press the key (if any) outside of the bracket.

To run a macro when you know its control code:

1. Move the cursor to where you want the macro to start running and select text if necessary.
2. Press the control code.

INTERRUPTING OR CANCELING A MACRO

If you need to interrupt or cancel a macro:

1. Press Esc. Word displays a message asking you if you want to continue or to cancel the macro.
2. Press Y if you want to continue running the macro where it left off, or press Esc if you want to cancel the macro.

CREATING YOUR OWN MACROS

There are two ways to create a macro:

1. Recording keystrokes and commands.

2.   Typing representations for keystrokes, commands, and instructions.

Because recording a macro is much easier than the second method, this book concentrates on the recording method. If you're interested in learning the typing method, see your Word documentation.

Basic Steps

Here are the basic steps in creating a macro:

1.   Plan the steps in a macro and decide on a name and a control code for your macro.
2.   Record the macro by performing the steps, then name the macro and assign a control code.
3.   Test the macro to see if it works.
4.   Record the macro again (if necessary), or edit a written copy of the macro.

Planning a Macro

Creating your own macro takes some planning. First and foremost, what do you want the macro to do? Write down the steps you want the macro to accomplish. Here's a few examples of steps for short macros:

Example: Steps for a Macro that Formats an Item in a Bulleted List

1.   Choose the Format Paragraph command and set the following indents for the selected paragraph:

    | Left indent: | 1 inch |
    | Right indent: | 1 inch |
    | First line indent: | -.5 inch |

2.   Insert a bullet character and a tab character in front of the selected paragraph.

Example: Steps for a Macro that Prints Three Double-Spaced Copies

1.   Press Shift+F10 to select the entire document.
2.   Press Alt+X2 to double-space the text. (The X has been added in case a style sheet is attached.)
3.   Choose the Print Options command and set the "copies" field to 3, the "paper feed" field to Auto, and the "range" field to All.

4. Choose the Print Printer command to begin printing.

Example: Steps for a Macro that Prints on Letterhead Stationery

1. Choose the Format Division Margins command and set the "top" field to 2.5 inches.
2. Choose the Print Options command, and set the "paper feed" field to Manual.
3. Choose the Print Printer command to begin printing.

These are just a few examples of what you can do. A macro can be very complex. For example, you have a consistent page format you like to use—legal-size paper, 2-inch margins top and bottom, 1-inch side margins, a running head that puts the page number in italic in the middle of the top margin, and a running foot that centers the date in the bottom margin. You could record all those actions in a macro, then just press a couple of keys when you want to use the macro to format your document.

To avoid having to start over, you may want to rehearse the steps you've planned for your macro before you begin recording.

Rules for Macro Names and Control Codes

When you've decided on the steps you want in a macro, decide on a name and a control code. The name should be descriptive, so that you can remember what the macro does. Macro names can contain up to 28 characters, and can include letters, numbers, underscores (_), hyphens (-), and periods (.). It's a good idea to use a MAC extension so that you'll be able to tell at a glance which glossary entries are macros. Here are some sample macro names: bullet-item.mac, print-2-copies.mac, bolditalic.mac.

Control codes are key combinations that are assigned to the macro. You can run a macro by typing the control code, thereby saving you the time of having to display a glossary and highlight the macro name. Control codes can consist of:

• The Ctrl key, followed by one or two characters. Examples: <Ctrlx>, <Ctrlx>a, <Ctrl 3>, <ctrl 3>b. (You don't need to type the brackets, as Word will put them in for you when you release the keys. If you want to use two characters, hold down the Ctrl key while you press the first key, then release both keys and press the second key.

- Function keys and function key combinations. Generally speaking, though, it's not a good idea to assign the function keys, because the macro assignment may replace a vital function already assigned to a key. For example, if you used the Shift+F10 combination as a macro control code, then Shift+F10 would no longer select the entire document. Examples: <Alt F8>, <Ctrl=F1>, <Shift F2>. You don't need to type the brackets, as Word will put them in for you after you release the keys.

Note: If you accidentally replace a Word-assigned function of a function key combination, such as Shift+F10, you can still use the previously assigned function by pressing Ctrl+X, then pressing the key combination. For example, if you've assigned Shift+F10 as a macro control code, you can still use Shift+F10 to select the entire document (Word's original assignment) if you press Ctrl+X, then pressed Shift+F10.

Both macro names and control codes must be unique, so you may want to check the entries in the current glossary to make sure the name and control code you're planning to use have not been used before.

Recording a Macro

Recording a macro is just like making a videotape of your actions—whatever you do is recorded, in exactly the same way you do it. After you've recorded the macro, you can run it to reproduce your actions, just like you would play a videotape. The difference is that Word responds to the macro just as if you were performing the actions yourself.

To record a macro:

1. Press Shift+F3 to begin recording.
   The letters "RM" (recording macro) appear in the status line to remind you that you're recording. Don't expect anything else—when you see "RM", the recorder is "on". Start going through the steps in your macro.
2. Type the keystrokes and commands you want to record.
3. Press Shift+F3 to stop recording.

Word automatically chooses the Copy command so that you can name the macro. The macro becomes a glossary entry in the glossary file attached to your document.

4. Type the macro name.

5. If you want to assign a control code, type a caret (^) immediately after the macro name, then press the keys you want to assign as the control code. Figure 22-2 illustrates naming a macro and assigning a control code.

6. Press Enter to store the macro in the attached glossary.
   If you've accidentally chosen a macro name or a control code that already exists in the glossary, Word displays a message asking you if you want to overwrite the glossary. Press N if you want to type a different name for your macro, or press Y if you want to replace a glossary entry with the macro name you just typed.

Just like any other glossary entry, a macro isn't saved until you save the glossary file with the Transfer Glossary Save command or the Transfer Allsave command.

Figure 22-2 . **Naming a macro and assigning a control code.**

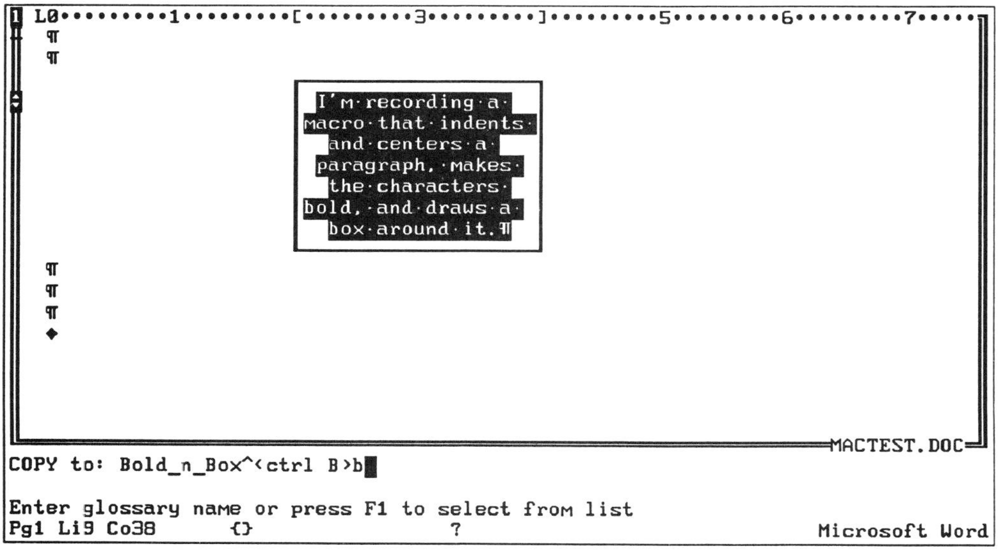

Testing Macros

When you've recorded a macro, you'll want to test it. There are two ways to test a macro:

1. Run the entire macro and check the results.
2. Run the macro in step mode to check each step before going on to the next.

To run the entire macro, follow one of the procedures listed under "Running a Macro" earlier in this chapter.

To run a macro in step mode:

1. Press Ctrl+F3 to start step mode. Word displays "ST" in the status line to remind you that you're using step mode.
2. Run the macro, using one of the procedures listed under "Running a Macro" earlier in this chapter. Word executes the first step of the macro, then pauses.
3. Press any key other than Esc or Ctrl+F3 to execute the next step.
4. Repeat step 3 to execute all the steps in the macro, or press Control+F3 to exit step mode or Esc to interrupt the macro.

Making Corrections

If your macro is short, but it didn't work right when you tested it, the easiest thing to do is to record it again. Give it the same name and control code, then press Y when Word asks you if you want to overwrite the current glossary.

If you recorded a long macro and you want to take the time to decipher the codes Word uses for macros, you can also put the text of the macro into a document, then revise the text . You might want to put the macro text in a file by itself so that you can easily save it and work on it over the course of several days.

Displaying Macro Text

To put the text of the macro into a document:

1. Move the cursor to where you want to insert the macro text.

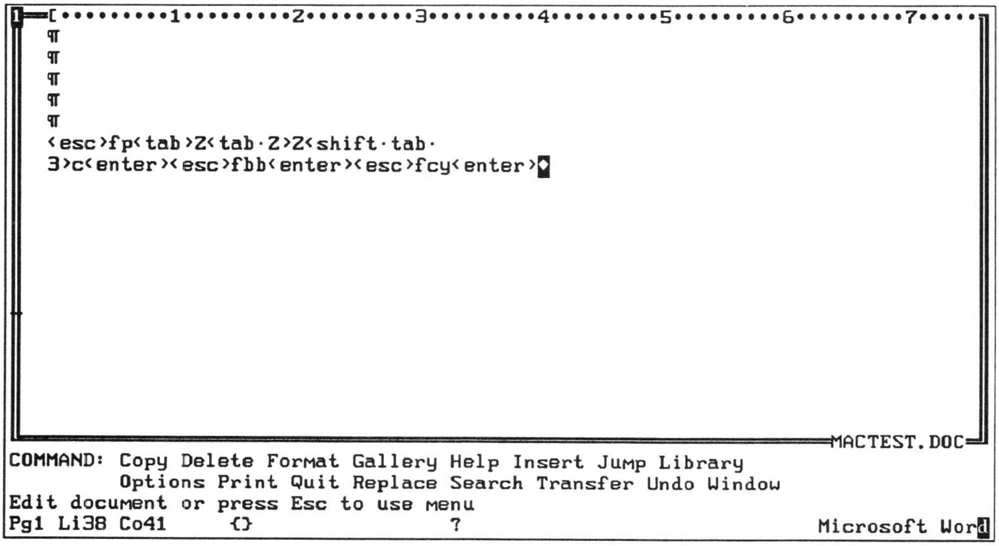

```
█━[•••••••••1•••••••••2•••••••••3•••••••••4•••••••••5•••••••••6•••••••••7•••••┓
  ¶
  ¶
  ¶
  ¶
  ¶
  <esc>fp<tab>Z<tab·Z>Z<shift·tab·
  3>c<enter><esc>fbb<enter><esc>fcy<enter>▌
```

```
                                                          ═MACTEST.DOC═
COMMAND: Copy Delete Format Gallery Help Insert Jump Library
         Options Print Quit Replace Search Transfer Undo Window
Edit document or press Esc to use menu
Pg1 Li38 Co41    {}            ?                        Microsoft Word
```

Figure 22-3.   **The text of a macro.**

2. Choose the Insert command.
3. Press F1 to display a list of glossary entries in the glossary file attached to your document.
4. Use the arrow keys to highlight the macro name. You may need to scroll down with the PageDown key to see all of the macros in the list.
5. Type a caret (^).
6. Press Enter or click the command name to insert the macro text (as shown in Figure 22–3).

Editing Macro Text

To edit and save the macro text:

1. Revise the macro text as necessary. For detailed instructions on how to write macros, see Chapter 24 of the *Using Word* manual.
2. Select all of the macro text.
3. Choose the Copy command (or the Delete command, if you want to remove the macro text).

4. Type the name of the macro, followed by its control code.

5. Press Enter to save the macro in the glossary. If you've used the same name for the macro, Word displays a message asking you if you want to overwrite the glossary. Press Y.

CHANGING WORD TO SUIT YOU

This Chapter Contains the Following:

Word comes with a myriad default settings that the programmers believe will suit the needs of the majority of users. However, there are many aspects of Word that you can change if you want. There are two general categories of changes you can make: changes to the way the Word program treats your documents, and changes to the way the program looks on your monitor screen. Almost all of the features that are customizable in Word are controlled through the Options command, whose command fields are shown in Figure 23-1. Word saves the settings you choose in the Options command fields when you quit Word, so the next time you start Word again, you'll be using the settings you want.

Many of these options were covered in appropriate sections in this book. This chapter covers some of the more powerful options that we didn't discuss in other chapters.

CHANGING THE WAY WORD TREATS YOUR DOCUMENTS

You can change the way Word treats your documents by changing the General Options fields of the Options command.

Figure 23-1.   **The Options command fields.**

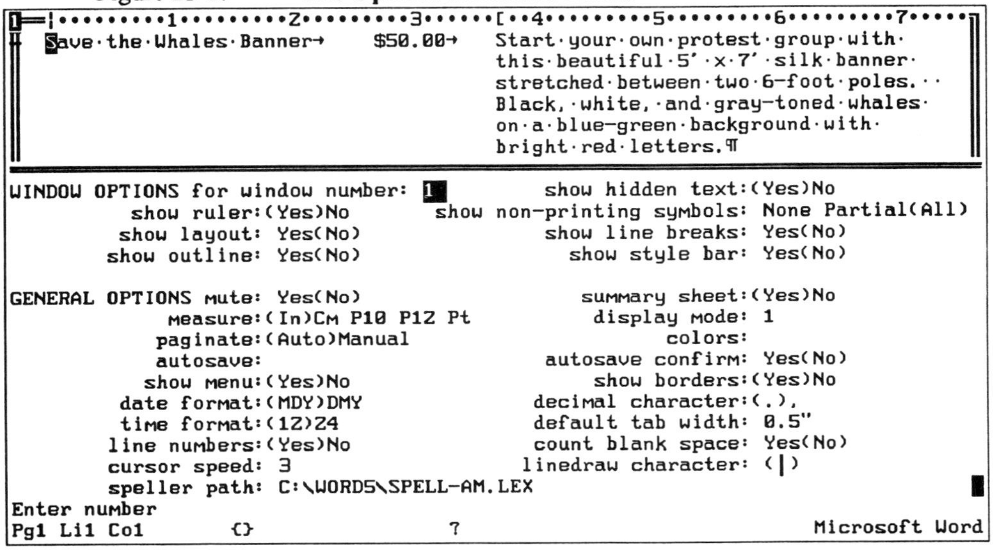

Figure 6.1: LIst of Files in the WP5 Directory (F(Shift-F7).

Changing the Default Unit of Measurement

By default, Word uses inches in most of the fields that require measurements. You can specify centimeters by typing *cm* after a measurement number in a field: *2.5 cm*, for example. You can also change the default unit of measurement from inches to centimeters points, or pica measurements. Not only does this make Word assume that all measurements are in centimeters points, or pica type it also makes the ruler reflect the default unit of measurement as well.

To change the default unit of measurement:

1. Choose the Options command.
2. In the "measure" field, choose one of the following options:

Option	Changes Default Measurement to
In	Inches
Cm	Centimeters
Pt	Points
P10	10-point Pica
P12 1	2-point Pica

3. Press Enter or click the command name.

Changing the Decimal Character

In the United States we commonly use a decimal point to separate whole numbers from fractions and dollars from cents, as in 3.099 and $12.78. Americans also use commas to separate thousands from hundreds, as in 9,388. However, most countries in the world use just the reverse. They use commas to separate whole numbers from fractions and dollars from cents like this: 3,099 and $12,78; and they use decimal points to separate thousands from hundreds, like this: 9.388. If you want to use this international system, use the following procedure to change the decimal character.

To change the decimal character:

1. Choose the Options command.
2. In the "decimal character" field, choose a comma or a decimal point.
3. Press Enter or click the command name.

If you choose a comma as the decimal character, you'll have to use a

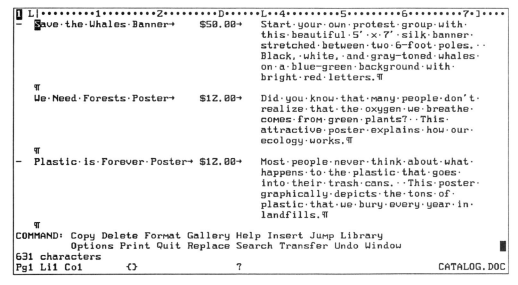

Figure 23-2.   **The Word screen without window borders.**

semicolon (;) to separate the names of fields in form letters and to separate tab positions when setting them with the Format Tab Set command.

Changing the Order of Dates

In the United States we usually write dates with the month first, followed by the day and the year, like this: December 1, 1989 or 12/1/89. However, most countries in the world put the day first, then the month and the year, like this: 1 December 1989 or 1/12/89. If you'd like to use this international order for dates, use the following procedure to change the default order of dates. This procedure won't change the order of any date that you type, but it will change the (date) glossary entries that insert the current date in your document.

To change the order of dates:

1. Choose the Options command.
2. In the "date format" field, choose DMY (Day/Month/Year) or MDY (Month/Day/Year).
3. Press Enter or click the command name.

CHANGING THE WAY WORD TREATS THE SCREEN

You can change the way the Word window looks by changing the Window Options fields of the Options command and the following fields in General Options: "show borders," "show menu," "colors," and "display mode."

Removing Window Borders

You can add two lines and three columns to the text area of the Word window by removing the window borders, as shown in Figure 23-2. If you're a mouse user, however, you probably won't want to do this because some mouse functions, such as window splitting, use the window borders.

To remove window borders:

1. Choose the Options command.
2. In the "show borders" field, choose No.
3. Press Enter or click the command name.

Hiding the Word Menu

You can make the text area of the Word screen three lines longer by hiding the Word menu, as shown in Figure 23-3. This feature doesn't mean that you can't use the menu. You can press Esc or click in the status line to display the menu whenever you want to use a command.

When the menu is hidden, only the status line gives you information about changes as they occur. When Word needs to display a message, it replaces the status line with the message. As soon as you respond to the message, Word erases the message and displays the status line again.

To hide the Word menu:

1. Choose the Options command.
2. In the "show menu" field, choose No.
3. Press Enter or click the command name to hide the menu.

Changing the Colors of the Word Screen

If you have a color monitor, you can change the colors of the Word win-

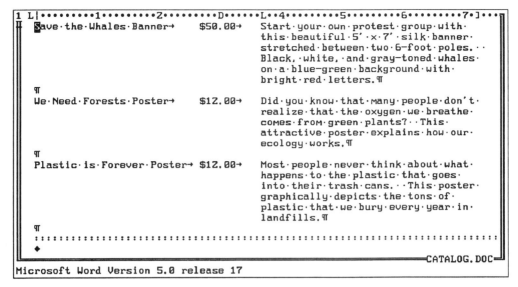

```
1 L|•••••••••1•••••••••2•••••••••D•••••L••4•••••••••5•••••••••6•••••••••7•]•••
 |  $ave·the·Whales·Banner→    $50.00→   Start·your·own·protest·group·with·
                                         this·beautiful·5'·x·7'·silk·banner·
                                         stretched·between·two·6-foot·poles.··
                                         Black,·white,·and·gray-toned·whales·
                                         on·a·blue-green·background·with·
                                         bright·red·letters.¶
    ¶
    We·Need·Forests·Poster→    $12.00→   Did·you·know·that·many·people·don't·
                                         realize·that·the·oxygen·we·breathe·
                                         comes·from·green·plants?··This·
                                         attractive·poster·explains·how·our·
                                         ecology·works.¶
    ¶
    Plastic·is·Forever·Poster→ $12.00→   Most·people·never·think·about·what·
                                         happens·to·the·plastic·that·goes·
                                         into·their·trash·cans.··This·poster·
                                         graphically·depicts·the·tons·of·
                                         plastic·that·we·bury·every·year·in·
                                         landfills.¶
    ¶
    :::::::::::::::::::::::::::::::::::::::::::::::::::::::::::::::::::::::::::::::
    ♦
                                                             ═CATALOG.DOC═
Microsoft Word Version 5.0 release 17
```

Figure 23-3.   **The Word screen with the menu hidden.**

dow, the messages, and the menu. For example, you might want to change the message line to bright red to make all messages stand out on the screen.

To change screen colors:

1. Choose the Options command.
2. In the "colors" field, press F1 to display a list of items for which you can set colors.
3. Use the arrow keys or the mouse to highlight the item for which you want to set the color.
4. If you want to look at all the available colors, press PgUp or PgDn to move through the color list until you see the one you want. If you know the color you want, press the letter for that color as displayed above the menu. For example, if the letter B at the top of the screen is bright blue, you can press B to get bright blue. The words "sample text" are displayed in the color you choose. Figure 23-4 illustrates choosing colors for items.
5. When the color you want is displayed in that field, use the arrow keys or the mouse to move to a different field, then set more colors if necessary.

```
                 B C D E F G H    J K L M N O P  * (ignore)
background for window 1:                      border: sample text
              menus: sample text            messages: sample text
       menu options: sample text         status line: sample text
 font 8.5 pts or less: sample text          uppercase: sample text
        9.0 to 10 pts: sample text        small caps: sample text
       10.5 to 12 pts: sample text         subscript: sample text
       12.5 to 14 pts: sample text       superscript: sample text
     more than 14 pts: sample text       hidden text: sample text
               bold: sample text       strikethrough: sample text
             italic: sample text      bold and italic: sample text
          underline: sample text     bold and underline: sample text
   double underline: sample text   italic and underline: sample text

          measure:(In)Cm P10 P12 Pt        display mode: 1
        paginate:(Auto)Manual                    colors:
        autosave:                      autosave confirm: Yes(No)
     show menu:(Yes)No                    show borders:(Yes)No
     date format:(MDY)DMY            decimal character:(.),
     time format:(12)24              default tab width: 0.5"
   line numbers:(Yes)No              count blank space: Yes(No)
     cursor speed: 3                 linedraw character: (|)
     speller path: C:\WORD5\SPELL-AM.LEX
Press F1 and select item. Press letter or use PgUp, PgDn to set color
Pg1 Li1 Col        {}                     ?                  Microsoft Word
```

Figure 23-4.   **Choosing colors for the Word screen.**

6. When you've set all the screen colors you want, press F1 to get back to the Options command fields, then set other options as necessary.
7. Press Enter or click the command name to carry out the command.

Switching Display Modes

Depending on whether or not you have a graphics card installed, you may have a choice of several display modes that control how Word displays the mouse cursor, character formats, and the number of lines in the window.

To switch between display modes:

1. Choose the Options command.
2. In the "display mode" field, press F1 to see a list.
3. Highlight the mode you want, then press Enter to switch to that mode.

You can also use various switches to start Word in specific display modes. See "Starting Word" in Chapter 2 for more information about that.

Appendix

SUMMARY OF SHORTCUTS

This Appendix Contains the Following:

File Management Shortcuts
  Loading Files
  Saving Files
Editing Shortcuts
  Checking Spelling
  Looking for Synonyms
  Moving Text with Keys
  Moving Text with the Mouse
  Copying Text with Keys
  Copying Text with the Mouse
  Using a Glossary
Formatting Shortcuts
  Character Formatting
  Paragraph Formatting
    Indenting
    Aligning
    Setting Line Spacing
Shortcut to Create Running Heads and Running Feet
Printing Shortcut
Repeating the Last Action
Repeating a Search

This appendix summarizes the shortcuts listed throughout the book.

FILE MANAGEMENT SHORTCUTS

Loading Files

To choose the Transfer Load command and display a list of .DOC files in the current directory at the same time:

• Press Ctrl+F7.

Saving Files

Instead of choosing the Transfer Save command, then pressing Enter to save a file with the same name, you can just press Ctrl+F10. Word will save the file without displaying the command fields.

EDITING SHORTCUTS

Checking Spelling

You can quickly check spelling without choosing a command:

• Press Alt+F6.

Looking for Synonyms

You can quickly look for a synonym without choosing a command:

• Press Ctrl+F6.

Moving Text with Keys

You can quickly move text without choosing commands. To insert new text in front of existing text:

1. Select the text you want to move.
2. Press the Del key.
3. Place the cursor where you want to insert the text.
4. Press the Ins key to insert the text.

Moving Text with the Mouse

To use the mouse to move text quickly without using the scrap:

1. Select the text to move.
2. Insert the text using the following table as a guide:

To Insert in Front of	Point Here	Hold Down the Ctrl Key and Click This Button
Character	In window	Left
Word		Right
Sentence		Both
Line	In selection bar	Left
Paragraph		Right
Beginning of document		Both

Copying Text with Keys

To copy text quickly without using a command:

1. Select the text.
2. Press Alt+F3.
3. Move the cursor to where you want to insert text.
4. Press the Ins key.

Copying Text with the Mouse

To use the mouse to quickly copy text without using the scrap:

1. Select the text to copy.

2.   Insert the text using the following table as a guide:

To Insert in Front of	Point here	Hold Down the Shift Key and Click This Button
Character	In window	Left
Word		Right
Sentence		Both
Line	In selection bar	Left
Paragraph		Right
Beginning of document		Both

Using a Glossary

If you know the name of the glossary entry you want, you can insert it without choosing any commands:

1.   Place the cursor where you want to insert the entry.
2.   Type the name of the entry. For example, if you want to put the date into your document, you could type *date*, or if you have your company logo stored in a glossary entry named "logo," type *logo*.
3.   Press F3.

FORMATTING SHORTCUTS

If you have a style sheet other than NORMAL.STY attached to your document, press X between the Alt key and the letter key listed in the sections below. For example, if you have a style sheet attached to your document and you want to make selected text bold, press Alt+XB.

Character Formatting

You can quickly apply character formats to selected text using the key combinations shown in the following:

Format	Key Combination
Bold	Alt+B
Italic	Alt+I

Underline	Alt+U
Double underline	Alt+D
Strikethrough	Alt+S
Small caps	Alt+K (affects only lowercase letters)
Hidden text	Alt+E
Superscript	Alt+ + (plus)*
Subscript	Alt+ - (hyphen or minus)*
Change case	Ctrl+F4 (keep pressing until you see what you want—uppercase, lowercase, or only first letter capitalized)
Back to plain text	Alt+Spacebar

* Use the key in the top row, not the key on the numeric keypad at the right of the keyboard.

Paragraph Formatting

Indenting
Select the paragraphs to indent, then use the key combinations shown below.

Press	To
Alt+N	Indent whole paragraph from the left margin to the next tab position (usually 1/2 inch).
Alt+F	Indent only the first line to the next tab position (usually 1/2 inch).
Alt+T	Indent all lines except the first line to the next tab position, creating a hanging indent.
Alt+M	Decrease left indent back to the previous tab position (usually 1/2 inch).
Alt+Q	Indent paragraph from both left and right margins to the closest tab position (usually 1/2 inch).

You can press all these key combinations several times to set the indent you want.

Aligning
Select the paragraphs, then use the key combinations shown below.

Press	To
Alt+L	Align text with left indent.
Alt+C	Center text.
Alt+R	Align text with right indent.
Alt+J	Justify text.

Setting Line Spacing

Select the paragraphs, then use the key combinations below.

Press	To
Alt+2	Double-space text.
Alt+1	Single-space text.
Alt+O (letter "O")	To "open" spacing (insert one blank line) before paragraphs.

SHORTCUT TO CREATE RUNNING HEADS AND RUNNING FEET

If you want to use Word's default formats for running heads or running feet that appear on both odd and even pages, you can quickly create them this way.

1. Move the cursor to the beginning of the division to which you want to add running heads or running feet.
2. Type and format a paragraph containing the text and fields you want to appear in a running head or in a running foot.
3. Select the paragraph.
4. If you want to format the paragraph as a running head, press Ctrl+F2. If you want to format the paragraph as a running foot, press Alt+F2.

PRINTING SHORTCUT

To begin printing your document without choosing a command:

• Press Ctrl+F8.

REPEATING THE LAST ACTION

To repeat the last formatting or editing action:

- Press F4.

REPEATING A SEARCH

To repeat a search to find the next occurrence:

- Press Shift+F4.

Index

Julian →

Weldon Sci.

235

6146

zu Ernest
Frankel